# Scottish Roads Law

# Scottish Roads Law

*Second edition*

**Ann Faulds** BA, LLB, Dip LP MIHT, RTPI
Legal Associate
Partner, Dundas & Wilson CS LLP

**Trudi Craggs** LLB, Dip LP
Partner, Dundas & Wilson CS LLP

**John Saunders** BSc, MSc, MBA, MCILT
Associate, MRC McLean Hazel

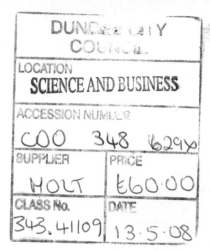
Published by
Tottel Publishing Ltd
Maxwelton House
41–43 Boltro Road
Haywards Heath
West Sussex
RH16 1BJ

Tottel Publishing Ltd
9–10 St. Andrew Square
Edinburgh
EH2 2AF

ISBN 978 1 84592 780 6
© Tottel Publishing Ltd 2008
First published by LexisNexis Butterworths 2000
Second edition 2008

**British Library Cataloguing-in-Publication Data**
A catalogue record for this book is available from the British Library

Typeset, printed and bound in Great Britain by
M & A Thomson Litho Ltd., East Kilbride, Glasgow, Scotland

# Contents

# Foreword

Within the transport system roads continue to cater for most of our movement. Even in our major cities road-based transport dominates the working environment. The increasing demands on the network and the range of issues around management and new construction make it essential that practitioners have a clear understanding of the legislative framework. The revised edition of Scottish Roads Law is timely. As with the first edition the ability to present the full framework in one publication is remarkably helpful for all practitioners, be they legal, academics or transport professionals.

The team of authors bring a wide range of knowledge and experience. Ann Faulds, the principal author of the first edition, is widely recognised as the most experienced solicitor in this field. Trudi Craggs also brings a wealth of legal experience to the book, including an involvement in some of the most significant recent cases around traffic management. John Saunders brings 30 years of practitioner experience in both public and private sector.

As one who has had a long-term involvement in these issues at various levels, I am clear that this book ought to be sitting, well-thumbed in every office. There are major issues and interests on all topics from construction through regulation to ownership of the road network. The practitioner who does not understand the legal framework of their involvement will rapidly find themselves out of their depth without this book. For academics and students, it provides an invaluable and instructive text book.

I have no hesitation is commending this book to all interests.

**Andrew M Holmes**
**Director of City Development**
**The City of Edinburgh Council**

**January 2008**

# Preface

Since the publication of the first edition of this text in 2000, interest in national transportation policy and practice has continued to grow in Scotland. As predicted, we have seen a period of significant investment in transport: such as the Government's heavy rail programme including the Waverley Line, the Edinburgh tram project, which is now under construction, and road construction and improvement schemes such as the M80 upgrade. However, some of the more radical solutions to deal with road congestion and public transport investment have not worked so far. Notably, Scotland's first road user charging scheme was successfully taken through a public inquiry process only to be rejected when submitted to a public referendum by the City of Edinburgh Council. It is doubtful whether there will be any political appetite for another road user charging scheme in the short term but public expenditure constraints coupled with continuing demand from business and the public for investment in our infrastructure may force Government to revisit some form of pricing or charging. The current debate on PFI/PPP and Scottish Future Trusts will shape future investment in our transport infrastructure. Funding the Replacement Forth Crossing will focus that debate in the short term.

The political landscape changed fundamentally in 2007 and there are many challenges facing the new Scottish Government and new local authorities as they pursue sustainable economic growth. We have also seen the creation of Regional Transport Authorities which provide the opportunity to deliver transport projects and initiatives at a regional level although their effectiveness will depend upon the willingness of local authorities to fund such projects. We wish them every success in implementing the National Transport Strategy, the Regional Transport Strategies and the Local Transport Strategies. Shared services will be a key management tool in local government – and roads and transport seems to be an ideal 'service' to be shared across boundaries.

The objective of the first edition was to provide a simple guide to roads law and we were pleased that it proved to be of assistance to practitioners. We hope that this edition provides more insight into some issues such as the identification of a road, as well as providing an update on areas such as New Roads and Street Works Legislation and Road Traffic Regulation Orders.

We are grateful to a number of friends and colleagues in the industry for their support and a special thank you to June Hyslop for her commitment and professionalism in co-authoring the first edition. A special thank you to Alastair Andrew of the Forth Estuary Transport Authority for permission to use the cover photograph of the Forth Road Bridge.

The law is stated as at 31 January 2008.

Ann Faulds
Trudi Craggs
John Saunders

# Table of Statutes

[References are to page number]

# Table of Statutory Instruments

[References are to page number]

# Table of Cases

## G

## H

## J

## L

## M

## N

## O

## P

# R

# S

# T

# U

# V

# W

# Table of EC Material

[References are to paragraph number]

# Table of Other Materials

# Abbreviations

**Reports**

| | |
|---|---|
| AC | Law Reports, Appeal Cases (House of Lords and Privy Council) 1890– |
| All ER | All England Law Reports 1936– |
| CMLR | Common Market Law Reports 1962– |
| Const LJ | Construction Law Journal |
| ECGS | Estates Gazette Case Summaries 1988– |
| EG | Estates Gazette 1858– |
| EGLR | Estates Gazette Law Reports 1985– |
| EHRR | European Human Rights Reports 1979– |
| Ex D | Law Reports, Exchequer Division (England) 1875–80 |
| GWD | Green's Weekly Digest 1986– |
| ICR | Industrial Case Reports 1972– |
| IH | Inner House (Court of Session) |
| JPL | Journal of Planning Law |
| KB | Law Reports, King's Bench Division (England) 1900–52 |
| LGR | Local Government Reports 1902– |
| M | Macpherson's Session Cases 1862–73 |
| Macph | Macpherson's Session Cases 1862–73 |
| Macq | Macqueen's House of Lords Reports 1851–65 |
| OH | Outer House (Court of Session) |
| PLR | Planning Law Reports 1988– |
| QB | Law Reports, Queen's Bench Division (England) 1952– |
| R | Rettie's Session Cases 1873–98 |
| R(HL) | House of Lords Cases in Rettie's Session Cases 1873–98 |
| RTR | Road Traffic Reports 1970– |
| RVR | Rating and Valuation Reports 1960– |
| SC | Session Cases 1907– |
| SC (HL) | House of Lords in Session Cases 1907– |
| SCCR | Scottish Criminal Case Reports 1981– |
| SCLR | Scottish Civil Law Reports 1987– |
| SLT | Scots Law Times 1909– |
| SLT (Notes) | Notes of Recent Decisions in Scots Law Times 1946–81 |
| SN | Session Notes 1925–48 |
| WLR | Weekly Law Reports (England) 1953– |

**Statutes**

| | |
|---|---|
| NRSWA 1991 | New Roads and Street Works Act 1991 |
| R(S)A 1984 | Roads (Scotland) Act 1984 |
| RTRA 1984 | Road Traffic Regulation Act 1984 |
| TCP(S)A 1997 | Town and Country Planning (Scotland) Act 1997 |
| T(S)A 2005 | Transport (Scotland) Act 2005 |
| T(S)A 2001 | Transport (Scotland) Act 2001 |

# PART ONE

# 1   Introduction

## 1.1   SCOTTISH ROADS: AN OVERVIEW

The Scottish public road network forms the core of the country's transport system. Its management and development are largely devolved matters and closely connected to the overall transport policies determined by the Scottish Government.

Transport has been the subject of considerable attention by Ministers, Parliament and the public since devolution. This continues a period of UK policy development that started in the mid-1990s, driven by concern about growing road traffic leading to increased congestion and environmental problems throughout the country. A series of policy reviews, White Papers and Acts of Parliament has significantly changed the level of activity over the last 10 years, resulting in a number of very major transport projects currently in the planning stages. In Scotland, the framework is set by the Transport (Scotland) Acts of 2001 and 2005, the 2004 Transport White Paper[1] 'Scotland's Transport Future' and the National Transport Strategy[2] published in December 2006.

Major innovations from this period of change include the provision of powers for local authorities to charge for road use, the establishment of a 'Road Works Commissioner' and the re-introduction of a regional dimension to transport strategy through statutory 'Regional Transport Partnerships'. However, transport policy, including the management of the public road network is likely to continue to be a focus of public and political debate. There is an underlying conflict that remains unresolved between public expectations to benefit from the freedoms provided by car ownership and use, and the economic and environmental costs of road use. The damaging effects of congestion on economic activity and of vehicle emissions on climate change are being increasingly recognised at the same time as vehicle use becomes increasingly essential to people's everyday lives. Moves by UK government to tackle congestion through road pricing policies, and climate change through controls on greenhouse gas emissions, may well have direct or indirect implications for Scottish road users in the future.

In the National Transport Strategy, the Executive identify three 'strategic outcomes' expected to set the context for transport decisions in Scotland for the next 20 years.[3] These are to:

1   Scotland's Transport Future – The Transport White Paper, Scottish Executive, June 2004.
2   Scotland's National transport Strategy, Scottish Executive, December 2006.
3   Scotland's National Transport Strategy, para 10.

- **Improve journey times and connections**, to tackle congestion and the lack of integration and connections in transport which impact on our high level objectives for economic growth, social inclusion, integration and safety;

- **Reduce emissions**, to tackle the issues of climate change, air quality and health improvement which impact on our high level objective for protecting the environment and improving health;

and

- **Improve quality, accessibility and affordability**, to give people a choice of public transport, where availability means better quality transport services and value for money or an alternative to the car.

This policy framework recognises the wide range of road users, who all need to be taken into account in the administration and management of the road network. Users include pedestrians as well as those using vehicles of all types including public transport. Roads also have different functions. They are not simply a means of communication, but form a basic infrastructure for economic activity, providing access to shops, businesses or farms for people on foot or in vehicles. They are the building blocks for towns and villages providing public space that allows them to function and gives them character. Today's policy challenge is to balance the competing needs of these different users and functions within wider policy commitments to support economic activity and protect the environment both locally and globally.

The legal framework provides the tools to support both the provision and the management of transport infrastructure. This volume is concerned primarily with the duties and powers of roads authorities to build, manage and maintain the road network, and the relationship between roads and development. This must increasingly be considered in the context of other functions relating to the regulation of traffic and parking, to public transport provision, and to the promotion of wider economic, social and environmental aims.

## 1.2    HISTORICAL PERSPECTIVE

A short review of the historical development of the public road network demonstrates how the authorities have addressed issues of public road policy in the past. Early statutory provisions placed the burden of local road maintenance on the local community. Under the Statute Labour provisions specified categories of local residents had to provide six days labour each year. These days were known as parish road days. Obviously a maintenance system based on forced labour by unskilled men was far from satisfactory and the practical inadequacies of the system led to the creation of turnpikes. As a result, the burden of funding road maintenance was transferred from the local community to users of the road and the standard of maintenance greatly improved.

Statute Labour was finally abolished by the Highway Act 1835.[3] This Act set a modern framework for road construction and maintenance, which became the responsibility of local authorities which financed the public road network through a system of rates.

The statutory framework for roads was extended throughout the nineteenth century, notably by the Roads and Bridges (Scotland) Act 1878. In 1910, the Road Fund was established to fund road construction from the proceeds of a tax on vehicles; it lasted until 1937 although some of the Fund was used for non-roads purposes from 1926. National government took over direct responsibility for roads of national importance under the Trunk Roads Act 1936; while this has been superseded by further legislation, the principle of trunk and local roads is still in place.

In the second half of the twentieth century, road traffic grew steadily. By the 1960s the need to manage the demand for road space became apparent as it became increasingly difficult to provide roadspace to match demand, especially in urban areas. Two seminal government reports at that time proposed measures to tackle the issue: the Buchanan Report[4] and the Smeed Report.[5] Buchanan identified four possibilities for influencing demand for road space:

1    A system of permits or licences to control entry of vehicles to certain defined zones.

2    A system of pricing the use of road space.

3    Parking policy.

4    Subsidising public transport so that it offers considerable financial advantage over the use of cars.

Smeed examined in considerably more detail the economic theory and technology options for pricing the use of road space to achieve a balance between supply and demand, using market principles. It is interesting to note the similarities between current debate and the conclusions of these 1960s reports.

## 1.3   ROADS (SCOTLAND) ACT 1984

In the 1960s, the Scottish Law Commission identified a need to modernise the statutory framework of roads law and this led to the enactment of the Roads (Scotland) Act 1970, which introduced new powers and duties, but did not consolidate the law of roads in Scotland. Consolidation came with the Roads (Scotland) Act 1984 – an act to make

3    For further reading see Road and bridge making on the main routes in and around Dalkeith 1750–1850 by Professor Roland Paxton MBE CEng FICE FRSE.
4    Traffic in Towns (the Buchanan Report) HMSO 1963.
5    Road Pricing: The Economic and Technical Possibilities (the Smeed Report) HMSO 1964.

provision as regards roads in Scotland and for connected purposes. In his annotations to the 1984 Act, Robert S Jack states:

'The principal effect of the Act is to bring to an end the anomalous situation in which a different set of legislative provisions applied to the former burgh areas than that which applied to the landward areas. This situation, which has its roots in the historical development of local government in Scotland, became increasingly intolerable after 1975 when the regional councils were established and became the local highways authorities for both the landward and the former burgh areas. The confusion and difficulties arising from such a situation are obvious, but, as if they were not enough, the situation was further complicated by various local enactments of the former local authorities dealing with roads and streets which applied only to certain defined areas.'

The 1984 Act is the current legislative framework for the construction, management, maintenance and use of the Scottish road network. It deals with the powers and duties of roads authorities in relation to both public and private roads. It also makes provision in relation to new road construction, road improvement and maintenance, works affecting roads, access and stopping up, bridges, tunnels and diversion of water, interference, damage and land ownership as well as dealing with various offences and administrative matters regarding roads.

When this Act came into force all statutory references to 'highways' were repealed. There are no longer highways or highways authorities in Scotland, only roads and roads authorities.

In 1996, regional councils with their strategic roads functions were abolished and the national road network became the responsibility of the new unitary authorities with the exception of the system of motorways and trunk roads. These are now the responsibility of Transport Scotland, an executive agency of the Scottish Executive established in January 2006.

The statutory Regional Transport Partnerships established in 2006 are not roads authorities. However, Ministers can, by order, transfer any function to be exercised by an RTP instead of or concurrently with the body currently holding it if considered necessary to fulfil the RTP's Transport Strategy.

## 1.4   OTHER SOURCES OF ROADS LAW

The law relating to roads in Scotland is primarily found in Acts of Parliament and delegated legislation. Principally Scottish roads law has a statutory basis. There are some court cases interpreting the statutory provisions but not as many as in other more frequently litigated areas, such as planning law. The one exception is case law relating to road traffic offences, some of which deal with relevant matters for roads law, such as the definition of a road. The common law also has an important role in relation to the liability of roads authorities.

## 1.4.1   LEGISLATION

The main statutes are:

1.   The Roads (Scotland) Act 1984

2.   The Road Traffic Regulation Act 1984

3.   The New Roads and Street Works Act 1991

4.   The Transport (Scotland) Act 2001

5.   The Transport (Scotland) Act 2005

6.   The Environmental Assessment (Scotland) 2005

7.   The Town and Country Planning (Scotland) Act 1997

8.   The Planning etc. (Scotland) Act 2006

9.   The Transport and Works (Scotland) Act 2007

**The Roads (Scotland) 1984 Act** is the most important Act in this context. It is the principal source of roads law in Scotland.

**The Road Traffic Regulation Act 1984** empowers local traffic authorities regulating the use of a road to address matters such as road safety, damage prevention or facilitating passage on the road of any class of traffic. To give effect to transport policies and objectives, including road safety, measures to manage the way in which a road is used by moving traffic or parked and waiting vehicles are frequently required. These may include measures such as speed limits, traffic signals, bus lanes, parking restrictions or access controls in town centres. The legal basis for introducing these is principally the Road Traffic Regulation Act 1984 which provides for 'Traffic Regulation Orders' to be promoted by traffic authorities.

**The New Roads and Street Works Act 1991** makes provision for the cost of new road construction to be recovered by charging tolls and it also deals in some detail with the need to ensure that road works carried out by statutory undertakers and others minimise disruption to traffic, do not jeopardise public safety and are properly reinstated.

**The Transport (Scotland) Acts of 2001 and 2005** both introduced further measures affecting the management of the road network. The 2001 Act provided powers for local authorities to introduce road user charges and enabling powers for the replacement of Joint Bridge Boards with new authorities responsible for a wider range of functions. The 2005 Act established a Scottish Road Works Commissioner, and a Register, aimed largely improving the effectiveness of the road works provisions of the 1991 Act discussed above.

**The Environmental Assessment (Scotland) Act 2005** was enacted by the Scottish Parliament pursuant to Council Directive No 2001/42/EC on the assessment of the effects of certain plans and programmes on the environment (the SEA Directive).[6] Under this Act, any plan or programme which is prepared or adopted or both by a 'responsible authority' must carry out an environmental assessment in relation to that plan or programme. A responsible authority is any person, body or office holder exercising functions of a public character. This means that the National Transport Strategy, Regional Transport Strategies and Local Transport Strategies must be the subject of an environmental assessment.

**The Planning etc. (Scotland) Act 2006** sets out the legislative framework for a fundamental review of the planning system. It does so by amending the provisions of the Town and Country Planning (Scotland) Act 1997, which is referred to in the 2006 Act as the "Principal Act". Amongst its provisions, it gives a statutory basis to the National Planning Framework,[7] which is a strategy for Scotland's spatial development, and imposes a statutory duty on the Scottish Ministers to exercise their functions in relation to the National Planning Framework with the objective of contributing to sustainable development. It replaces the phrase 'development control' with 'development management' and it introduces a hierarchy of developments known as 'national developments', 'major developments' and 'local developments'.[8] In the past, roads authorities may have used the Notice of Intention to Develop procedure[9] to obtain deemed planning permission for a new road proposal. However, with effect from 1 April 2007, that procedure was discontinued by The Planning Etc (Scotland) Act 2006 (Consequential Provisions) Order 2007. The effect is that local authorities must now apply for planning permission for their own developments where relevant.[10] Any NID process, which had commenced and been the subject of published public notices on or before 31 March 2007, is allowed to continue. Applications for local authority development now fall to be notified to the Scottish Ministers if the development proposal would be contrary to the development plan or has been the subject of a substantial body of objections.[11] If an application for local authority development falls to be notified to the Scottish Ministers, the authority must submit, in addition to application and supporting documents set out in the Circular 5/07[12] a statement relating to non-inclusion in the development plan and details of alternative development. It is assumed that the Scottish

6    See Circular 2/1004: Strategic Environmental Assessment for Development Planning; the Environmental Assessment of Plans and Programmes (Scotland) Regulations 2004.
7    Section 3A of the Town and Country Planning (Scotland) Act 1997.
8    Section 26A of the 1997 Act.
9    The Town and Country Planning (Development by Planning Authorities) (Scotland) Regulations 1981.
10   See The Scottish Executive Development Department Circular 3/2007.
11   The Town and Country Planning (Notification of Applications) (Scotland) Direction 2007.
12   The Scottish Executive Development Department Circular 5/2007: Notification of Planning Applications.

Transport Appraisal (STAG) prepared to support any major road or transport proposal would rely on the option appraisal and selection process to satisfy the second requirement. However, this might raise interesting questions about the relationship between STAG and the development plan process.

Roads may also be affected by the introduction of street-running trams. These will be subject to an order procedure under the Transport and Works (Scotland) Act 2007, similar to that of the 1984 Roads (Scotland) Act for new roads.

In addition to statutes, there is a significant amount of delegated or secondary legislation. These are known as statutory instruments and take the form of orders or regulations which are made by the Scottish Ministers under powers devolved by statute. Since the setting up of the Scottish Parliament, there have been some Scottish Statutory Instruments[13] dealing with roads matters. For example, the Environmental Impact Assessment (Scotland) Regulations 1999,[14] various orders relating to the Skye Bridge culminating with an order[15] which revoked the toll charges on the bridge, The Forth Estuary Transport Authority Order 2002[16] establishing new management arrangements for the Forth road bridge, and an order under the 2005 Act establishing seven statutory Regional Transport Partnerships covering the whole of Scotland.[17]

There are also some statutory and non-statutory Codes of Practice made under the 1991 Act. For example, the 'Specification for the Reinstatement of Openings in Highways' published in June 1992.[18]

From 1997 onwards both the drafts and the full text of legislation and statutory instruments are available via the Internet.[19] Proposals for legislation and discussion documents can be found on the Westminster Parliament Website.[20] It is also worth browsing the open government site. For Scottish proposals visit the Scottish Parliament or Scottish Government websites.[21]


## 1.4.2  EUROPEAN LAW

The United Kingdom, as a member of the European Union,[22] is bound by European law. In addition, the Scotland Act 1998 specifically provides

13  SSIs.
14  SSI 1999/1.
15  SSI 2005/167.
16  Forth Bridge – SSI 2002/178.
17  RTPs – SSI 2005/622.
18  SI 1992/1498; SI 1992/1499; SI 1992/1500 and SI 1992/1501.
19  UK legislation (primary and secondary) can be found at http://www.opsi.gov.uk/legislation/about_legislation.htm
20  www.parliament.uk/
21  www.scottish.parliament.uk/; www.scotland.gov.uk/
22  European Communities Act 1972, s 2.

that the Scottish Parliament cannot competently enact legislation, nor can a member of the Scottish Executive make delegated legislation, or do anything else, which is incompatible with the European Convention on Human Rights (ECHR) as imported into UK law by the Human Rights Act 1998, or with EU law generally.[23] Unquestionably, the influence of European law will continue to develop and grow in relation to Scottish roads law.

EU law related specifically to roads and transport aims to support basic EU Treaty obligations for the removal of barriers to a single European market and the reinforcement of European economic and social cohesion. EC Directives have been introduced in the field of environmental assessment of both transport plans[24] and of individual road construction projects,[25] in the definition of certain strategic routes as part of the 'Trans-European transport networks' (TEN-T).[26] Decision 1692/96/EC of the European Parliament and of the Council on Community Guidelines for the development of the trans-European transport network on the interoperability of electronic tolling schemes,[27] and for any road user charges applied to goods vehicles over 3.5 tonnes (the 'Eurovignette directive').[28] There has also been a requirement to charge Value Added Tax (VAT) on bridge tolls in the UK as a result of a European Court ruling.

### 1.4.3   CASE LAW

There are relatively few court cases interpreting the legislative provisions relevant to roads. Unlike planning legislation, this area has not been the subject of a great deal of litigation although both roads and planning involve the discharge of duties and the exercise of powers by public authorities whose decisions may be challenged in the courts. It is possible that a legal challenge of a decision of a roads authority is simply not viable in commercial terms, unlike many planning decisions. Whatever the reason, there is little case law available to interpret the wording of the legislation.

### 1.4.4   ENGLISH LAW

The law of roads in England and Wales is similar to that in Scotland but it is not the same. As in Scotland, there is a statutory basis for much of the law, but the legislation is different. The equivalent of the 1984 Act is

---

23   Scotland Act 1998, ss 29 and 57(2).
24   Directive 2001/42/EC of the European Parliament and of the Council on the assessment of the effects of certain plans and programmes on the environment.
25   See further Chapter 5, pp 73 ff.
26   Decision 1692/96/EC of the European Parliament and of the Council on Community Guidelines for the development of the trans-European transport network.
27   Directive 2004/52/EC (OJ L166, 30.4.2004, pp. 124–143).
28   Directive 99/62/EC as amended by Directive 2006/38/EC (OJ L 157, 9.6.2006, pp. 8–23).

the Highways Act 1980. In England and Wales the term 'highway' is used instead of road. While the New Roads and Street Works Act 1991 applies north and south of the border, different parts of the Act relate to England and Wales.

### 1.4.5 THE HUMAN RIGHTS ACT 1998

The Human Rights Act 1998 came into force on 2 October 2000. This Act introduced the European Convention on Human Rights into UK domestic law. The Act provides that it is unlawful for a public body to act in a way that is incompatible with a Convention right. The Convention rights which may be of relevance in relation to roads and transportation are:

- A fair hearing in civil and criminal proceedings (Article 6).

- Protection of Property (Article 1).

- Respect for family and private life (Article 8).

Article 6 of the Convention provides '[i]n the determination of his civil rights and obligations or of any criminal charge against him, everyone is entitled to a fair and public hearing within a reasonable time by an independent and impartial tribunal established by law.' In the case of *Bryan v United Kingdom*,[29] the European Court held that the requirements of Article 6 would be met even if the tribunal were restricted to questions of law. The court considered whether the availability of a court review was sufficient to allow a planning procedure to comply with Article 6 and concluded that it was sufficient on the facts of that case.[30] Although that principle was challenged in the case of *County Properties Limited v The Scottish Ministers*,[31] it now appears to be settled following the decision of the House of Lords in the case of *R (Alconbury Developments Ltd and others) v Secretary of State for the Environment, Transport and the Regions [2001] 2 WLR 1389*. This means that the existence of a right of appeal to the Court of Session as set out in Schedule 2 to the 1984 Act should render the making and confirming of orders and schemes covered by Schedule 2 compliant with the relevant provisions of the European Convention on Human Rights.

---

29  Bryan v United Kingdom 21 EHRR 342.
30  For further reading see article by John M Watchman (1996) 53 SPEL, 10–11.
31  25 July 2000 unreported.

# 2 Roads Administration

## 2.1 INTRODUCTION

Responsibility for the road network is allocated between national and local government. Section 1 of the Roads (Scotland) Act 1984 specifies the powers and duties of 'local roads authorities' whilst section 2 sets out the responsibility of the Secretary of State for Scotland as a 'roads authority'. The functions of the Secretary of State for Scotland were transferred to the Scottish Ministers by section 53 of the Scotland Act 1998.[1]

## 2.2 THE SCOTTISH PARLIAMENT

The Scottish Parliament assumed its full legislative powers on 1 July 1999. In relation to devolved matters, it can enact new legislation and amend or repeal existing legislation.[2] In some instances, there is what is known as executive devolution. This means that, although the power to legislate remains with Westminster, the Scottish Executive will carry out ministerial functions in connection with the operation of that legislation in Scotland. Certain road traffic functions are within the scope of executive devolution.[3]

The Scottish Parliament has overall responsibility for roads law in Scotland. The Scotland Act 1998 does not specify the responsibilities of the Scottish Parliament but instead specifies the powers that are reserved to the United Kingdom Parliament. These reserved powers are listed in Schedule 5 to the Act. The relevant reserved powers in relation to roads are listed under the heading of 'Road Transport' and principally deal with road traffic matters. The following powers are reserved:

- the issue of international driving licenses and recognition of foreign licenses;

- the licensing of public service and goods vehicle operators;

- various aspects of road traffic law such as traffic regulation on special roads;

- pedestrian crossings;

- traffic signs;

- speed limits;

1 Scotland Act 1998 (c 46).
2 Ie legislation enacted by the United Kingdom Parliament.
3 SA 1998, s 63; Scotland Act 1998 (Transfer of Functions to the Scottish Ministers etc) Order 1999 SI 1999/1750.

- road safety;
- construction and use of vehicles;
- driver licensing;
- driving instruction;
- aspects of liability and insurance;
- road traffic offences;
- revocation of probationary drivers' licences, as well as the licensing and registration of vehicles;
- the regulation of hours or periods of work by bus and goods drivers;
- the conditions for international transport of passengers or goods; and
- the regulation of driving instructors.[4]

There is provision for consultation with the Scottish Ministers in relation to these matters.[5]

There are two exceptions to these reservations, namely road safety information and training[6] and payment for the treatment of road traffic casualties.[7] This means that the Scottish Parliament can legislate in relation to these two areas.

### 2.2.1   THE SCOTTISH EXECUTIVE

The Scottish Executive comprises the First Minister, other Ministers appointed by the First Minister,[8] the Lord Advocate and the Solicitor General for Scotland.[9] The members of the Scottish Executive are collectively known as the Scottish Ministers.[10] The Scottish Ministers are collectively responsible for any acts or omissions of any member of the Scottish Executive.[11] However, this collective responsibility does not apply to functions conferred upon the First Minister alone or to the retained functions of the Lord Advocate.[12] Junior ministers are not members of the Scottish Executive but are members of the Scottish Administration. In September 2007, the Scottish Executive was renamed the 'Scottish Government'; however, this was a policy decision to clarify the governmental role of the Scottish Executive. Legal references to the Scottish Executive remain correct.

4   SA 1998, Sch 5, Section E1.
5   SI 1999/1750.
6   Which is exercised concurrently with UK Ministers under SA 1998, s 56.
7   SA 1998, Sch 5, Section E1.
8   Under SA 1998, s 47.
9   SA 1998, s 44(1).
10   SA 1998, s 44(2).
11   SA 1998, s 52(4).
12   SA 1998, s 52(5). As to 'Retained functions', see s 52(6).

## 2.2.2   THE SCOTTISH MINISTERS

The Scotland Act 1998 provides for the transfer of functions formerly exercised by Ministers of the Crown to the Scottish Ministers.[13] Any legislation, instrument or document prior to the commencement of the Act which refers to a Minister of the Crown is taken to refer to or include a reference to the Scottish Ministers, where this is necessary in connection with the exercise of a function by a member of the Scottish Executive within a devolved area.[14] This includes the Roads (Scotland) Act 1984, the Scottish provisions of the New Roads and Street Works Act 1991 and the Town and Country Planning (Scotland) Act 1997 together with delegated legislation made under these Acts. Any member of the Scottish Executive may exercise the statutory functions of the Scottish Ministers.[15]

## 2.2.3   THE SCOTTISH ADMINISTRATION

The Scottish Administration comprises the Scottish Ministers and their staff[16] as well as some holders of non ministerial offices such as the Registrar General of Births, Deaths and Marriages.[17]

The Scottish Administration largely inherited the functions formerly exercised by the Scottish Office. The staff remain members of the Home Civil Service.[18]

The detailed management structure within the Administration is subject to continuous review and adjustment. A major restructuring took place following the Parliamentary elections of May 2007, with the former departmental structure replaced by a larger number of Directorates responsible to a corporate Strategic Board consisting of the Permanent Secretary (Head of the Scottish Administration) and five Directors-General.

The roads responsibilities of the Scottish Ministers are administered by a Transport Directorate, responsible for:

- Coordinating the National Transport Strategy for Scotland

- Liaison with regional transport partnerships, including monitoring of funding

- Sustainable transport, road safety and accessibility

- Local roads policy and casework

13   SA 1998, s 53.
14   SA 1998, s 117.
15   SA 1998, s 52(3). But see p14 above re the First Minister and the Lord Advocate.
16   SA 1998, s 126(6).
17   SA 1998, s 126(7), (8).
18   SA 1998, s 51(2).

- Aviation, bus, freight and taxi policy

- Ferries, ports and harbours

An Executive Agency, Transport Scotland, was established in 2006 to manage the trunk road network, as well as the rail system within Scotland. An aim of the new arrangements is to achieve better integration across transport modes. Transport Scotland has five Directorates:

- Rail Delivery

- Strategy and Investment

- Trunk Road Infrastructure and Professional Services (TRIPS)

- Trunk Road Network Management

- Finance and Corporate Services

The Scottish Ministers are responsible for the national through traffic routes, which include trunk roads or special roads provided by them or other roads built by them but not entered on the local roads authority's list of roads.[19] The Scottish Ministers must maintain a list of roads[20] for which they are responsible and this list is open for public inspection free of charge at such reasonable times and places as they may determine.[19] Every road under the responsibility of the Scottish Ministers vests in them for the purposes of their functions as roads authority. However, any such vesting does not confer upon them any heritable right in relation to the road.[19]

### 2.2.4   MANAGEMENT AND MAINTENANCE OF THE NATIONAL ROAD NETWORK

Although the Scottish Ministers are the roads authority in respect of certain designated roads, the Roads (Scotland) Act 1984 permits them to enter into agreements with local roads authorities for the discharge of their functions.[21] It is specifically provided that this is an agency agreement and does not affect the status of the Scottish Ministers as roads authority. Since 1996 the contract for the management and maintenance of the national road network has been subjected to competitive tender.

### 2.2.5   DEVELOPMENT MANAGEMENT

In the development industry, most people will be involved with the Scottish Executive as statutory consultees in the development management system.[22] Although the Scottish planning system is

19   See Chapter 4.
20   Section 2 of the RSA 1984.
21   R(S)A 1984, s 4.
22   See Chapter 7.

undergoing fundamental review following the enactment of the Planning Etc.(Scotland) Act 2006, the role of the Scottish Executive, as a consultee, is unlikely to change. Following the enactment of the 2006 Act, the Scottish Executive will be issuing a wide range of secondary legislation and policy statements in support of the new planning system.

Under the Town and Country Planning (General Development Procedure) Order 1992, the Scottish Ministers must be consulted if the proposed development constitutes development of land within sixty-seven metres of the middle of a road within their responsibility. They must also be consulted if the development consists of or includes the formation, laying out or alteration of any means of access to such a road. Transport Scotland, an Executive Agency, acts on behalf of Ministers in this process.

Transport Scotland generally manages this process by the appointment of private transportation consultants who review the Transport Assessments submitted by applicants for planning permission for development which may affect a road under the responsibility of the Scottish Ministers. SPP 17[23] states that direct access to a motorway or motorway slip road is not permitted from a private development other than a motorway service area approved by the Scottish Executive. Where a local authority or developers propose a new or expanded motorway junction a full STAG[24] appraisal will be required by Transport Scotland. Following full Transport Assessment, SPP 17 states that the residual traffic impact of developments on the strategic road network should be mitigated to achieve 'no net detriment' to the flow and safety of traffic on the network. For further reading see Planning Advice Note 66 'Best Practice in Handling Planning Applications Affecting Trunk Roads' (2003)

The term consultant's report on the application and its supporting documentation will form the basis of Transport Scotland's formal consultation response to the planning authority. In practice, the applicant's transportation consultants will liaise with the term consultants, who may request additional information on the application. In recent years Transport Scotland's role in the development management process has been increasing. They now become involved in the development appraisal which may, at their request, include a STAG approach to transport options for the proposed development. They also scrutinise proposals for compliance with national transport policy and provide input to proposed Travel Plans. If a public inquiry is held, the term consultants will usually present evidence on behalf of Transport Scotland.

If the agency is not satisfied with the potential impact or effect of a proposed development on the operation of the trunk road system, they are likely to recommend refusal of planning permission. Although their consultation response is a material consideration to be taken into account by the local planning authority when determining the application, it is

23   SPP17: Planning for Transport paragraph 71.
24   Scottish Transport Appraisal Guidance.

not binding upon the authority. However, if a planning authority decides to grant planning permission, contrary to the recommendation of Transport Scotland, the Scottish Ministers may exercise their power to call in the application for determination at national level.[25]

Planning Circular 5/07[26] provides guidance on the circumstances in which the Scottish Ministers may intervene to call in an application for planning permission. These circumstances include:

"Where the planning authority proposes to grant planning permission against the advice of relevant national advisers (e.g. SNH, SEPA, HSE, Transport Scotland, etc) and where the Ministers have not been convinced by the authority's justification for doing so."

### 2.2.6   PROPOSED PLANNING CONDITIONS TO AVOID CALL IN

Another legislative tool was introduced by the Town and Country Planning (General Development Procedure) (Scotland) Amendment Order 2007. Article 2(4) enables the Scottish Ministers to direct planning authorities to consider attaching conditions when granting planning permission. This tool will be useful in circumstances in which the Scottish Ministers think that planning permission could be granted if a particular condition or conditions were to be imposed by the planning authority. On receipt of the Direction, the authority will consider the matter and then inform the Ministers either that it has decided to impose the condition or that the condition is not necessary. If the proposed condition is to be imposed or if the Minister is convinced that it is not necessary, the authority could proceed to grant planning permission. This is a useful tool which hopefully will not be needed too often, if the consultation process is effective and thorough. However, it provides a more straightforward procedure than having to resort to call in, and possible public inquiry, just to add a condition on to the planning permission.

## 2.3   LOCAL ROADS AUTHORITIES

Each Scottish local authority[27] is a local roads authority for the purposes of the Roads (Scotland) Act 1984.[28] Each one is the local roads authority for all roads or proposed roads in its area, other than roads falling within the responsibility of the Scottish Ministers.

---

25   Town & Country Planning (Scotland) Act 1997, s 46.
26   Notification of Planning Applications.
27   Each council constituted under the Local Government etc (Scotland) Act 1994, s 2.
28   R(S)A 1984, s 151.

## 2.3.1 MANAGEMENT AND MAINTENANCE OF THE LOCAL ROAD NETWORK

The powers and duties of the local roads authority are set out in section 1 of the 1984 Act. These are as follows:

1. *The management and maintenance of all roads currently entered in its list of public roads.* This is the principal duty of the local roads authority. Its scope includes the physical maintenance and improvement of the road network as well as a range of other measures designed to ensure road safety. (As to the list of public roads, see Chapter 4, p 59 ff. See also Chapters 10, 11.)

2. *A wide power to reconstruct, alter, widen, improve or renew any road on the public list.* If such works constitute development, planning permission is necessary. However, certain road works are expressly excluded from the statutory definition of development, which means that planning permission is not required.[29]

3. A power to determine the means by which the public right of passage may be exercised over the public road, or any part of it. This power includes the power to redetermine by order the means of exercise of the public right of passage.[30]

## 2.3.2 DEVELOPMENT MANAGEMENT

Another important function of the local roads authority is its role in development management. Before the creation of unitary local authorities in 1996, there was a formal requirement for the planning authority to consult the local roads authority before determining an application for planning permission. This is no longer a formal requirement but planning officers continue to ask for a written consultation response from their colleagues dealing with the Council's roads functions.

There has been a good deal of change within local government since the creation of unitary authorities in 1996 and it appears that there will be further change within the new administrations, which were elected in May 2007. A significant number of members of Scottish local authorities are new members so training will be no doubt be a priority, especially when the provisions of the Planning Etc (Scotland) Act 2006 come into full effect. The new planning system should see an increasing number of planning decisions being delegated to officers. Effective consultation between officers charged with managing the roads function and the planning case officer will become even more important.

---

29  Town and Country Planning Act 1997, s 26. See further Chapter 5.
30  R(S)A 1984, s 152(2). See further Chapter 9.

### 2.3.3    REGIONAL TRANSPORT PARTNERSHIPS

The Transport (Scotland) Act 2005 introduced statutory Regional Transport Partnerships, of which seven cover the whole of Scotland as from April 2006. Powers available to the Partnerships were initially limited, with a first duty of each Partnership being to produce a Regional Transport Strategy (see Chapter 3). The exceptions are the West of Scotland RTP to which all non-rail powers of the former Strathclyde PTA were transferred, and the South West Scotland and Shetland RTPs which took on or shared the statutory transport powers of their single coterminous local authorities.[31]

The Act allows for further transfer of transport-related functions to the RTPs [TSA 2005 s14], to be exercised either in place of or concurrently with the body or bodies currently exercising them, subject to Ministerial approval. In most cases this would involve transfer from constituent local authorities, but could potentially include the Scottish Executive or other public agencies. It would be possible for RTPs to become the roads authority for some or all of the roads within their area under this legislation.[32]

RTPs will also have a role in development management supplementing that of local roads authorities. For major new developments, the location of the development, the application of parking standards and the transport-related conditions attached to planning permission can have a significant impact on transport services and infrastructure. It is likely that RTPs will become involved both in developing appropriate policies and in consultation on specific developments.

31    SSI 2006 No 106 The Transfer of Functions from the Strathclyde Passenger Transport Authority and the Strathclyde Passenger Transport Executive to the West of Scotland Transport Partnership Order 2006; SSI 2006 No 527. The Transfer of Functions to the Shetland Transport Partnership Order 2006; SSI 2006 No 538 The Transfer of Functions to the South-West of Scotland Transport Partnership Order 2006.

32    See for example SESTRAN RTP 2007 Policies 8, 20, 21.

# 3 The Policy Context

## 3.1 AIMS OF TRANSPORT POLICY

Roads, and transport in general, are provided for the pursuance of wider goals, not for their own sake. They are essential to allow the movement of people and goods necessary for our everyday economic and social activities, within the spatial framework of locations where these activities are based. The beneficial effects of the transport system in facilitating activity can be counterbalanced, however, by damaging secondary effects such as congestion and pollution. The benefits may also be unevenly distributed, leaving groups in the population excluded from access to activities, or bearing the burden of the indirect negative impacts of the transport system.

Transport needs are constantly evolving to reflect the changing world. Their consideration is therefore a dynamic process taking into account changing economy and wealth, demography, technology and social mores. A key factor over the last decades has been the growth in car ownership, which has given rise to major changes in activity patterns. This pattern of change is still taking place: car ownership in Scotland has grown by 25% over the last ten years, but remains well below the European average, and around half that of the USA.

However, there are already concerns about traffic congestion and damage to the local and global environment from current levels of traffic. Much of the policy framework described below is aimed at tackling these problems now and in the future while at the same time maintaining a favourable environment for economic growth and social justice. The key to reconciling these potentially conflicting aims is adoption of the principle of 'sustainable development'.

### 3.1.1 SUSTAINABLE DEVELOPMENT

A widely accepted definition of sustainable development was provided in a 1987 report from the World Commission on Environment and Development entitled *Our Common Future*. It is 'development that meets the needs of the present without compromising the ability of future generations to meet their own needs'. In the years since 1987, the UK government has established a wide-ranging policy framework supporting this principle, most recently in its strategy document 'Securing the Future' published in March 2005.[1] A Scottish strategy 'Choosing our Future' was published in December 2005. Sustainable Development

1   Securing the Future – delivering UK sustainable development strategy, Con: 6467 HMSO March 2005.

principles underpin the National Transport Strategy, as well as other strategies relevant to roads and transport including the Framework for Economic Development in Scotland,[2] Scotland's Climate Change Programme,[3] the Air Quality Strategy for England, Scotland, Wales and Northern Ireland[4] and the National Planning Framework for Scotland.[5]

Future updates to these strategies will be influenced by two major, complementary reviews commissioned by UK government and completed in late 2006: the Stern Review[6] and the Eddington Transport Study.[7] The Stern Review considered the impacts of climate change on the nation's economy, and the Eddington Study considered transport's role in sustaining the UK's economic productivity and competitiveness. Some key conclusions of the Eddington Study are that:

-    Transport matters for the economic performance of countries and regions.

-    In mature economies like the UK, the main focus should be on the performance of the existing network, particularly where capacity is stretched, as demonstrated, for instance, through congestion or unreliability.

-    The efficiency with which existing transport networks are used can be just as important as the underlying investment.

While the recommendations of the Eddington study are not directly applicable to Scotland, the analysis is relevant, and will inevitably influence Scottish as well as national UK decision-making.

The Stern Review does have a UK-wide perspective, and has been followed by a UK Climate Change Bill that includes a target to reduce Carbon emissions by 60% by 2050. The Transport sector, and Scotland, will have to play their parts in achieving this target, and consultation on a Scottish Climate Change Bill is expected to start in early 2008. In 2004 the transport sector contributed 22% of Scottish carbon emissions, with 86% of this coming from road transport. Carbon emissions from transport are increasing, in contrast to all other sectors other than households.[8]

2    Scottish Executive, Framework for Economic Development in Scotland, September 2004.
3    Scottish Executive, Changing Our Ways: Scotland's Climate Change Programme, March 2006.
4    Cm 4548, Air Quality Strategy for England, Scotland, Wales and Northern Ireland, January 2000.
5    Scottish Executive, National Planning Framework for Scotland, April 2004. See also NPF2 Consultation Draft published January 2008.
6    HM Treasury, Stern Review on the Economics of Climate Change, November 2006.
7    HM Treasury and Department for Transport, The Eddington Transport Study, December 2006.
8    Scottish Executive, National Transport Strategy, December 2006: pages 15–16.

### 3.1.2 STRATEGIC ENVIRONMENTAL APPRAISAL

For many years, individual projects have been subject to Environmental Impact Assessment.[9] More recently, EU legislation[10] has led to a requirement for Strategic Environmental Appraisal (SEA): formal environmental appraisal of plans and programmes of work whose future implementation could have an impact on the environment. Roads and transport plans are included in the list of topics for which such appraisal is required. The Scottish legislation[11] requires views to be sought at various points in the development of such a plan from Scottish Natural Heritage, the Scottish Environmental Protection Agency, Scottish Ministers (in particular Historic Scotland) and from the public. An environmental report describing potential impacts, actions to mitigate them and the responses to consultation and consequent changes to the plan must be published together with the plan or programme. A detailed SEA 'toolkit' is available from the Scottish Executive on the internet.[12]

## 3.2 SPATIAL PLANNING

Transport is required because economic and social activity requires the movement of people and goods between locations, for example from producers to shops, or from home to school. Decisions about the location of activities therefore have a critical impact on transport demand. Similarly the existence of transport supply can itself influence location decisions. An obvious example is the desire of logistics companies to locate warehouses and distribution centres close to motorway interchanges, allowing easy access to the strategic road network. Spatial planning policies attempt to manage these interactions to obtain the best balance of locational decisions to achieve sustainable development objectives.

### 3.2.1 NATIONAL PLANNING POLICY

The first National Planning Framework (NPF) was published by the Scottish Executive in 2004, and is to be refreshed every four years. It is intended to give effect to the principles of sustainable development[13] and provide a mechanism for ensuring the delivery of national policy and investment programmes. In the White Paper: *Modernising the Planning System*, published in June 2005, the Executive suggest that "we want the second NPF to place more emphasis on implementation than its predecessor... The NPF will identify responsibilities and outputs for

9   See Chapter 5 for details of Environmental Impact Assessment.
10  Council Directive No 2001/42/EC.
11  The Environmental Assessment (Scotland) Act 2005, SSI 2004 No. 258, The Environmental Assessment of Plans and Programmes (Scotland) Regulations 2004.
12  SEA Toolkit, http://www.scotland.gov.uk/Publications/2006/09/13104943/3.
13  Scottish Executive, National Planning Framework, 2004: para 54.

locally-delivered services and facilities in key policy areas such as health, education, affordable housing and waste management. The NPF will be closely linked to the Infrastructure Investment Plan and the investment programmes of public agencies and infrastructure providers. The next NPF[14] will provide a stronger context for development plans and planning decisions. This will help establish and deliver a clear strategy for Scotland's spatial development in the long term." Combined with the changes to the development plan system summarised below, this represents a significant change to the overall planning context in Scotland. The Planning Etc. (Scotland) Act 2006 gives effect to amendments to the planning system proposed in *Modernising the Planning System*. It updates some aspects of the Town & Country Planning (Scotland) Act 1997. Parts 1, 2 and 3 of the Act are particularly relevant in the context of transport and planning issues. Part 1 gives a statutory basis to the National Planning Framework, while Part 2 revises the development plan structure, including giving Planning authorities a new duty to contribute to sustainable development. Part 3 covers changes to development management (formerly 'development control') arrangements. Of particular interest is S23 which amends S75 of the 1997 Act concerning planning agreements – now to be known as 'Planning Obligations'. These may include the provision of road improvements or other transport measures.

A suite of planning policy statements and advice notes is published by the Scottish Executive.[15] The first of these, SPP1[16] 'The Planning System', highlights the importance of the planning system in delivering a sustainable, effective and integrated transport system: "Development Plans and transport strategies must work to a common agenda".

Detailed guidance on the relationship between planning and transport is provided in SPP17. This sets out how integration of land use, economic development, environmental issues and transport planning can contribute to sustainable development, in particular through development at locations readily accessible by public transport, walking and cycling networks, where car dependency is mitigated. SPP17 provides advice on both the provision of transport infrastructure, and the management of transport aspects of new development. Tools to ensure that new development maximises scope for use of sustainable modes of transport are emphasised, including transport assessment, travel plans and standards for parking provision. A guide to Transport Assessment[17] is published in parallel to SPP17 setting out a procedure to be undertaken as part of the submission of a planning application.

Other Guidance supports a co-ordinated approach between specific types of locational decision and existing and planned transport

14  Consultation Draft of NPF2 was published in January 2008.
15  An index of these is available at http://www.scotland.gov.uk/Topics/ Planning/PolicyLegislation/Policy.
16  Scottish Planning Policy 1: The Planning System.
17  Scottish Executive, Transport Assessment and Implementation: A Guide, August 2005.

infrastructure, for example SPP 2 **Economic Development**, SPP 3 **Planning for Housing**, SPP 4 **Planning for Minerals** and SPP 15 **Planning for Rural Development**. Location specific policy statements may also be produced relating to sites considered to be of national strategic importance.

Planning Advice Notes (PANs) provide more detailed advice on specific issues. For example PAN75 "Planning for Transport", August 2005 aims to create greater awareness of how linkages between planning and transport can be managed, building on the policy framework of SPP17. PAN76 New Residential Streets November 2005 provides advice on the design of better quality residential streets and clarifies the roles and responsibilities of those involved.

## 3.2.2 LOCAL AND REGIONAL PLANNING POLICIES

As indicated, the Planning Etc. (Scotland) Act 2006 sets out a revised framework for development plans. Structure Plans are replaced by 'Strategic Development Plans' covering Scotland's four city regions and dealing with key land and infrastructure issues which cross planning authority boundaries. Local Development Plans will cover the whole country, and will have to be in conformity with the strategic plans where these exist. Elsewhere they form a unitary development plan. A more streamlined approach to plan making and review is set out. In relation to transport, there will be a particularly close relationship between the new Strategic Development Plans for urban areas and the Regional Transport Strategies (see below) covering those areas.

The definition and designation of the new Strategic Planning Authorities and regulations concerning the new form of development plans are due to be in place in late 2008.[18]

Locations considered to be of national strategic importance may be identified in the National Planning Framework, and a statutory planning framework prepared. To date only one area, West Edinburgh, has been identified in this way. A 'West Edinburgh Planning Framework' (West Edinburgh Planning Framework (2003) ISBN: 07559 07965) has been prepared and published, and development plans will need to be consistent with this.

Development plans set the framework for individual developments, including policies relating to transport impacts and access provision aimed at supporting overall transport strategy based on the prinicples of SPP17. Certain types of development will require Transport Assessments to be undertaken and appropriate mitigation measures to be implemented as a condition for planning permission to be granted.[19]

18  See http://www.scotland.gov.uk/Publications/2007/06/19143600/1.
19  This topic is covered in detail in Chapter 5.

## 3.3   TRANSPORT STRATEGY

### 3.3.1   NATIONAL TRANSPORT STRATEGY

The first Scottish National Transport Strategy (NTS) was published in December 2006. This follows a number of White Papers, and two Transport Acts.[20] There is now a complex structure of national, regional and local policy-making for transport in Scotland, with a range of new powers introduced since devolution. The NTS sets the strategic agenda, identifying three 'strategic outcomes' to be the focus of transport policy over a 20 year period. These are to:

'Improve journey times and connections'

'Reduce emissions' and

'Improve quality, accessibility and affordability'.

A number of commitments are identified relating to each of these, and a range of indicators are 'to be developed', together with a carbon balance sheet for transport. Specific targets are not incorporated in the NTS, and the target to reduce traffic levels to 2001 levels by 2021 included in the earlier White Paper[21] is given reduced emphasis.

In managing the road network, a balance has to be struck between managing demand for road use, and targeted enhancement of capacity. Given financial and environmental constraints, much of the focus is on managing demand for roadspace, for which there are a wide range of tools available. These include investment in alternative forms of transport, land use policies to reduce the need for travel, limiting road access or parking availability in certain areas, and financial measures including parking and road use charges. Much of the transport legislation of recent years is aimed at facilitating such measures, for example the enabling legislation for road user charging included in the Transport (Scotland) Act of 2001.

All measures requiring Scottish Executive approval and funding have to be appraised using Scottish Transport Appraisal Guidance (STAG) developed by the Executive.[22] This sets out a common framework for assessing the implications of a transport intervention in relation to economic, environment, social justice and wider policy objectives.

Consideration of measures to reduce road traffic remains an obligation under the Road Traffic Reduction Act 1997. This Act requires local authorities to review and report on current and future traffic levels and targets and measures adopted to reduce traffic levels and traffic growth, as necessary. These reports can be incorporated into local transport strategies.

20   Transport (Scotland) Act 2001; Transport (Scotland) Act 2005.
21   Scottish Executive, Scotland's Transport Future: The transport white paper, June 2004.
22   See www.scot-tag.org.uk for details of the STAG process.

### 3.3.2 LOCAL AND REGIONAL TRANSPORT STRATEGY

Other than the trunk road network, much of the responsibility for delivering transport outcomes lies at the local or regional level although the bulk of capital funding is provided centrally. Since 1999 local authorities have been able to set out their transport policies in Local Transport Strategies (LTS). Although not mandatory, these are intended to provide policy support for project funding bids made by local authorities to the Scottish Executive, and all authorities have prepared them. In the first round of LTSs, authorities were invited to produce interim strategies by July 1999 and full strategies by October 2000. A second round were invited in 2005, taking into account the changes introduced by the Transport (Scotland) Act 2001.

Since the establishment of the statutory Regional Transport Partnerships (RTPs) in 2006 the picture has changed. RTPs must prepare statutory Regional Transport Strategies to be approved by Ministers. The first round of RTSs were submitted in April 2007. The ongoing role of the LTSs may also be uncertain.

RTSs are key documents supporting the NTS. Detailed guidance on their preparation was issued by the Executive[23] setting out guiding principles, based on the national aims and objectives for transport and on the Executive's overall policy goals, that should underpin the content of the regional transport strategies. Further reporting is also required, the guidance suggesting a hierarchy based on timescale:[24]

-   **RTS:** 10–15 year strategy reviewed, revised and refreshed every 4 years in line with the local government electoral cycle.

-   **Investment Plan:** investment plan covering the first 5 to 10 years of the strategy that sets out a programme of capital investment required for the successful implementation of the RTS. This would need to be updated when the RTP judged it appropriate.

-   **Delivery of business plan:** 3-year plan for the implementation of the RTS, updated annually to reflect local and central government planning and funding cycles. Includes plans for revenue and capital spending and borrowing.

-   **Annual report:** Yearly update of progress

RTPs are required to identify what functions they require to deliver their RTSs effectively. In practice, this is likely to involve a balance of different approaches depending on the service or project. SEStran[25] defines the options as:

---

23  Scottish Executive, Scotland's Transport Future: Guidance on Regional Transport Strategies, March 2006.
24  RTS Guidance, para 112.
25  SESTRAN, Regional Transport Strategy, 2006, s 10.3.

- **Influencing** – SEStran can seek the support, influence and persuade other partners, particularly where SEStran is not the funding body;

- **Guidance** – SEStran can provide guidance and advice to other partners tied in with funding provision to achieve consistency and best practice across the region;

- **Co-ordination** – the co-ordination of partners in the development and implementation of projects and initiatives is a potential role for SEStran; and

- **Direct Delivery** – this is the function that may require SEStran to take on additional statutory powers depending on the implementation powers required.

No firm proposals for transfer of powers are included in the first round of RTSs submitted to Ministers, although SEStran in particular suggest further consideration and consultation to be undertaken in a number of areas.


### 3.3.3   ROAD USER CHARGING

This topic is highlighted as it remains a key policy tool for managing demand for road use, but has proved a very difficult measure to introduce in practice. Congestion charging schemes exist in London, and on a small scale in Durham, with a limited number of schemes elsewhere in Europe. Both UK and Scottish governments are supportive of the principle, and are promoting trials of such measures focused in local, most likely urban, areas[26]. The onus for introducing such schemes is on local authorities (and potentially now RTPs), supported by enabling powers introduced by the Transport (Scotland) Act 2001. There are no powers to introduce road user charges on trunk roads. There are also no powers in Scotland for Workplace Parking Levies. This arrangement imposes charges on privately owned parking and has been proposed as a demand management measure. Powers do exist for its introduction in England, although these have not been used to date.[27]

A congestion charging scheme was promoted in Edinburgh but was rejected in a referendum in 2005, and currently no further schemes are being developed. Nevertheless the combination of increasing traffic and congestion, and financial pressures are likely to keep this topic on the agenda.

26   Scottish Executive, National Transport Strategy, 2006: paras 113/4.
27   Nottingham City Council considering implementation of a Workplace Parking Levy scheme.

# PART TWO

# 4 The Definition of a Road?

## 4.1 INTRODUCTION

Roads are and always have been an essential part of society's infrastructure and the public right to use the road network has been respected over the centuries; from the early drove roads, to General Wade's system of military roads, to Telford's roads and bridges, to the construction of turnpike roads with tolling regimes, to the modern day network of public and private roads and bridges. What might have started as some form of servitude or right to drive cattle across private land to market has evolved into a complex statutory framework of modern roads law centred on the legal concept of a 'public right of passage.'

The legal concept of a public right of passage is enshrined in the Roads (Scotland) Act 1984. ("the 1984 Act") Although the latest statutory definition of 'road' is based on this legal concept of a 'public right of passage', a wide range of terms arise in relevant case law, including: a right of passage, a servitude of road, a right of highway, a right of public road, a public right of way as well as a public right of passage. It is not always clear whether different terminology implies different legal principles or merely a different turn of phrase. The 1984 Act removed all references to 'highways' from the Scottish statutory framework. There are no longer any 'highways' or 'highway authorities' in Scotland.

Despite the long history of our road network, there remains uncertainty about the interpretation of the statutory definition of 'road' as set out in section 151 of the 1984 Act. Perhaps because of that uncertainty, the correct identification of a 'road' is an issue that arises frequently in public law and in the context of private development. Distinctions between public and private roads and between private roads and accesses are often misunderstood in attempts to apply the facts in any particular case to the legal definition. And it is well established that, in assessing whether a particular route or track or way is a 'road', the statutory definition of 'road' must be applied to the facts of the case. When considering the statutory definition for the purposes of the Road Traffic Act 1988, the House of Lords hesitated to formulate a comprehensive definition whereby a place might be identified as a road. Whether a particular area of land is or is not a road eventually comes to be a matter of fact.[1] Defining what is meant by a 'road' and a 'public right of passage' remains one of the most contentious areas of roads law and there is some degree of tension between the provisions of the 1984 Act and judicial decisions on their interpretation.

1    Clark v Kato; Cutter v Eagle Star Insurance Co Ltd [1998] 4 All ER 417, HL.

## 4.2    THE STATUTORY DEFINITION

The 1984 Act[2] defines a road[3] as follows:

"any way (other than a waterway) over which there is a public right of passage (by whatever means and whether subject to a toll or not) and includes the road's verge; and any bridge (whether permanent or temporary, over which the road passes; and any tunnel through which the road passes; and any reference to a road includes a part thereof."[4]

A road is the generic term for the way over which the public have a right of passage. Carriageways, footways, footpaths and cycle tracks are all roads for the purposes of the 1984 Act. Where the public right of passage is by foot only, the road is either a footway or a footpath. A footway is associated with a carriageway, that is, a traditional pavement. A footpath is independent of a carriageway. Where the public right of passage is by pedal cycle only or by pedal cycle and foot only, the road is a cycle track. Where it includes a right by vehicle, other than by pedal cycle only, the road is a carriageway.

### 4.2.1    WHAT IS A WAY?

The first aspect to consider in the statutory definition of a road is the meaning of a 'way'. The 1984 Act does not provide a definition of 'way'. Nor does it provide a standard or specification for a way, so different ways might have been formed or constructed to different standards. A way need not be formed or constructed to a standard suitable for adoption by the statutory roads authority. It need not be a traditional carriageway with associated footways and verge. As the 1984 Act provides no definition or assistance on what constitutes a way, it is necessary to look to case law for guidance. The basic principle deriving from the relevant case law is that the definition or identification of a way is a matter of fact in each case. In Clark v Kato,[5] Lord Clyde said:

"I would hesitate to formulate a comprehensive definition whereby a place might be identified as a road, but some guidance should be found by considering its physical character and the functions which it exists to serve..."

In another case, the court held that a 'way' was an area in which some form of travel takes place and that whether an area was a way was essentially a question of fact.[6] A test of practicality was introduced in the case of Mackinnon v Argyll and Bute Council[7] when Lord Osborne said:

2    R(S)A 1984, 151(1).
3    Subject to subsection 3 of Section 151 – see also 4.3.3 below.
4    R(S)A 1984, s 151.
5    Clark v Kato [1984] 4 All ER 417, HL per Lord Clyde at 431.
6    Aird v Vannet 1999 SCCR 322.
7    2001 SLT 725.

"It appears to me that prescriptive rights have no necessary part to play in the resolution of the issue of whether a way is a "road". Furthermore, much depends on the question of whether the public use of the way is or is not practicable."

In Dick v Walkingshaw,[8] the court considered whether a quayside ramp lowered onto the car deck of a ferry constituted a road for the purposes of the 1984 Act. It was argued that the car deck was not a road because it could not be a 'way' when the ferry was at sea and the public had no right of passage over it. The court rejected this argument. The Lord Justice Clerk said:

"Thus [counsel] said that a road could not be a road at one time and not at another. We are not persuaded that that is so. If a road for some reason was taken out of use, for example, during repairs, we can see that it might cease to be a road within the meaning of the definition. Likewise in the present case it was accepted … that the ramp mechanism was part of the quay which was a road and that accordingly the ramp itself was a road in terms of the legislation. But the ramp could only be a road within the meaning of the definition at times when it was in the down position and connected to the vessel. When the ramp was in the perpendicular position, although it is part of the quay, it could not at that stage … be a road."

It is interesting that the Lord Justice Clerk appeared to accept that a road might cease to be a road within the meaning of the statutory definition if the road had been taken out of use, for example, for repairs. It should be borne in mind that the public right of passage over any 'way' is not without statutory control. The right to pass is to be exercised subject to the general provisions of road traffic law (such as speed restrictions) and the provisions of any extant traffic regulation orders[9] (such as waiting restrictions or banned turns). Likewise the exercise of the public right of passage over a public road may be determined or redetermined by the roads authority.[10] If the public right of passage had to be suspended for a period to allow road works to be carried out, then the roads authority would make a temporary traffic regulation order[11] to regulate the public right of passage over the road for the period of the road works. Such regulation could prohibit entry to the locus of the road works with a planned diversion route. Therefore it might have been more reasonable to conclude that the road would continue to be a road during the period of roadworks even although the public right of passage would have been suspended or diverted by order under roads legislation. A particular difficulty with concluding that the road would no longer be a road in such circumstances is that the carrying out of road works is regulated by statute. If the relevant section of road was no longer a road, then the legal basis for undertaking the

8    1995 SLT 1254.
9    Orders made under the provisions of The Road Traffic Regulation Act 1984. See Chapter 22.
10   Section 1(1) of the 1984 Act.
11   Section [14] of the Road Traffic Regulation Act 1984.

road works and regulating the public right of passage would be under-mined and could have the unintended result of rendering the relevant statutory orders and consents ultra vires. The Lord Justice Clerk's con-clusion on the facts in the ferry case appear to be consistent with the regulation of the public right of passage during the operation of a swing bridge, a draw bridge or a bascule bridge when that bridge is positioned to allow the passage of boats. Similarly, in the case of a road crossing a railway when the barrier is in position to allow the passage of trains.

Although the identification of a 'way' may be obvious in most cases, there may be situations in which the position is not clear. In such cases the principles endorsed in the relevant case law may assist; those principles are as follows:

- whether or not a place is a 'way, is a matter of fact in each case[12]

- prescriptive rights are not necessary[13]

- function and physical character are relevant[14]

- Is it an area in which some form of travel takes place?[15]

- Is the public use of the way practicable or not?[16]

- A car deck in the down position and connected to the vessel could be a road[17]


## 4.3    WHAT IS A PUBLIC RIGHT OF PASSAGE?

### 4.3.1    INTRODUCTION

The second and more difficult aspect of the statutory definition is the meaning of a 'public right of passage'. Do members of the public have the right to pass along the way? As the 1984 Act does not define a 'public right of passage', it is once again necessary to look to relevant case law for guidance. However, case law on this issue is far from straightforward and appears to raise as many questions as it answers. In the 2006 case involving Dumfries and Galloway Council,[18] Lord Kingrath noted that there is limited judicial authority on this matter and, therefore, some uncertainty as to what is meant in Section 151 by a "public right of passage". In order to consider the modern legal concept of a public right of passage, it is helpful to look back at its origins in both statute and common law.

---

12  Clark v Kato [1984] 4 All ER 417.
13  Mackinnon v Argyll and Bute Council 2001 SLT 725.
14  Clark v Kato.
15  Aird v Vannet 1999 SCCR 322.
16  Mackinnon v Argyll and Bute Council 2001 SLT 725.
17  Dick v Walkingshaw 1995 SLT 1254.
18  Brian Gregory Hamilton v Dumfries and Galloway Council [2006] CSOH 110.

## 4.3.2   ORIGINS OF A PUBLIC RIGHT OF PASSAGE

Before the enactment of the 1984 Act, the legal concept centred on 'a right of public road or highway' rather than a public right of passage. Going back to the early principles of Scots Law, it was Erskine's view[19] that "the right of a public road, or King's highway, is not properly a servitude, but *public juris* – common to all members of the State, whether they are or are not proprietors of any tenement." This clear distinction between a public right to be enjoyed by all 'members of the State' and a private right in property was still evident in the nineteenth century. In 1868, a 'right of highway' was considered in a judicial decision[20] as follows:

"A right of highway confers on the public a right to use the surface for the ordinary purposes of locomotion. It is the kind of right that has existed in this country and elsewhere from the infancy of civilisation. Means of travelling from one part of the country to another is absolutely essential to the very existence of society. Unless rights of highway belong to the public, the power of locomotion would be completely annihilated. In all civilised nations we find such a right belonging to the public. It was known in the Roman law as *res publica.* With us, also it is *res publica,* and is vested in the Crown as a branch of the Regalia, for behoof of the public. The nature of the right is to use the surface for the purpose of locomotion by carriage or on foot, but not to exercise any other rights of property."

At this stage, the public right – *res publica* – was considered to be fundamental to 'the very existence of society' recognising its precedence over private rights of property, but only insofar as entitling the public to use the road for travel by carriage or on foot – there was no public entitlement to any other rights of property, all of which presumably remained vested in the owner of the solum of the road.

This public right of highway was endorsed in 1914[21] in the case of McRobert v Reid by Lord Skerrington who looked at it in the context of a public right of way. Lord Skerington said:

"It would be unsafe to argue that a public right of way is a highway, and then to assume that in Scotland there is no difference between one class of highway and another. Rights of way undoubtedly stand in a class by themselves – per Lord President Dunedin in Reilly v Greenfield.[22] In particular, the public must take them as they find them and not alter their character – per Lord President Inglis in Mackenzie.[23] So too, I should expect to find some legal difference between (1) a highway included in the list made up under the Roads and Bridges (Scotland) Act

19   Erskine (II.ix.12).
20   Waddell v Earl of Buchanan (1868) 6 M 690.
21   McRobert v Reid 1914 SC 633.
22   1909 SC 1336 (or 8 – see page 648 footnote 2).
23   (1868) 6 Macph 936.

1878 and (2) a highway once a turnpike or statute labour road but no longer maintained at the public expense; and (3) what Lord Dunedin in the case of Reilly described as "one of those still older roads in Scotland for which there is no actual *nomen juris*, and which, though neither statute labour roads nor turnpike roads, have still been public roads from time immemorial. In the south of Scotland stretches of the great Roman road and of other artificial roads of venerable but unknown origin are still used by the public even for cart traffic though their surface has become entirely overgrown. There is not much authority in Scotland as to the nature and limit of the right enjoyed by the public in the different classes of highways, but, in my view, there is one quality which is essential and which must be common to all of them, viz, that the surface of the highway and every square inch of it belongs to the public, not, of course, as property, but in order that it may be used for certain purposes. Hence, there is no room as to any question as to public termini, because at each step one passes from one public place to another. The primary right of the public in a highway is that of passage, but if this point be kept in view, one may say, as Lord Curriehill did in Waddell v Buchan[24] that 'the nature of the right is a right to use the surface for the purpose of locomotion.' In short, a member of the public has a *jus spatiandi* within the limits of a highway which he may exercise as he thinks fit, provided the eccentricity of his course does not disturb the public traffic or the public peace."

This case reiterated that the primary right of the public in a highway was the right of passage. Lord Skerrington confirmed that, whatever other legal differences might exist, all roads and highways had one essential quality – that the surface of the highway and every square inch of it belongs to the public, not as property but for use to travel – a public right of passage. The only qualification was that, in exercising this right, a member of the public could not disturb the public traffic or the public peace.

In this case, His Lordship distinguished between highways included in the list made up under the Roads and Bridges (Scotland) Act 1878 and highways 'no longer maintained at the public expense'. But this distinction, based on the responsibility for maintenance, did not affect His Lordship's conclusion that what was common to both categories of highway was that 'the surface of the highway and every square inch of it belongs to the public'; not as property but 'in order that it may be used for certain purposes.' His Lordship said that 'The primary right of the public in a highway is that of passage'.

His Lordship's view on the public right of passage in the highway, whether it is maintained by the public purse or not, reflects the current statutory provisions under the 1984 Act. The 1984 Act deals with roads over which there is a public right of passage and the Act distinguishes between public roads and private roads on the basis of responsibility for maintenance of the road. Section 151 of the 1984 Act defines a 'public

24    6 Mach 690 at p. 699.

road' as 'a road which a roads authority have a duty to maintain' and it defines a 'private road' as any road other than a public road'. As both are roads, they are ways over which there is a public right of passage. Likewise, in Lord Skerrington's view, there was a public right of passage in relation to all highways, whether or not the highway was included in the public list under the Roads and Bridges (Scotland) Act 1878. Of course, His Lordship expected there to be some legal difference between the different categories of highway but, whatever that difference was, it was not a difference affecting the public right of passage.

Of course, it should be borne in mind that Lord Skerrington was talking about both highways and other roads. Prior to the 1984 Act, statutory definitions of 'road' tended to distinguish between the 'highway' and 'any other road to which the public had access' or between the 'highway' and a road or bridge 'open to be used by the public'. Therefore, before 1984, there appeared to be some legal distinction between the highway over which there was a public right of passage and other roads to which the public has access.

Some ten years before Lord Skerrington delivered his judgement in McRobert v Reid[25], the phrase 'bridges open to be used by the public' was considered by Lord Kinnear in the decision in the case of The Magistrates of Edinburgh v North British Railway Co.[26] Lord Kinnear said:

> "But it is said that, so far at least as the railway bridge is concerned, it is covered by the words 'bridges open to be used by the public'. These are words of ordinary language, and they do not appear to be very difficult of interpretation. A bridge is not open to the public, if the public is prevented from making use of it by any physical or legal obstruction; and the definition must therefore mean that it is physically accessible, and that the public is either entitled or allowed to enter upon it. But the words of the definition describe a condition of fact, without any implication of legal right or liability. So long as that condition of fact continues, the definition applies. If it is lawfully altered, the definition applies no longer. There is nothing in words that are merely descriptive to import a transference of rights of property from one person to another, or from a private owner to the public."

This is a straightforward interpretation of the statutory provision based on ordinary language. As a condition of fact, the road or bridge is either open to the public or it is not. If it is closed to the public, it does not fall within the statutory definition assuming that the closure is lawful. On this right of closure by the party with the legal control of the road or bridge, Lord Kinnear added:

> "If the ground is not already subject to a public right, there is no positive enactment that touches the inherent power of the

25 1914 SC 633.
26 (1904) 6 F 620.

private owner to exclude the public, and if the public has been allowed to pass, out of mere goodwill and so long only as their passage is not inconsistent with the use and occupation by the proprietor of his own property, there is nothing in the statute to prevent the proprietor from taking his road or bridge outside the definition by appropriating it to purposes inconsistent with public use. But the pursuers' argument is that if they once allow the public to enter upon a road or bridge, although not for long enough to found a prescriptive right, and without creating an adverse right in any other form, the supereminent right of the magistrates comes in to compel them to keep their property open to the public for all time, This is confiscation of private property for the benefit of the community, without compensation, and without previous notice which is generally exacted before power is given by Parliament even to purchase without the owner's consent."

Lord Kinnear appears to be distinguishing between highways, which are subject to the public right of passage and which 'belong to the public', and other roads or bridges which are 'open to be used by the public' but do not 'belong to the public'. His Lordship is clear that the latter category is based on a condition of fact and not a public right so the road or bridge opened to be used by the public remains within the control of the private owner of the road or bridge unless it is already subject to a public right. This distinction is important in road traffic legislation. As the enforcement of road traffic legislation underpins road safety, convictions in the public interest should not be avoided on the basis of a narrow statutory definition of a road. For this reason, statutory definitions of highway or road usually include a 'catch all' phrase which describes a 'condition of fact', such as, "and any road opened to be used by the public" or "and any road to which the public has access."

For instance, the Road Traffic Act of 1960 defined a road as 'any highway and any other road to which the public has access'. This definition encapsulates roads over which the public have a right of passage, that is, the highway, and any other road to which the public have access, as a condition of fact rather than under a legal right. This 'catch all' phrase is similar to the one considered by Lord Kinnear. The inclusion of a 'catch all' phrase in the statutory definition of a 'highway' or a 'road' should reduce the risk of road traffic offenders avoiding conviction on the basis of the statutory definition of a road. Prior to the enactment of the Road Traffic Act of 1991, the current definition of a road under the 1984 Act created such a difficulty.[27] The solution was for the 1991 Act to extend the definition of 'road', as defined in the 1984 Act, by adding the 'catch all' phrase "and any other way to which the public has access". The effect is to widen the application of road traffic legislation to all roads, as defined in the 1984 Act, and to other ways to which the public has access.

---

27  See Lord Cameron's comments in Viewpoint Housing Association Ltd v Lothian Regional Council 1993 SLT 921 at 927 B.

The 'catch all' phrase in the definition in the Road Traffic Act 1960 was 'any other *road* to which the public has access'. At that time, the term 'highway' was used to describe roads over which there was a public right of passage. The 'catch all' phrase in the 1991 Act is 'any other *way* to which the public has access'. Since 1984, the term 'road' has been used to describe roads over which there is a public right of passage. If the term 'road' had continued to be used in the catch all phrase after 1984, there would have been some confusion between the interaction of the public right of passage, which right is now a pre-requisite of a road, and the private rights of property which underpin the other 'ways' covered by the 'catch all' phrase.

The 1960 'catch all' phrase was considered by Lord Justice Emslie in 1973 in the case of Cheyne v MacNeill.[28] Lord Justice Emslie said:

"The statute does not in terms require that the access upon which the issue of liability to the statutory provisions depends shall be in respect of any legally enforceable rights of passage. Further the definition contrasts 'highway' with the words 'road to which the public has access'. Upon a 'highway' the public right of passage is secured by law and its maintenance is the responsibility of a statutory authority. A 'road' within the meaning of the definition would therefore seem to include a way which need not possess either of these qualities. From this contrast, it is not difficult to infer that the words 'to which the public has access' are necessarily referable to a situation in which it is found-in-fact that the public has access – access for the purpose of which a road is intended or designed, i.e. passage on foot or in a vehicle. But when the statute refers to access it cannot be assumed that this means access which is obtained unlawfully, e.g. by climbing over or opening gates, or by surmounting walls or fences, designed to exclude potential intruders. In our opinion, 'access' as the word is used in the definition, covers access for passage by permission express or implied from, or acquiescence or toleration by, the person or persons with legal right to control the use of the road. The degree or extent of use necessary to bring a particular road within the definition will necessarily be a question of fact in every case. Where there is such permission, acquiescence or tolerance demonstrated by use or otherwise it can properly be said that there is nothing illegal or unlawful in such access as the public has proved to enjoy, and therefore that the public has access lawfully to the road. "

Like Lord Kinnear in North British Railway Company, Lord Justice Emslie distinguished between 'highways' and 'roads to which the public had access'; the former having a public right of access 'secured by law' and being maintained by the public purse but the latter 'need not possess either of these qualities". If His Lordship's analysis were to be applied to the current 'catch all' phrase in the definition for the purposes of the

28   Cheyne v MacNeill 1973 SLT 27.

Road Traffic Act 1991, he would have to distinguish between (1) a 'road' over which there is a public right of passage and which may or may not be maintained by the public purse and (2) any other way to which the public has access. His approach applies equally to the definition in the 1991 Act – a way need not possess either of the qualities of a road – there could be a way over which there is no public right of passage but to which the public has access. That way would not be a road for the purposes of the 1984 Act but it would fall within the definition of the 1991 Act and hence it would be subject to road traffic legislation.

Although the terminology may be confusing at times, the basic common law public right of passage over Scottish highways and roads can be traced over the centuries. What has been established at common law and in statute is the distinction between (1) highways or roads over which there is a public right of passage and (2) other roads or ways to which the public has access as a condition of fact rather than by public right. This distinction was clearly set out by Lord Kinnear in 1904, is consistent with Lord Skerrington's judgement in 1914 and with Lord Justice Emslie's judgement in 1973. Prior to the 1984 Act, the first category was referred to as 'highways' and the second category was referred to as other 'roads' to which the public had access. However, the 1984 Act rationalised the definition of road and removed all references to 'highways'. Since 1984, the first category is referred to as 'roads' and the second category is referred to as other 'ways' to which the public has access.

### 4.3.3    THE PUBLIC RIGHT OF PASSAGE SINCE 1984

The 1984 Act introduced the new statutory definition of a 'road',[29] as set out in paragraph [4.2] above. The new statutory framework deals only with roads, both public roads and private roads. A public road[30] is "a road which a roads authority has a duty to maintain' and a private road[31] is 'any road other than a public road'. The distinction between a public road and a private road relates solely to maintenance liability. A public road is maintained by the roads authority and a private road is not. To put it another way, a public road is a way over which there is a public right of passage and which the roads authority has a duty to maintain. A private road is a way over which there is a public right of passage but which the roads authority has no duty to maintain.

The 1984 Act deleted all references to 'highways'. This raises the question of what Parliament intended with the new definition including the deletion of 'highway' from Scottish roads law. It also raises the question of whether there was a Parliamentary error in the omission of the phrase "and any other way to which the public has access", the so called 'catch all' phrase which was retrospectively added for the purposes of road traffic legislation by the Road Traffic Act 1991.

29    RS(A) 1984 Section 151.
30    RS(A) 1984 Section 151.
31    RS(A) 1984 Section 151.

Prior to 1984, there were two parts to the statutory definition:

1.   A highway, and

2.   Any other road to which the public has access

Case law distinguished between these two parts of the statutory definition as discussed above.[32] This distinction was significant. The first part involved a public right of passage as a matter of law whereas the second part involved access to property by the public as a condition of fact, which access was subject to control by the owner of the property. Perhaps unsurprisingly, given the lack of these two distinct parts in the 1984 Act definition, no such distinction has been drawn in case law since 1984. As a result the courts have applied the legal principles of private property law underpinning the second part of the definition to the first part of the definition, which is based on a public right. The interaction of these two approaches is particularly focussed in the context of road traffic law, which was of concern to Lord Cameron in 1991[33] who said:

> "I am not certain there is truly any distinction in this difference. It is true that the definition which now applies in Scotland for the purposes of the Road Traffic Act 1988 is that in the Roads (Scotland) Act 1984, and that the earlier definition which makes reference to 'highway and any other road to which the public has access' is no longer applicable. However, the new definition makes no reference to the word highway which, as noted in Cheyne v MacNeill, was a road upon which the public right of passage was secured by law and whose maintenance was the responsibility of the statutory authority. In these circumstances it was not surprising that Parliament employed the phrase 'public right of passage' in the substituted definition. If counsel for the pursuer contended the word 'right' to be read as a real legal right, and not something which is obtained by virtue of permission express or implied from, or acquiescence or toleration by person or persons with legal right to control the use of the road, the consequences would be startling. It would mean, for instance, that where a road was not a public road but a private road, unless and until the public right of passage had been demonstrated by continuance over the prescriptive period, no such road would fall within the definition and thus a person driving on such a road, albeit the public had access to it, could not be convicted on evidence which would secure his conviction in England and Wales."

Lord Cameron's concern about the implications for road traffic law was resolved by the Road Traffic Act 1991 which extended the 1984 Act definition of 'road' for the purposes of road traffic law by adding the phrase 'or any other way to which the public has access'. Lord Cameron also said:

32   See Origins of a Public Right of Passage para 4.3.2.
33   Viewpoint Housing Association.

"I am content to decide the case on the more limited basis for which counsel for the pursuers contended, namely that the change in definition of a road in the 1984 Act made no difference to the manner in which a public right of passage could be constituted and that the law remained the same as it had done prior to the passage of the 1984 Act."

Lord Cameron was deciding a case involving a housing association which had constructed a sheltered housing development in Edinburgh. In planning their development, they had applied to the roads authority for two street orders under the Edinburgh Corporation Order Confirmation Act 1967 authorising the construction of a street. The orders were granted and the street was constructed to a standard necessary for adoption by the roads authority. The development was completed in 1976 and from 1976 to 1990 the public were allowed to use the street without hindrance. The Association made two applications to the roads authority to have the road adopted but both applications were refused. In 1990, the Association erected a barrier[34] across the street. The roads authority ordered the Association to remove the barrier in terms of Section 59(3)[35] of the 1984 Act. The Association refused to remove the barriers claiming that the street had remained 'private' despite the fact that members of the public had been allowed access. The roads authority accepted that there was no public right of way but argued that a public right of passage had been created and this entitled them to invoke Section 59 of the 1984 Act.

The court held that permission by the owner of the street to its use by the public for a period short of the prescriptive period[36] could be terminated by the owner. In deciding this case, Lord Cameron said that the substantial issue was that, even if the street had acquired the character of a road for the purposes of the 1984 Act by virtue of "the unrestricted and tolerated use made of it for a period by the public" was the owner deprived thereafter of restricting the class entitled to use it by means of a barrier? He followed the reasoning of Lord Kinnear in the Magistrates of Edinburgh case.[37] His Lordship said that he found nothing in the cases presented to him to suggest "that once it is established that the road is one to which the public has access, the owner of the road with legal right to control the use of the road, ceases to be entitled to exercise such legal right."[38] However, Lord Cameron's statement appears to be referring to the 'catch all' phrase – a road to which the public has access – rather than to a 'road' as a statutory successor to a 'highway' – a way over which there is a *public right* of passage rather than public access as a condition of fact.

In the circumstances of this case, it might have been more appropriate to consider whether this 'street' fell within one of two categories:

34   Two posts and a removable chain.
35   Control of obstructions in roads.
36   See discussion on public rights of way at [4.4.2] below.
37   the Magistrates of Edinburgh v North British Railway Co (1904) 6 F 620.
38   page 926 G.

(1)  a 'road' as defined in the 1984 Act, or

(2)  a 'way to which the public had access' as considered in earlier cases.

Presumably this approach was not submitted to Lord Cameron because the second category was not part of the definition of 'road' within the 1984 Act. However, it was part of the reasoning of Lord Kinnear in 1904 and Lord Skerrington in 1914 and Lord Justice Emslie in 1973.[39] Lord Cameron went on to apply Lord Kinnear's reasoning in relation to second 'catch all' category to the first category. Lord Cameron said that he "found nothing in these cases to suggest that once it is established that the road is one to which the public has access, the owner of the road with legal right to control the use of that road, ceases to be entitled to exercise such legal right" That proposition follows the decisions of Lord Kinnear, Lord Skerrington and Lord Justice Emslie as they applied it to the second category – the 'catch all' phrase which described a condition of fact rather than a public right of highway, which evolved into a public right of passage under the 1984 Act. Perhaps the substantial issue in this case should have been – whether the street had acquired the character of a road for the purposes of the 1984 Act, in which case it fell within the jurisdiction of the roads authority, or whether it remained a way to which the public had access, in which case it remained within the control of the property owner?

The effect of the Viewpoint case has been to create doubt about the powers and duties of the roads authority under the 1984 Act because of the application of the principles of private property law to a public right. For instance, is it intended that owners of the solum of roads, whoever is responsible for their maintenance, can at any stage short of the prescriptive period restrict or remove the public right of passage? That could allow every house builder to ransom householders after entry had been taken to new homes. However, in the case of Hamilton v Dumfries and Galloway Council[40] a local landowner laid claim to the solum of a road and approached local residents who used the road requiring them to make payment for the right to use part of the road that had been the subject of a stopping up order some years before. The roads authority reacted by adopting the road to the list of public roads. The local landowner sought judicial review of the Council's decision to adopt the road on the basis that it was not a road. Lord Kingrath held that the relevant section of the road was a private road within the meaning of the 1984 Act.

Lord Kingrath said:

> "I am not persuaded (any more than the Lord Ordinary in *Viewpoint Housing Association Ltd v Lothian Regional Council*) that, although the language used in the definition of road in the 1984 Act is different, there was truly intended to be any material distinction from previous definitions such as that in the Roads

---

39  See paragraph [4.3.2] above.
40  2006 S.C.L.R. 839.

(Scotland) Act 1970, which referred to ways 'to which the public had access'. These words were, of course, understood to refer to more than mere access in fact as was said by Lord Justice General Emslie in Cheyne v MacNeill[41] at p30

"[It] is not difficult to infer that the words 'to which the public has access' are necessarily referable to a situation in which it is found-in-fact that the public has access – access for the purpose of which a road is intended or designed, i.e. passage on foot or in a vehicle. But when the statute refers to access it cannot be assumed that this means access which is obtained unlawfully, e.g. by climbing over or opening gates, or by surmounting walls or fences, designed to exclude potential intruders. In our opinion, 'access' as the word is used in the definition, covers access for passage by permission express or implied from, or acquiescence or toleration by, the person or persons with legal right to control the use of the road. The degree or extent of use necessary to bring a particular road within the definition will necessarily be a question of fact in every case. Where there is such permission, acquiescence or tolerance demonstrated by use or otherwise it can properly be said that there is nothing illegal or unlawful in such access as the public has proved to enjoy, and therefore that the public has access lawfully to the road. "

So Lord Kingrath agreed with Lord Cameron that there was no parliamentary intention to change the meaning of the definition of 'road' notwithstanding the difference in terminology – that is, using the word 'road' rather than 'highway'. Lord Kingrath then applied previous judicial reasoning on the 'catch all' phrase to justify the existence of the public right of passage, which is, of course, a pre-requisite of establishing a road in terms of the definition in the 1984 Act. In order to conclude that the public right of passage was in existence, His Lordship founded on the condition of fact of public access, which, according to previous judicial reasoning, should have been subject to private property law.

The result appears to be contradictory: in Viewpoint, it was decided that, although the 'way' was a road to which the public had access, it did not prevent the owners from restricting the class of persons entitled to use it, whereas in Dumfries and Galloway Council it was decided , following Viewpoint, that although the 'way' was a road to which the public had access, it did prevent the owners from restricting the class of persons entitled to use it – because the public right of passage outweighed the private property rights.

## 4.3.4   CONCLUSION

So what has changed with the enactment of the 1984 Act? Lord Cameron said the 1984 Act 'made no difference to the manner in which a public

---

41   1973 SLT 27.

right of passage could be constituted and that the law remained the same as it has done prior to the passing of the 1984 Act." In 2006 Lord Kingrath agreed with Lord Cameron saying ""I am not persuaded (any more than the Lord Ordinary in *Viewpoint Housing Association Ltd v Lothian Regional Council)* that, although the language used in the definition of road in the 1984 Act is different, there was truly intended to be any material distinction from previous definitions such as that in the Roads (Scotland) Act 1970, which referred to ways 'to which the public had access'.

If nothing has changed, where do we find the pre-1984 distinction between the public right of highway or passage and access by the public based on permission, express or implied from, or acquiescence or toleration by the owner? And what are the consequences for the 1984 Act of the application of the legal proposition that private property rights apply, not just to the 'catch all' category of 'ways to which the public have access', but also to private roads as defined by the Act?

One example involves consideration of private rights of property in the context of a decision by the roads authority[42] to add a private road to their list of public roads. Or, indeed, to delete a road from their list, which would change the road's status from public to private, having the effect of transferring responsibility for maintenance from the authority to the road owner. Before a road can be competently added to the statutory list, it must already be a road, which means that a public right of passage must already exist in respect of the 'way' that is to be added to the list.[43] Apart from the provisions of the 1984 Act, as a matter of public policy, one would have to question why a roads authority should adopt a way that is not a road? Why should public funds be committed to maintaining a 'private' way over which there is no public right of passage? If the existence of a public right of passage is a pre-requisite of adoption of a road, then it must follow that the legal process of adoption of the road cannot create the public right of passage over it. Of course, adoption should provide evidence of the roads authority's view that the 'way' in question is a road.[44]

Any such decision by the roads authority to add to or delete from their list of public roads is subject to a requirement to notify affected frontagers.[45] The roads authority must serve notice of their intention to adopt a private road on the frontagers[46] who may submit representations to the authority. If the authority proceeds to adopt the road, notwithstanding an objection from the frontagers, there is provision for the requisite number of frontagers to make application to the Sheriff, whose decision

---

42   Section 1 of the 1984 Act.
43   See Brian Gregory Hamilton v Dumfries and Galloway Council [2006] CSOH 110.
44   See Brian Gregory Hamilton v Dumfries and Galloway Council [2006] CSOH 110.
45   See chapter [4.8.2] below.
46   Section 1(4) of the 1984 Act.

is final.[47] Any road which is entered in the statutory list vests in the roads authority for the purposes of their functions as a roads authority.[48]

However, the right to be notified, to submit representations and to apply to the Sheriff applies to frontagers, who are defined as 'the owner of any land fronting or abutting' the road. These provisions do not apply to the owner of the solum of the road, who may well wish to object to the vesting of his private property in the roads authority.

These provisions contrast with the requirements under Section 21 of the 1984 Act for an application for road construction consent. A Section 21 application requires notice to be served on the owners of all land which would front, abut or be comprehended in the new road. However, the person who owns the solum of a private road could be faced with the proposed adoption of that road without having a right to be notified of that proposal. Even if the owner were to see a public notice of the proposed listing of his private road and he objected to the listing, the authority is still entitled to proceed to list the road on following due process.

Moreover, the owner of the solum might not fall within the definition of 'the requisite number of frontagers' so he might not have the right to apply to the Sheriff. If he were to fall within that definition and, consequently, he had the right to apply to the Sheriff, it has to be assumed that the Sheriff's decision is not pre-determined in favour of the owner due to his private right of property in the road?[49] If the roads authority proceeds to list the road, it would vest in the authority without payment of compensation. As listing transfers the liability for maintenance of the road from its owner to the roads authority, it seems reasonable that the owner should not be compensated for this loss of a liability. Nor is he compensated for the 'creation' of a public right over his property because that public right must already be in existence before the listing.

The lack of inclusion of the owner of the solum of the road in the statutory process for listing contrasts with his inclusion in the statutory process for making an application for road construction consent. This difference might be explained by the proposition that the construction of a road under the 1984 Act creates a public right of passage, once the road has been constructed in accordance with the statutory consent and opened to public use. If the public right of passage takes precedence over the private right in property, it seems reasonable that the owner of the property that will be 'comprehended within' the proposed road should be notified of the application and given the opportunity to make representations to the roads authority. In contrast, a private road, as defined in the 1984 Act, is already burdened by a public right of passage,

47    Section 1(5) of the 1984 Act.
48    Section 1(9) of the 1984 Act.
49    See Brian Gregory Hamilton v Dumfries and Galloway Council [2006] CSOH 110.

which takes precedence over any private right in property. Therefore the authority's proposed listing or delisting of the private road only affects the maintenance liability not the diminution of any private right. However, that maintenance liability directly affects frontagers of a private road as they carry a risk that at any stage the authority could serve notice under Section 13 of the 1984 Act requiring them, at their expense, to upgrade the road. The removal of this risk on listing or its creation on delisting is of direct relevance to frontagers. So the operation of these statutory provisions sits somewhat uncomfortably with the proposition that the owner retains his fundamental property right in the road, which proposition draws no support from the decision in Dumfries and Galloway.

Furthermore, what happens if the owner decides to control the use of a private road in a way that is inconsistent with an extant traffic regulation order? How does a member of the public wishing to exercise his right to pass, reconcile conflicting private law conditions with extant statutory provisions? The statutory power to make a traffic regulation order applies to all roads – not just to public roads. Does this private right mean than any such order can only properly be made with the consent of the owner who has the common law right to control the use of the road? If so, why is there no provision to consult the owner on a draft traffic regulation order?

## 4.4    CREATION OF A PUBLIC RIGHT OF PASSAGE OVER A WAY

Unfortunately it is not at all clear how a public right of passage is to be established. If a landowner applies under Section 21 of the 1984 Act for consent to construct a road and he subsequently constructs the road in accordance with that consent and then opens it to public use, would those acts create a public right of passage? If the owner applies to have that road listed by the roads authority after expiry of the statutory twelve month period,[50] the authority must adopt the road so, by that stage, the public right of passage must already be in existence. So it must be possible for a public right of passage to be created in relation to a newly constructed road within that 12 month period to make any sense of those provisions. The steps are as follows:

1.    submit application for road construction consent having notified the owner of the solum and others;

2.    obtain road construction consent;

3.    construct road in accordance with the road construction consent;

4.    on completion of road, open road to public use;

5.    expiry of 12 month period from completion;

50   Section 16(2) of the 1984 Act.

6.    statutory right to have the road added to list of public roads thereby transferring maintenance liability

If the provisions are to make sense, the public right of passage must be established between steps 4 and 5. The public right of passage may be created (1) at the outset on opening the road to public use or (2) on application to adopt after the expiry of the 12 month period or (3) on some intervening date? Number (2) is flawed because the application must be in respect of a road, therefore the public right of passage must already have been created by the date of the application. If choosing between (1) and (3), the former seems more credible because it relates to the specific actings of the party who has control of the land on which the road has been constructed. That person could construct the road and then decide not to open it to public use. If the right is not triggered on the first day that the new road is open to public use, how does one draw any legal distinction between second day or the third day or any other subsequent day up until day 365?

There are two other ways in which a public right of passage may be created:

1.    By statute;

2.    By creation of a public right of way

### 4.4.1   BY STATUTE

Section 151(1A) of the Act requires a way to which the public has access and which passes over a bridge constructed pursuant to a Private Act is to be treated as if there were a public right of passage over it. The trigger in this statutory provision is the public having access, not public access being exercised for a specified period.

This provision refers to the 'catch all' phrase of "a way to which the public has access" suggesting that this category is distinct from the category of road over which there is a public right of passage, as discussed above in paragraph [4.3.1].

### 4.4.2   BY CREATION OF A PUBLIC RIGHT OF WAY

A public right of passage is not the same thing as a public right of way. Both rights may exist over the same 'way' but the establishment of a public right of way is not a pre-requisite of the creation of a public right of passage. That said, if a public right of way has been established, then there will be a public right of passage over that way.

In 1986,[51] the Lord President Emslie said that "the definition of 'road' in the Roads (Scotland) Act 1984 does not require that there must exist over

51   Cowie v Strathclyde Regional Council 8 July 1986 – unreported.

the 'way' a public right of way. Parliament has not chosen to define 'road' with reference to the well understood concept of a public right of way at common law. ...all that is required, therefore, in order to establish that the lane is a 'road' within the meaning of the Roads (Scotland) Act 1984 is to show that there exists over it 'a public right of passage'. It does not, for example, have to be shown that the passage is between one public place and another. Since it is well known that 'roads' within the meaning of the Act include cul de sacs,[52] and that some exist to provide access and egress to private properties it is evident that the 'right of passage' mentioned in the definition of the word 'road' involves less exacting considerations than those which govern the existence of a public right of way over private land."

This decision is helpful as it confirms that a public right of passage is not to be equated with the common law public right of way as the former involves "less exacting considerations". There are four essential requirements for the creation of a public right of way under common law:

- The route must run from one public place to another public place.[53]

- There must be a definite route.[54]

- Members of the public must have used the route openly and peaceably, without the permission, express or implied, of the landowner.

- Members of the public must have used the route without interruption for a period of 20 years or more.[55]

How do these requirements for a public right of way relate to the requirements for a public right of passage? In a case[56] in 2006, Lord Kingrath considered Lord President Emslie's views on the" less exacting requirements for a public right of passage". Lord Kingrath said:

52  At common law there were doubts about whether a cul-de-sac was a highway (Bateman v Black (1852)18 QB 870). Those doubts resulted in the statutory definition of 'street' in the Public Utilities Street Works Act 1950 being extended to include the words: '...irrespective of whether the highway, road or other thing in question is a thoroughfare or not.' In considering the meaning of this phrase in the case of Strathclyde Regional Council v British Railways Board 1978 SLT (Sh Ct) 8, Sheriff Principal R Reid QC accepted that its purpose was to exclude doubts which had arisen in the common law regarding cul-de-sacs. However, he was of the view that it was not intended to have the effect that a length of highway which had been blocked off at both ends should continue to be regarded as a highway. Such an interpretation would set aside the decision in *Bailey v Jamieson(1876) 10 CP 329* and make 'a considerable statutory inroad into the idea of a highway as a place over which all persons may pass.'
53  Campbell v Lang (1853) 1 Macq 451.
54  Mackintosh v Moir (1871) 9 M 574, (1872) 10 M 517.
55  For further reading see Rights of Way – A Guide to the Law in Scotland published by the Scottish Rights of Way Society Ltd.
56  Brian Gregory Hamilton v Dumfries and Galloway Council 2006 S C L R 839.

"It is clear from Cowie v Strathclyde Regional Council that the definition 'involves less exacting considerations than those which govern the existence of a public right of way over private land'. In that case it was recognised that although there required to be a 'way', since it was well known that roads within the meaning of the Act included cul-de-sacs and that some existed to provide access and egress to private property, at least two of the requirements for the acquisition of a public right of way – use from end to end on a continuous journey and public termini – were not involved. What of the remaining conditions for the constitution of the public right of way, namely continuous use as of right and use for the prescriptive period? It is possible to envisage that Parliament intended that something similar to the former of these conditions apply – that is that there should have been substantial, as opposed to occasional, use as of right – as opposed to use by tolerance or by permission. In relation to public rights of way, it is well known that while occasional use might be tolerated, regular open use, if not challenged, is generally taken to imply a right (See Gordon, Scottish Land Law (2nd edition) at p 775)."

Lord Kingrath added:

"I am not persuaded that it can have been intended that any such use as of right required to be for the prescriptive period... Prescriptive use was not apparently thought to be necessary in Beattie v Scott. I was not referred to any authority in which it was. The 1984 Act itself make no specific requirement to this effect. Section 3(3) of the Prescription and Limitation (Scotland) Act 1973 relates specifically to public rights of way only."

In Mackinnon v Argyll and Bute Council,[57] Lord Osborne said "It appears to me that prescriptive rights have no necessary part to play in the resolution of the issue of whether a way is a "road"".

A public right of way may also be created by statute. The Countryside (Scotland) Act 1967 empowers planning authorities to create, maintain,[58] divert and distinguish public rights of way. This may be done by two means – by the creation of a public path agreement with the landowner or under a public path creation order, which involves the exercise of compulsory powers. The agreement or order may specify the terms and conditions under which members of the public can exercise the right of way. The exercise of the right of way subject to conditions is the main distinguishing feature between a statutory public right of way and one created under common law. A statutory public right of way need not therefore necessarily end in a public place unlike a right under common law. However, in the case of public paths created under the Countryside (Scotland) Act 1967. Such paths fall within the scope of section 151 (3) of

57   2001 SLT 725.
58   Cumbernauld and Kilsyth District Council v Dollar Land (Cumbernauld) Ltd 1993 SLT 1318 HL.

the 1984 Act.[59] This means that the 1984 Act does not confer any powers or impose any duties as regards a road which is a public path created under the Countryside (Scotland) Act 1967. So, although both common law and statutory public rights of way should fall within the statutory definition of 'road', the statutory public right of way would be outwith the scope of the Act's powers and duties by virtue of section 151(3).

It is settled that a public right of way may be a footpath, a carriage road[60] or a motor road.[61] It would appear therefore that all common law public rights of way are roads for the purposes of the Roads (Scotland) Act 1984.[62] They are all ways over which the public has a right of passage.

### 4.4.3   CONCLUSIONS

In comparing the public right of passage with the common law public right of way, the conclusions that can be drawn from case law are:

- A public right of passage need not run from one public place to another[63]

- There must be a 'way' over which the public right of passage is exercised[64]

- A public right of passage may be exercised over a cul de sac[65]

- A public right of passage may provide access to and egress from private property[66]

- A public right of passage need not be used from end to end on a continuous journey

- A public right of passage need not be exercised for the prescriptive period of 20 years

- Actual public use is an important consideration and much depends on whether public use of the way is or is not practicable[67]

Although these principles may be of some assistance in assessing the facts in any given case, they do not provide the same kind of useful framework which is now established for the creation of public rights of way. This is particularly the case in relation to the running of the prescriptive period. It is settled that the right of way must be exercised by the public in accordance with the relevant principles for a period of at

---

59   See para [4.10] below on Section 151(3).
60   Mackenzie v Banks (1868) 6 M 936.
61   Smith v Sexton 1927 SN 92, 142.
62   With the exception of any road covered by Section 14 of the Local Government and Planning (Scotland) Act 1982.
63   Cowie v Strathclyde Regional Council, 8 July 1986 – unreported.
64   Cowie v Strathclyde Regional Council, 8 July 1986 – unreported.
65   Cowie v Strathclyde Regional Council, 8 July 1986 – unreported.
66   Cowie v Strathclyde Regional Council, 8 July 1986 – unreported.
67   Mackinnon v Argyll and Bute Council 2001 SLT 725 page 84.

least 20 years; in contrast, although we know that a public right of passage need not be exercised for the 20 year period, there is no settled alternative minimum period of use for the establishment of a public right of passage. Lord Kingrath said that it was possible to envisage that Parliament intended..." that there should have been substantial, as opposed to occasional, use as of right"

The one certainty is that each case will turn on its own facts. Of course that may be of little practical assistance so, perhaps it should be borne in mind that the purpose of the 1984 Act is to allow the road network to be built, maintained, managed and used safely. In any particular circumstances, one should perhaps consider whether or not the 'way' in question should benefit from such statutory protection.

## 4.5   REDETERMINATION OF THE PUBLIC RIGHT OF PASSAGE

Section 1 of the 1984 Act empowers the roads authority to determine the means by which the public right of passage over a public road, or over any part of it, may be exercised and Section 151 (2) sets out the three means of exercise of the public right of passage:

1.    By foot only

2.    By pedal cycle only or by pedal cycle and foot only, and

3.    By vehicle other than by pedal cycle only

Section 152 of the 1984 Act makes provision for the means of exercise of the public right of passage to be determined or redetermined by order. For instance, the exercise of the public right of passage by foot only over a footpath may be redetermined by order to a public right of passage by pedal cycle and foot only, which would convert the footpath to a cycle track.

## 4.6   PUBLIC RIGHTS OF PASSAGE AND THE PUBLIC STATUS OF A ROAD

There is no relationship between a public right of passage and the public status of the road. The public status of a road relates only to responsibility for maintenance. It does not create or sustain a public right of passage over the road. Deletion of a road from the list of public roads does not extinguish the public right of passage. The right of passage can only be extinguished by confirmation and implementation of a stopping up order in terms of the 1984 Act or the Town and Country Planning (Scotland) Act 1997.[68]

68   See chapter 9.

In the *Bute* case,[69] Lord Moncrieff said:

'Once a road has been made public, I know of no way in which the rights of the public in the road can be excluded, or the road itself closed, except by following one of the three alternative methods of closing a public road which are available in law. These methods are (1) resort to statutory procedure under the Turnpike Roads (Scotland) Act 1831: (2) resort to statutory procedure under the Roads and Bridges (Scotland) Act 1878; and (3) application to Parliament for a particular enactment.'

'I am clearly of the opinion that a public road cannot be closed by mere failure on the part of the road authority to expend money on its maintenance; nor do I think that the public can lose their right of passage as a result of the failure or refusal of a road authority to include in the list of highways, as directed in the Roads and Bridges (Scotland) Act, 1878, what may be proved or admitted to have been a public road.'

'The mere non-inclusion of a road in the county list of highways cannot, however, in my opinion, be conclusive against the public in a question of their right to use the road.'

In giving this opinion, his Lordship was using the term public road in the sense of the current statutory definition of 'road', which is a way over which the public have a right of passage. His Lordship clearly makes the point that responsibility for maintenance of the road does not affect the public right of passage.

### 4.6.1  NO PUBLIC RIGHT OF PASSAGE OVER PRIVATE ACCESSES

Care must be taken when considering the difference between a private road and a private access. A private access is a way over which there is no public right of passage. If such a right were in existence, the way would be a private road, not a private access. The roads authority has no control over the construction of a private access, although planning permission may be necessary. Private accesses cannot be adopted to the list of public roads. A roads authority is empowered to adopt roads to their list of public roads.[70] Private accesses are not constructed in terms of a construction consent and they are outwith the scope of section 16 of the Roads (Scotland) Act 1984, which deals with applications for private roads to become public roads. Furthermore, why should a roads authority take on the responsibility for maintenance of a 'way' unless there is a public right of passage over that 'way'? Listing or delisting of a road under section 1 of the Act transfers maintenance liability for that road; it does not create or extinguish any public rights of passage over the road.

---

69  Marquis of Bute v McKirdy and McMillan 1937 SC 93 at 126–127.
70  R(S)A 1984, s 1 and s 16.

In John McNicol (Farmers) Limited v Scottish Ministers,[71] the owners of a farm challenged the making of a road traffic regulation order under the Road Traffic Regulation Act 1984. The Order affected a section of the M90/A90 trunk road. Their farmland lay on either side of the trunk road and they had a private means of access from their land onto the trunk road on each side. There was a gap in the central reservation which allowed farm traffic to cross trunk road from one part of the farm to the other part as well as turning right or left or making a U-turn. The effect of the Order was to prevent the crossing movement as well as banning some of the turns. The appellants argued that the effect of closing the gap in the central reservation was to stop up their private access. They argued that the Ministers should have made a stopping up order in which event they would have been entitled to compensation. The Inner House held that the gap in the central reservation was part of the public road and, since there was no scope in the statutory framework for a place to be simultaneously part of a public road and a private means of access to land, when the appellants used it for cross traffic they were exercising their public right of passage as members of the public. Accordingly, no private means of access would be stopped up by the closure of the gap. Their Lordships said that it was not necessary for them "to decide whether closing the gap would amount to stopping up a road (though we have no reason to think that it would)." This is a useful indication of the court's possible approach to the legal distinction between closures made under a road traffic regulation order and the stopping up of a road under a stopping up order.

## 4.7    IDENTIFICATION OF A ROAD

Although the identification of a road is straightforward in most cases, there can be circumstances in which it is more difficult to establish that the way is a road and not a private access or some other area of land. If the way has been constructed in accordance with a valid road construction consent and planning permission, these documents could provide evidence of its status. Likewise, it may have been added to the list of public roads by the local roads authority, which could provide evidence of its status.

### 4.7.1    CAR PARKS

In *Clarke v Kato*[72] in 1998, the House of Lords held that a car park is not a road for the purposes of the Road Traffic Act 1988. Their Lordships rejected the decision of the Court of Appeal that regular and incontrovertible use of a car park as a pedestrian route to a parade of shops was sufficient for the route to qualify as a road for the purposes of the Road Traffic Act 1988. Lord Clyde stated that he would:

71    [2006] CSIH 25.
72    The Times Law Report October 23 1998.

'hesitate to formulate a comprehensive definition whereby a place may be identified as a road, but some guidance should be found by considering its physical character and the functions which it exists to serve. ... In the ordinary use of language a car park does not [qualify as a road]. In character and more especially in function they are distinct. ... The proper function of a road is to enable movement along it to a destination. ... The proper function of a car park is to enable vehicles to stand and wait. A car may be driven across it; but that is only incidental to the principal function of parking. A hard shoulder may be seen to form part of a road. A more delicate question could arise with regard to a lay-by, but where it is designed to serve only as a temporary stopping place incidental to the function of the road it may well be correct to treat it as part of the road'.[73]

Although the House of Lords ruled that a car park was not a road, in 1999[73] the High Court of Justiciary held that an area of ground used principally as a car park for employees of Strathclyde Regional Council was a 'way' over which the public had access. This car park was controlled by a barrier during office hours but otherwise open to use by the public. It was also used by pedestrians as a short cut and to provide access to a railway station. The appellant, having been charged with driving without a licence and insurance in this car park, argued that it was not a road. Nevertheless, she was convicted and she appealed to the High Court. The court held that a 'way' was an area in which some form of travel takes place and whether an area was a 'way' was essentially a question of fact; that the circumstances of this case left out of account any question of public rights of passage, the question being whether as a matter of fact the public had access by the way, whether permitted or not, that there was nothing in the definition[74] which confined the user of the way to vehicular traffic and that there were sufficient facts and circumstances to entitle the magistrate to have reached the view that the car park was a way over which the public had access.

These cases demonstrate how the courts will approach a consideration of the facts to establish the existence or otherwise of a 'road' or a 'way over which the public has access'. Another such example is found in the case of Rita Joan May v Director of Public Prosecutions.[75] M was convicted of careless driving after colliding with five cars parked in a car park belonging to a car dealership. The car park was only open during the day with a sign advising that its use was for customers only. The car park was accessed off a public road. M appealed her conviction on the basis that the car park was not a public place for the purposes of the Road Traffic Act 1988. On appeal, the court held that the car park in effect joined a public place and there were no restrictions placed on members

73 Aird v Vannet(Procurator Fiscal, Glasgow) 1999 SCCR 322.
74 Section 192(1) of the Road Traffic Act 1988 as amended by paragraph 78 of Schedule 4 to the Road Traffic Act 1991, which defines a road as, inter alia, 'any other way to which the public has access.'.
75 [2005] EWHC 1280.

of the public on entry to the car park although it was intended for use by customers only. They found that it was a public place for the purposes of the 1988 Act. However, the court warned against treating this type of decision as if it contained 'hard' law stressing that the court must look at the particular facts in each case.

## 4.7.2   ROAD VERGES

The statutory definition of a road includes the verge, which means that the public right of passage extends to the verge. Identification of the extent of the road verge is often not without some difficulty. It is a cardinal rule of property development to ensure that the land take for the proposed development falls within the control of the developer or within the boundary of the road to ensure that they can provide access from the development to the road network without risk of ransom.[76]

Like the identification of a road, the identification of the extent of the road verge is a question of fact.[77] If the road is on the list of public roads, then the roads authority is responsible for maintenance of the verge, which is part of the road.[78] If the roads authority has appropriate maintenance records, they may be able to demonstrate the extent of the road verge. Likewise, it may be possible to establish the extent of the verge from the statutory list of public roads if that list contains maps or dimensions of the road. Some authorities who manage roads in rural areas apply a standard area to the road verge. In the absence of any such evidence or assistance from the roads authority, the identification of the extent of the road verge will be a question of fact in each case.

In the case of Perth and Kinross County Council v Magistrates of Crieff,[79] Lord Murray said:

> "In its natural meaning and construction...'road' or 'highway' means and includes the whole area dedicated to public passage from 'fence to fence' (or as may be 'building line to building line') including the area, if any, occupied by footways of any kind."

In the Runciman case[80] the petitioners argued that the existence of a hedge meant that the public could not have exercised their right of passage over that part of the verge obstructed by the hedge. However, the court held that it was not necessary for the right of passage to exist

---

76   See Strathclyde Regional Council v Persimmon Homes (Scotland) Limited 1994 SLT 176.
77   See Stansfield v Findlay 1998 SLT 784 for consideration of private road verges.
78   Cameron v Central Regional Council 16 January 1995.
79   1933 SC 751.
80   David Runciman & Sons v Scottish Borders Council 2003 SLT 1405.

over every part of the way because the roads authority had the power to place bus shelters and other such 'barriers' in the road, even although such barriers would impede the right of passage. The appropriate boundary in this case was held to be the roadward side of the trunks of trees that made up the hedge. Lord Drummond Young said:

> "In relation to features on the ground, the position is reasonably straightforward where a road is bounded by an established wall or fence or by a building. In such cases the boundary of the verge will normally be taken as the roadward face of the wall, fence or building; this situation is discussed by Lord Murray[81] and it seems clear that the same analysis applies to the 1984 Act. In such cases there exists an obvious physical barrier that stretches up from the ground and is obviously designed to separate the road and its verge from the property beyond. At the other extreme are cases where there is no barrier of any sort… in the absence of a barrier, the verge must clearly be reasonable in extent and what is reasonable will depend on function rather than any physical barrier on the ground."

There appears to be merit in the approach of roads authorities in rural areas who apply a set distance from the edge of the carriageway or footway to the edge of the verge to delineate the boundary of the road. This approach also has the merit of consistency.

An interested party may undertake a property search to identify ownership of the land in question to establish, if possible, the extent of the public road. If the land is owned by the roads authority, that may point to the area under scrutiny being part of the road. However, it would not be conclusive. Ownership by the local authority would not necessarily mean that the land was part of the public road. Conversely, ownership by a third party would not necessarily mean that the land was not part of the public road. The solum of the road may be owned by a third party although the roads vests in the roads authority for the purposes of the 1984 Act. It depends upon the circumstances of the case.

In the case of Elmford Ltd v City of Glasgow Council[82] the court considered whether the petitioners were entitled to take vehicular and pedestrian access and egress across a certain strip of land between land belonging to the petitioners and a link road owned by the Council as roads authority. The land comprising the road and the disputed strip had been acquired compulsorily by the Council's statutory predecessors, who had constructed the road and made an entry in the list of roads under Section 1 of the 1984 Act. The petitioners argued that the land had been acquired for road purposes and, as it had not been appropriated by the Council for any other purpose, it must be deemed to be part of the land constituting the road and, accordingly, the petitioners as the owner of land fronting the road had a right of access over the strip. The Council

81    In Perth and Kinross County Council v Magistrates of Crieff 1933 SC 751.
82    2001 S.C. 267.

argued that the strip of land was not part of the road and that they were entitled to charge to obtain value from the petitioners in respect of taking such access. Lord Clarke held that the acquisition by an authority of land under section 29 of the 1970 Act[83] in connection with the construction of a road was not the equivalent of declaration of that land in its entirety to public passage and since the petitioners had failed to demonstrate any subsequent actings or circumstances which amounted to such dedication, the Council was justified in law in seeking to obtain consideration from the petitioners in exchange for granting any rights of access. At a superficial level, it might seem harsh that land could be taken by compulsion to construct a road with the former owner then having to pay to access that road. However, it should be borne in mind that an authority pays the market value for any land taken under compulsory purchase powers. Furthermore, if there were to be surplus land which could be offered back to the former owner, it would only be transferred back at a consideration reflecting the market value. This is reasonable as it is a transfer of a public asset to a private party and the authority must ensure that any disposal of public assets stands up to scrutiny and audit. Any private landowner faced with a compulsory purchase order would be well advised to consider such risks and enter into appropriate contractual terms with the acquiring authority.

## 4.8   PUBLIC ROADS

A public road is "a road which a roads authority has a duty to maintain."[84] A private road means "any road other than a public road".[85] The roads authority's statutory duty to maintain a road is contained in Section 1 of the 1984 Act.[86] Section 1 provides that the authority "shall manage and maintain all such roads in their area as are for the time being entered in a list (in this Act referred to as the "list of public roads") prepared and kept by them under this section; and for the purposes of such management and maintenance … they shall have the power to reconstruct, alter, widen, improve or renew any such road or to determine the means by which the public right of passage over it, or any part of it, may be exercised." Every road which is entered into the list of public roads shall vest in the roads authority for the purposes of their functions as roads authority.[87] However, such vesting does not confer any heritable right in relation to the road.[88]

---

83   Section 29 of the Roads (Scotland) Act 1970 provided that a highway authority may acquire by agreement or compulsorily, land required in connection with the construction of a highway.
84   R(S)A 1984 s 151.
85   R(S)A 1984 s 151.
86   See Transco plc v Glasgow City Council 2005 S.L.T. 958.
87   R(S)A 1984 s 1(9).
88   R(S)A 1984 s 1(9).

## 4.8.1 LIST OF PUBLIC ROADS

The list of public roads is open for inspection free of charge at times and places determined by the local roads authority.[89] In practice, professional agencies provide a reporting service on the status of roads for solicitors and other professionals. Electronic access might also be available in some areas.

## 4.8.2 AMENDMENTS TO THE LIST OF PUBLIC ROADS

The local roads authority may add to or delete roads from its list of public roads.[90] If it wishes to add an existing private road to the list or delete an existing entry from the list, it must follow a specified procedure. This involves the service of a notice of its intention on the frontagers of the relevant road and the publication of a notice in a local newspaper. It must then consider any representations made within twenty-eight days of service and publication of the notices. Its final decision must be served on the frontagers and any person who made representations. It does not have to follow this procedure if it is reacting in response to:

1.  The decision of a sheriff on summary application by the frontagers in response to the authority's proposed addition to or deletion from the list.

2.  Any deletion in consequence of a stopping up of a public road.

3.  Any deletion on transfer of a public road to another roads authority.[91]

## 4.8.3 APPLICATION TO THE SHERIFF

Following service of a notice in relation to an amendment to the list, the requisite number of frontagers may within twenty-eight days of service, refer the matter by summary application to the sheriff.[92] The sheriff's decision is final and must be given immediate effect by the local roads authority. The notice served by the authority does not take effect until the expiry of the twenty-eight day period within which the matter can be referred to the sheriff. If the matter has been referred to the sheriff, the notice cannot take effect until his decision is known. The sheriff's decision does not prohibit the local roads authority from proceeding with a future proposal to add or delete the same road to or from the list if there is a material change in circumstances.

---

89  R(S)A 1984 s 1(3).
90  See MacKinnon v Argyll and Bute Council 2001 SLT 1275 and Brian Gregory Hamilton V Dumfries and Galloway Council 2006 CSOH 110.
91  R(S)A 1984 s 1(4) As to 'frontager' see Section 151(1).
92  R(S)A 1984 s 1(4) provisos i–iii.

### 4.8.4    THE REQUISITE NUMBER OF FRONTAGERS

'The requisite number' of frontagers is defined as a majority or such number as together own land which includes not less than half of the boundary between the land fronting or abutting the relevant road and that road.[93]

### 4.8.5    DE-LISTING OR STOPPING UP?

The power to delete a road from the list of public roads may be useful if local circumstances change. For instance, use of a public road may have become less popular and may be restricted to use by one party or by a restricted group of interests. The local roads authority may no longer wish to maintain a road which is no longer serving the public at large. Some authorities have been known to respond to such situations by promoting a stopping up order. However, de-listing would be a simpler and less expensive procedure. Of course, it is open to the requisite number of frontagers to oppose a proposal to de-list a road. Moreover, under section 16 of the 1984 Act, the requisite number of frontagers may make application to the local roads authority to adopt a private road to the list of public roads. (A road does not include a footpath for the purposes of this provision). If the private road is of the standard required in a section 13 notice[94] or, if there is no such notice, it is of a standard satisfactory to the local roads authority, the road must be adopted within twelve months of the application. It is reasonable to assume that a road which is on the list of public roads is of a standard that is satisfactory to the local roads authority because it is responsible for the road's maintenance. If the requisite number of frontagers oppose a proposed de-listing and find that their representations fail to persuade either the authority or the sheriff, there would appear to be no legal bar to prevent a subsequent application by them under section 16 to have the newly de-listed road re-adopted by the local roads authority.

### 4.8.6    MANDATORY ADDITIONS TO THE LIST OF PUBLIC ROADS

The local road authority's general power to add a road to its list is contained in section 1 of the 1984 Act. There are two situations in which the authority is required to add a private road to its list on application:

   1.    One is where an application is made by the requisite number of frontagers in terms of Section 16 of the 1984 Act. The authority must add the road[95] to their list within twelve months of application if the road is of a standard specified in a

---

93   R(S)A 1984 s 1(7) (amended by the Abolition of Domestic Rates Etc (Scotland) Act 1987.
94   See [4.9.1] below.
95   but not a footpath.

section 13 (1) notice or, in the absence of such a notice, if it is of a standard satisfactory to the authority. No such application is required if the local roads authority has undertaken and completed the works specified in a section 13 notice. In those circumstances, the authority must add the road to the list forthwith.

2.    The second situation is where a person has completed the construction of a private road in accordance with a construction consent granted by the roads authority in terms of Section 21 of the 1984 Act. If, on completion of the road, the person granted the construction consent applies to have the road added to the list, the roads authority must do so within twelve months of the application.

There is an arbitration provision to settle any dispute between the local roads authority and the person making the application. In the event of a failure to agree upon an arbiter, either party may apply to the sheriff to make an appointment.

If a party makes an application under Section 16, the roads authority may refuse to add the road to their list because the road is not of a standard satisfactory to the authority.[96] In practice, the authority will advise the applicant of the remedial works necessary to bring the road up to a standard that is satisfactory to the authority. Some authorities treat this 'response' as the roads authority's consent to undertake those remedial works. However, the provisions of Section 16 of the 1984 Act relate to applications for a private road to become a public road; they do not authorise the construction of a new road, or part of a new road or other works to a road. If a person other than a roads authority wishes to construct a new road or extend and existing road then that person must obtain the written consent of the roads authority in terms of Section 21 of the 1984 Act. It should be borne in mind that any reference to 'road' includes part of the road.[97] So works to part of the road fall within the scope of Section 21. It is an offence to construct a road or to extend an existing road without construction consent. Any person who undertakes remedial works to an existing private road on the basis of the roads authority's response under Section 16 risks having committed an offence under Section 21 of the 1984 Act.

## 4.9   PRIVATE ROADS

A private road is any road other than a public road.[98] Although the local roads authority is not responsible for the management and maintenance of private roads, they do have specific powers in relation to them, including:

96   Section 16(1) (b) of the R(S)A 1984.
97   Section 151 of the R(S)A 1984.
98   Section 151 of the R(S)A 1984.

- making a financial contribution to the cost of making up or maintaining a private road[99]

- carrying out repairs to a private road[100]

- carrying out emergency works to a private road[101]

- installing refuse or storage bins in roads[102]

- powers in relation to dangerous road works[103]

- control of obstructions in roads[104]

- temporary prohibition or restriction of traffic for reasons of public safety or convenience[105]

- regulation of horsedrawn carts etc[106]

- maintenance of vaults and cellars etc[107]

- power to direct that doors do not open onto a road[108]

- stopping up of roads by order[109]

- prevention of obstruction of view at corners, bends and junctions[110]

- control of builders' skips on road[111]

- removal of structures from roads[112]

- removal of projections which impede or endanger road users[113]

- removal of accidental obstructions from roads[114]

- restriction on placing bridges, beams, rails etc over roads[115]

- prevention of danger to road from nearby vegetation and fences or retaining walls being inadequate[116]

- restriction of planting of trees etc near carriageway[117]

99   Section 14 (1) of R(S)A 1984.
100 Section 14 (1) of R(S)A 1984.
101 Section 15 of R(S)A 1984.
102 Section 54 of R(S)A 1984.
103 Section 57 of the R(S)A 1984.
104 Section 59 of R(S)A 1984.
105 Section 62 of R(S)A 1984.
106 Section 65 of R(S)A 1984.
107 Section 66 of R(S)A 1984.
108 Section 67 of R(S)A 1984.
109 Section 68 of R(S)A 1984.
110 Section 83 of R(S)A 1984.
111 Section 85 of R(S)A 1984.
112 Section 87 of R(S)A 1984.
113 Section 88 of R(S)A 1984.
114 Section 89) of R(S)A 1984.
115 Section 90 of R(S)A 1984.
116 Section 91 of R(S)A 1984.
117 Section 92 of R(S)A 1984.

- protection of road users from dangers near a road[118]

- deposit of mud from vehicles[119]

- control of stray and other animals on a road[120]

- prevention of flow of water onto a road[121]

- offences relating to road damage[122]

These provisions address issues of road safety, which are relevant to both public and private roads because members of the public have a right of passage over each category of road. Likewise, roads authorities are empowered under the Road Traffic Regulation Act 1984 to make traffic regulation orders in respect of both public and private roads. In practice, however, such orders tend to be made in respect of public roads because they form the main part of the road network and are more likely to require regulation. If a private road were to become so heavily trafficked that it required regulation, the roads authority might well consider adding the road to their list of roads, which would extend their powers to matters such as the provision of street lighting.[123] One example where a traffic regulation order might be required in relation to a private road is in relation to a controlled parking zone. If a private road in a proposed zone were to be omitted from the traffic regulation order, it could undermine the objectives of the scheme by permitting uncontrolled or 'free' parking within the controlled zone. This might be particularly sensitive in situations where 'new build' residential developments have provided residents' parking spaces on private roads associated with the development. For this reason, it is in the interests of both the roads authority and the developer/residents to be clear about whether the development includes a private access or a private road in urban areas. The roads authority should be clear about their view in their consultation responses to the planning authority.

## 4.9.1  MAKING UP AND MAINTENANCE OF PRIVATE ROADS

*Section 13 notices*

Under section 13 of the 1984 Act, the local roads authority may serve a notice on the frontagers of a private road requiring them to make up the road to a reasonable standard, as specified in the notice, and thereafter to maintain the road. The works that can be required include levelling, paving, lighting and drainage. The Section 13 notice must specify:

118  Section 93 of R(S)A 1984.
119  Section 95 of R(S)A 1984.
120  Section 98 of R(S)A 1984.
121  Section 99 of R(S)A 1984.
122  Section 100 of R(S)A 1984.
123  Section 35 of R(S)A 1984.

1.    The local roads authority's estimate of the costs of the required works.

2.    A scheme apportioning the cost among the frontagers. The scheme must be equitable in the opinion of the authority and it must describe for each frontager the proportion of the cost to be paid by him.

3.    The dates by which the works shall be commenced and completed. The authority has the power to postpone commencement or completion, or both, by a subsequent notice.

If the frontagers fail to comply with the dates for commencement and completion specified in the notice, the authority has the power to carry out the work or to complete unfinished works. The authority also has the power to carry out the requirements of the notice with the agreement of the requisite number of frontagers.[124] In both situations, the expenses incurred by the local roads authority are recoverable in accordance with the scheme contained within the notice. This procedure has the practical advantage of providing a cost benchmark for frontagers in receipt of a notice. If the local authority's estimate is less than those of private contractors, the requisite number of frontagers may ask the authority to undertake the work in terms of the scheme on their behalf.

Any person receiving a section 13 notice may appeal by summary application to the sheriff within twenty-eight days of the date of service of the notice. The sheriff's decision on the matter is final.

The risk of being served with a Section 13 notice is carried by all frontagers of private roads in Scotland. In practice, local roads authorities do not serve such notices without good cause. Presumably the benefit to the general public of carrying out the works would have to outweigh the cost to the frontagers of paying for the works before Members would sanction service of the notice. The effect of a Section 13 notice is to impose a liability on the frontagers of the private road, not on the owner of the solum of the road.

### 4.9.2    FINANCIAL CONTRIBUTION BY THE LOCAL ROADS AUTHORITY

The local roads authority has an additional power which enables it either to make a financial contribution to private road maintenance works or to carry out such works.[125] Such a decision is entirely within its discretion. It may pay the whole or any part of expenditure incurred by a person in making up or maintaining a private road. It may also at its own expense carry out any repair to a private road which it considers necessary after giving such notice as is reasonable in the circumstances. This power is in

---

124  The requisite number of frontagers has the same meaning as in R(S)A 1984, s 1(7): R(S)A 1984, s 13(8).
125  Section 14 (1) of R(S)A 1984.

addition to and without prejudice to its separate power to carry out emergency work in relation to private roads.[126] If it decides to make a financial contribution or to carry out works to a private road, it does not as a result incur responsibility for making up or maintenance of the road. Future maintenance of the road remains the responsibility of the landowner. In the absence of a clear title to the solum of the private road, the frontagers could be liable for its maintenance if a Section 13 notice were to be served. The carrying out of such works by the local roads authority does not create any implication that the private road, on completion of the works, is of a standard satisfactory to the authority for the purposes of adopting a private road to the list of public roads.[127]

### 4.9.3   EMERGENCY WORKS TO A PRIVATE ROAD

The local roads authority may undertake works to a private road that, in its opinion, are necessary because circumstances have arisen that constitute an emergency. It is not required to give any notice of its intention to carry out the works. It may however give such notice as is appropriate in the circumstances. Any such works are carried out at the expense of the authority. For the purposes of this provision, an emergency excludes dangers relating to vegetation, fences or inadequate retaining walls.[128]

## 4.10   ROADS OUTWITH THE SCOPE OF THE ROADS (SCOTLAND) ACT 1984

The 1984 Act does not confer any power or impose any duty on a roads authority regarding a road or proposed road that falls within the following categories:

1.  A public path created under section 30 of the Countryside (Scotland) Act 1967. Such paths are created under powers conferred upon planning authorities and responsibility for them rests with planning authorities not local roads authorities.

2.  A footpath, which forms part of a long distance route approved by the Scottish Ministers under section 40(1) of the 1967 Act. Proposals for long distance routes are submitted to them by Scottish Natural Heritage and must contain proposals for the provision, maintenance and enjoyment of the route. Such routes are not the responsibility of the local roads authority.

3.  A road which forms part of land owned or managed by a local authority for the provision of recreational, sporting, cultural

---

126  Section 15 of R(S)A 1984.
127  Section 16(1)(b) of R(S)A 1984.
128  Section 91 of R(S)A 1984 and Chapter 11.

or social activities in terms of section 14 of the Local Government and Planning (Scotland) Act 1982.

In 1984 there was a two tier structure of local government in Scotland. This provision would have had the effect of separating the powers and functions of regional councils, as roads authorities, and district councils, which, as leisure and recreation authorities, were responsible for the management and maintenance of certain roads, such as park roads. This provision would have prevented a district council from applying to have a park road added to the list of public roads maintained by the regional council. The provision may be of less importance today but it continues to remove the jurisdiction of the roads authority in relation to roads that fall within the three categories. However, it does not follow that a public right of passage does not exist over the categories of road specified in subsections (a), (b) and (c) of Section 151 (3). The 'road' in question must be a road for the purposes of the 1984 Act in order to fall within these provisions. So they are ways over which there is a public right of passage. If a decision were to be taken to extinguish the public right of passage, a stopping up order would be necessary. However, that order could not be promoted by the roads authority under the 1984 Act because of the terms of Section 151 (3). The stopping up order would have to be promoted under a different statutory process. For instance, an order could be made under planning legislation.

## 4.11   TRUNK ROADS

The trunk road network is a national system of routes for through traffic in Scotland. The Trunk Roads Acts of 1936 and 1946 defined trunk roads as the principal roads constituting the national system of routes for through traffic. The actual roads are listed in Schedules to the Acts. All existing trunk roads maintained their status when the Road Traffic (Scotland) Act 1984[129] came into force.

## 4.11.1   TRUNK ROAD AUTHORITY

The Scottish Ministers are responsible for the management and maintenance of the trunk road network which will include any special roads for which they are special road authority and which have been designated as trunk roads.[130] The Ministers have the power to reconstruct, alter, widen, improve or renew trunk roads and can also determine the means by which the public right of passage may be exercised over the road. The day to day administration of the trunk road network is now carried out on behalf of the Scottish Ministers by the new national transport agency, Transport Scotland.[131] The Directorate within Transport Scotland is

129 Section 5 (1) of R(S)A 1984.
130 Section 2 of R(S)A 1984.
131 See Chapter 2.

known as the Trunk Roads Infrastructure and Professional Services Directorate (TR:IPS).

There is a list of roads which are managed and maintained by Transport Scotland. This list includes all trunk roads. It is open for public inspection free of charge.[132] Every trunk road vests in the Ministers for the purposes of their functions as roads authority but such vesting does not confer any heritable right in relation to the road.[133] The Ministers have an obligation to keep the trunk road system under review.[134] As part of that review, they may decide that an existing road, or any road to be constructed by them, should become a trunk road or that an existing trunk road should cease to be a trunk road. In making any such decision the Scottish Ministers must take into account the requirements of national and local planning, including the requirements of agriculture and industry. The Scottish Ministers may direct that a road, or a proposed road, should become part of the trunk road in order to relieve the trunk road from local traffic. They may do so even if there is intervening land between those roads.[135]

## 4.11.2   TRUNK ROAD ORDERS

The legal procedure to be followed by the Scottish Ministers to direct that a road shall become or cease to be a trunk road is set out in Schedule 1 to the 1984 Act.[136] They may have to publish an environmental statement in relation to certain road improvement projects.[137]

The procedure involves public advertisement with provision for submission of objections within a specified period being not less than six weeks from the date of publication of the statutory notice of the draft order. The Schedule contains a table of statutory consultees who must be served with a copy of the order, the statutory notice and any relevant map or plan. If a statutory consultee submits and maintains an objection, the Scottish Ministers must hold a local inquiry. If a party, other than a statutory consultee, submits and maintains an objection, the Scottish Ministers may hold a local inquiry. After considering outstanding objections and the report of the local inquiry, the Scottish Ministers may make the order with or without modifications.

The validity of Scottish Ministers' decision to make the order may be challenged in the Court of Session by an aggrieved person within six weeks of the date of public notice of the decision. The existence of this statutory right of appeal may have the effect of rendering this procedure

132  Section 2(3) of R(S)A 1984.
133  Section 2(4) of R(S)A 1984.
134  Section 5(2) of R(S)A 1984.
135  Section 5(3) of R(S)A 1984.
136  Section 5(4) of R(S)A 1984.
137  Section 55A of R(S)A 1984 (added by the Environmental Impact Assessment (Scotland) Regulations 1999, SSI 1999/1) See also Chapter 5.

compatible with the provisions of the Human Rights Act 1998 in relation to Article 6(1) of the European Convention on Human Rights which enshrines a right to a fair hearing.[138]

The Scottish Executive adopts this procedure in relation to the construction of side roads.[139] The Local Government etc (Scotland) Act 1994 introduced certain transitional powers of the Secretary of State to deal with existing and proposed trunk roads in relation to the establishment of new local government areas on 1 April 1996. Those powers allowed him to make trunk road orders in respect of existing or proposed roads directing that the roads should become or cease to be trunk roads.

### 4.11.3   SPECIAL PARLIAMENTARY PROCEDURE

A trunk road order may relate to a road which is, or will become, the responsibility of the local roads authority. The former involves a proposal to designate part of the local road network as a trunk road. This would effectively remove control of the road from the local roads authority. The second situation involves the 'de-trunking' of a trunk road to local road status thereby transferring the maintenance responsibility for the road from Transport Scotland to the local roads authority. In either case, the submission of a valid objection from the local roads authority means that the order will be subject to special parliamentary procedure, if the objection is not withdrawn.[140]

### 4.11.4   STATUS OF A ROAD WHICH CEASES TO BE A TRUNK ROAD

If, for the purposes of reorganising or improving the network, the Scottish Ministers decide that a road should no longer be a trunk road, they have the power to make a trunk road order, which specifies that the road shall cease to be a trunk road. Such an order may also direct that the local roads authority for the area shall become the roads authority for the road. The order must specify the date from which the local roads authority assumes responsibility for the road. The order may also direct the authority to enter the road in the list of public roads.[141]

### 4.11.5   CYCLE TRACKS AND FOOTPATHS ASSOCIATED WITH TRUNK ROADS

The Scottish Ministers have a general power to improve trunk roads by the construction of associated cycle tracks and footways.[142] They may also

138 See para 1.4.5.
139 See Chapter 5.
140 Section 5(5) of R(S)A 1984.
141 Section 5(2)(b)of R(S)A 1984.
142 Section 5(8) of R(S)A 1984.

make an order directing that cycle tracks or footpaths, which they propose to construct in association with a trunk road, albeit separated from the road by intervening land, will be part of the trunk road network.[143]

## 4.11.6 FINANCIAL CONTRIBUTIONS BY LOCAL ROADS AUTHORITY

A local roads authority may make a financial contribution towards the costs incurred by the Scottish Ministers in the construction or improvement of any trunk road.[144]

## 4.11.7 PROVISION OF PICNIC SITES FOR TRUNK ROADS

The Scottish Ministers have the power to provide and maintain picnic sites and associated facilities for trunk roads.[145] The associated facilities include public conveniences and facilities for the provision of meals and refreshments. They are not empowered to provide a catering service or to arrange for the local authority to provide that service although they may make arrangements for some other person to do so. They may acquire land voluntarily or compulsorily for the construction of a picnic site. The scope of land take authorised by a compulsory purchase order is restricted to 800 metres from the middle of the relevant trunk road.[146]

## 4.12  SPECIAL ROADS

A special road is one that is for the use of prescribed classes of traffic as specified in a special roads scheme.[147] Schedule 3 to the 1984 Act sets out the nine classes of traffic for this purpose. The Scottish Ministers may by order vary the classes of traffic and the composition of any such class. Special roads include, for example, motorways. All special roads provided under the Special Roads Act 1949 maintained their status when the 1984 Act came into force.[148]

## 4.12.1  SPECIAL ROAD AUTHORITY

A special road authority is a roads authority authorised by a special road scheme to provide a special road. A special road authority may be the Scottish Ministers or a local roads authority. One example of a local

143 Section 5(8) of R(S)A 1984.
144 Section 6 of R(S)A 1984.
145 Section 55 of R(S)A 1984.
146 Section 109 of R(S)A 1984, Sch 5, Pt 1, para 5.
147 Section 7of R(S)A 1984.
148 Section 7(1) of R(S)A 1984.

roads authority as special road authority was Strathclyde Regional Council in relation to the section of the M8 motorway within the boundaries of the former Glasgow District Council area.

## 4.12.2    SPECIAL ROAD SCHEMES

The legal procedure to designate an existing or proposed road as a special road involves the making of a special road scheme.[149] A special road scheme will be made by the Scottish Ministers in the case of a road to be provided by the Transport Scotland. If the road is to be provided by the local roads authority, the scheme will be made by that authority and confirmed by the Scottish Ministers.[150] There is a statutory obligation upon the Minister to give due consideration to the requirements of national and local planning, and to the requirements of agriculture and industry, before making or confirming a scheme.[151] Two or more local road authorities may jointly submit a scheme to the Scottish Ministers for confirmation. Any such scheme may determine which of the promoting authorities shall be the special road authority for the special road. In the case of a joint submission, one of the authorities can transfer its statutory roads function in relation to the road to the special road authority. The scheme can also make provision for the roads authority to make a contribution to the special road authority in respect of expenditure incurred in the performance of those functions.[152] With the establishment of Regional Transport Partnerships,[153] it would be possible for a Transport Partnership to enter into arrangements with the Scottish Ministers or the local roads authority in relation to a special road scheme.[154]

The procedure for making and confirming special road schemes is set out in Schedule 1 to the 1984 Act.[155] The procedure involves public advertisement and statutory consultation with the opportunity to submit objections within a specified period of not less than six weeks. One of the statutory consultees is the council in whose area any part of the route of the special road is situated. If the relevant council objects and does not withdraw its objection, the Ministers must hold a local inquiry.[156] Such an objection may arise from a function of the council other than its roads function, such as its planning function. If an objection is sustained by a person other than a statutory consultee, the Scottish Ministers have the discretion to dispense with the local inquiry if satisfied that an inquiry is unnecessary in the circumstances of the case.[157] Although they have a statutory discretion in these circumstances, they must nevertheless act

149  Section 7 of R(S)A 1984.
150  Section 7(6) of R(S)A 1984.
151  Section 7(7) of R(S)A 1984.
152  Section 7(10) of R(S)A 1984.
153  Transport (Scotland) Act 2005 Part 1.
154  Section 14 of the Transport (Scotland) Act 2005.
155  R(S)A 1984 Sch 1, Pt 1.
156  R(S)A 1984 Sch 1, Pt II, para 11.
157  R(S)A 1984 Sch 1, Pt II, para 12.

reasonably in reaching a proper decision. Failure to act reasonably may leave the decision open to legal challenge by means of judicial review.[158] Care will also have to be taken to ensure that the adopted procedure does not deny a relevant party their right to a fair hearing in terms of the Human Rights Act 1998. After considering any outstanding objections and, if applicable, the report of the local inquiry, the Scottish Ministers may make or confirm the scheme without modification or subject to such modification as they think fit. As soon as may be after making or confirming the scheme, they must publish notice of their decision. The scheme may be challenged in the Court of Session by an aggrieved person within six weeks of the date of public notice of the decision to make or confirm the scheme.[159]

### 4.12.3   SPECIAL PARLIAMENTARY PROCEDURE

The submission of following categories of objection will result in the scheme being subjected to special parliamentary procedure:[160]

1.   A valid objection made by the roads authority for any road (or proposed road) comprised in the route of the special road authorised by the scheme. This situation deals with a dispute between the roads authority for the road which is the subject of the scheme and the promoter of the scheme.

2.   A valid objection from any navigation authority or Scottish Water, on the ground that the scheme provides for any bridge or tunnel over or under navigable waters that is likely to impede the performance of their statutory functions. This situation deals with disputes between other statutory bodies and the promoting authority.

### 4.12.4   SUPPLEMENTARY ORDERS RELATING TO SPECIAL ROADS

A range of supplementary orders can be made in relation to special roads.[161] These orders may cover:

*   Appropriation of any road or proposed road in the course of construction as part of the special road.

*   Transferring any road or proposed road in the course of construction to the special road authority.

*   Authorising the special road authority to stop up, divert or improve any road which crosses or enters the route of a special road.

158  Associated Provincial Picture Houses Limited v Wednesbury Corporation [1948] 1 KB 223, CA.
159  R(S)A 1984, Sch 2: See Lithgow v Secretary of State for Scotland Court of Session Outer House Oct 18 1972.
160  Section 7(8) of the R(S)A 1984.
161  Section 9 of the R(S)A 1984.

- Construction of any new road related to such improvements.

- Transferring to the roads authority any new road constructed by the special road authority.

- The exercise by the special roads authority of the roads authority functions in relation to the special road.

- Any other purpose incidental to the special road scheme.

- Payment of contributions by or to the special road authority.

### 4.12.5   RELATIONSHIP WITH THE TRUNK ROAD NETWORK

Until 1991 special roads for which the Secretary of State was special road authority, were designated as trunk roads.[162] In administrative terms, this ensured that all of the roads that were under the responsibility of the Secretary of State were part of the trunk road network. They would therefore be part of any trunk road maintenance contract let by the Secretary of State. They would also benefit from the statutory provisions in respect of trunk roads. Now the special roads scheme may specify that the special road, or any part of it, shall not be a trunk road.[163] The Scottish Ministers retain the power to reclassify the special road as a trunk road at a future date.[164]

## 4.13   CROWN ROADS

A crown road is a road to which the public has access by permission granted by the appropriate Crown authority or otherwise granted by or on behalf of the Crown.[165]

162  Section 10(1) of the R(S)A 1984.
163  R(S)A 1984, s 10(3) added by the New Roads and Street Works Act 1991, s 46.
164  R(S)A 1984, s 5(2)(a).
165  Section 131(7)(b) of the Road Traffic Regulation Act 1984.

# 5   Road Construction

## 5.1   CONSTRUCTION BY SCOTTISH MINISTERS AS ROADS AUTHORITY

Transport Scotland, acting on behalf of the Scottish Ministers, is empowered to construct new roads. These may be special roads, trunk roads or other roads. In practice, Transport Scotland is only involved with the construction of special or trunk roads. It does not undertake the construction of local roads although it does have a specific power to construct 'other roads'.[1] This power is generally used for the construction or improvement of side roads, which will become part of the local road network.[2] Side roads are constructed to connect the local road network to the special or trunk road network. They are a necessary link to integrate the two networks.

The construction of a road constitutes development for the purposes of Section 26 of the Town and Country Planning (Scotland) Act 1997. However, the construction of a new road for which the Scottish Ministers are roads authority is permitted development under Class 73 of the Town and Country Planning (General Permitted Development) (Scotland) Order 1992.

This does not mean that there is no opportunity for public scrutiny of a proposed national road project. Transport Scotland must follow a statutory procedure that involves the promotion and implementation of trunk road orders[3] or special road schemes,[4] as appropriate. This procedure involves a consultation process that provides an opportunity for the local authority and members of the public to comment upon the project.

Road proposals by Transport Scotland will also be subjected to public consultation if they fall within the categories of projects that require publication of an environmental statement.[5]

A decision by the Scottish Ministers to make or confirm a roads order will be contained in a Scottish Statutory Instrument.[6]

1   R(S)A 1984, s 19.
2   Decisions to issue notices to transfer responsibility for managing and maintaining de-trunked roads and new side roads to a local roads authority are susceptible to judicial review: *Dumfries and Galloway Council v Scottish Ministers* 2 August 2000, unreported.
3   See Chapter 4, pp 67 ff.
4   See Chapter 4, pp 70 ff.
5   Ie in terms of R(S)A 1984, s 20A (added by the Environmental Impact Assessment (Scotland) Regulations 1999, SSI 1999/1, reg 49. See pp 86 ff.
6   R(S)A 1984, s 43.

## 5.2    CONSTRUCTION BY LOCAL ROADS AUTHORITY

A local roads authority enjoys a wide power to construct within its area any new road, which it considers to be necessary.[7] This general power expressly excludes the construction of special roads, which must be authorised by a special road scheme.[8]

### 5.2.1    PLANNING PERMISSION

As the construction of a new road constitutes development for the purposes of the Town and Country Planning (Scotland) Act 1997 planning permission is required. An application for planning permission may have to be supported by an environmental statement.[9] Circular 15/1999 states that this is more likely to be required for the construction or improvement of local roads where the new development is over 2km in length. If the project only involves maintenance of an existing road by the local roads authority, planning permission is not required if the works are contained within the boundaries of the road.[10] Such maintenance works do not constitute development and planning permission is not therefore necessary. Likewise, any works for the improvement of the road carried out by the local roads authority within the boundary of the road do not constitute development unless those works may have significant adverse effects on the environment. If the improvement works might adversely affect the environment, then they fall within the definition of development for the purposes of the 1997 Act. However, Class 31 (a) of the Town and Country Planning (General Permitted Development) (Scotland) Order 1992[11] provides that such improvement works constitute permitted development which means that there is no need to apply for planning permission.

### 5.2.2    PERMITTED DEVELOPMENT RIGHTS

The Town and Country Planning (General Permitted Development) (Scotland) Order 1992 permits certain specified classes of development to be carried out without a formal grant of planning permission. The Order applies to Scotland as a whole but certain areas may be excluded by the terms of an Article 4 direction which enables the Scottish Ministers or the planning authority to restrict permitted development. Before undertaking any development classified as permitted under the Order, it would be prudent to check with the planning authority to ensure that the development rights have not been restricted by an Article 4 direction. It is also important to check the relevant terms of the Order, which imposes conditions on the implementation of the specified classes of development.

7    R(S)A 1984, s 20.
8    See Chapter 4, pp 70 ff.
9    R(S)A 1984, s 20A. Environmental Assessment of certain road construction projects see p 86 below. See also s 20B – Projects with significant transboundary effects.
10    Town and Country Planning (Scotland) Act 1997, s 26.
11    SI 1992/223.

In terms of Class 31 of the Order, a local roads authority enjoys permitted development rights to carry out works on land outwith but adjoining the boundary of an existing road if those works are required for or incidental to the maintenance or improvement of the road. They also enjoy permitted development rights for those improvement works that involve development for the purposes of Section 26(2)(b) of the 1997 Act. Permitted development rights are unlikely to apply in conservation areas.

Under Class 30 of the Order a local authority enjoys permitted development rights to erect, construct, maintain, improve or alter lamp standards, refuse bins, public shelters and similar structures or works required in connection with the operation of any public service administered by them.

Class 73 of the Order permits development by the Scottish Ministers as roads authority in relation to:

(a)    the construction of a new road for which the Scottish Ministers are roads authority

(b)    the improvement of a road authorised by an order under Section 5, 9, 12, 75 or 77 of the 1984 Act

(c)    the improvement of a road without such an order

Class 74 of the Order permits the carrying out by the Scottish Ministers of development (other than development falling within Class 73) in exercise of their functions under the 1984 Act, or development in connection with, or incidental to, the exercise of those functions.

### 5.2.3   APPLICATIONS FOR PLANNING PERMISSION BY LOCAL ROADS AUTHORITIES

Before local government reorganisation in 1996, a regional council, as statutory roads authority, would submit an application for planning permission to construct a new road to the relevant district council, as planning authority. Since the introduction of unitary authorities in April 1996, the roads and planning functions have been vested in the same local authority. Until 1 April 2007 development by planning authorities was regulated by the Town and Country Planning (Development by Planning Authorities) (Scotland) Regulations 1981.[12] Under those Regulations, the planning authority followed the Notice of Intention to Develop procedure (NID) which raised particular constraints for commercial development and other forms of development undertaken as part of the PFI/PPP initiatives. However, the NID procedure was discontinued on 1 April 2007.[13] The effect is that a local authority, including the local roads authority, will now have to apply for planning permission for their own developments, where relevant.[14]

12   SI 1981/829 (amended by SI 1984/238).
13   Circular 4/1997 *Notification of Applications* para 14.
14   PFI and the Planning Process: Guidance Note dated 29 April 1998.

## 5.2.4   NOTIFICATION OF APPLICATIONS FOR PLANNING PERMISSION BY LOCAL ROADS AUTHORITIES

Applications for planning permission for local authority development fall within Category 13 of The Town and Country Planning (Notification of Applications) (Scotland) Direction 2007. This Direction came into force on 1 July 2007. Category 13 deals with development in which planning authorities have an interest. If the application relates to development for which the planning authority is the applicant/ developer and the proposed development is contrary to the development plan or has been the subject of a substantial body of objections, then it must be notified to the Scottish Ministers if the authority is minded to grant planning permission. Planning Circular 5/07: Notification of Planning Applications sets out the documents to be submitted to the Scottish Ministers with the relevant application. In cases of local authority development, the authority must also submit the following:

1.    A statement relating to non-inclusion in the development plan – that is a statement to explain why the development has not been planned for through the development plan; and

2.    Details of alternative development – that is information as to any alternatives considered by the authority.

## 5.3   CONSTRUCTION BY OTHERS: CONSENT REQUIRED

Any person other than a local roads authority wishing to construct a new road or to extend an existing road requires a construction consent from the local roads authority.[15] This requirement does not apply to roads authorities. It would appear that a construction consent is personal to the applicant. In event of default, the authority's remedy is to serve notice on the person holding the consent.[16] It would not appear to be open to someone with a construction consent to transfer the permission to a third party without the express consent of the roads authority. The construction consent does not enure for the benefit of the land like planning permission.

The construction of a new road or the extension of an existing road involves engineering operations, which constitute development. Planning permission is therefore required in addition to a construction consent. However, planning permission is not a legal prerequisite of a grant of construction consent. There is no legal requirement for the local roads authority to take into account the existence or the lack of any other statutory consent. The local roads authority must act within the powers of the Roads (Scotland) Act 1984. It should not be influenced by any

15   R(S)A 1984, s 21.
16   R(S)A 1984, s 21(5).

other statutory function of the local authority. For instance, it should not withhold a construction consent to remedy a breach of planning control. Nor should the issue of a construction consent be pre-determined by the local authority in relation to a separate matter, such as a land contract. The grant of planning permission for a road to be constructed on land owned by the authority does not infer the consent of the authority as heritable proprietor.[17]

## 5.3.1   APPLICATION FOR CONSTRUCTION CONSENT

An application for construction consent must be made in writing in a form to be determined by the local roads authority. In processing applications, the authority is concerned with a technical appraisal of the proposal. Its planning merits are irrelevant in this process as they will be taken into account by the planning authority when deciding whether or not to grant planning permission for the road. If the application for construction consent demonstrates to the satisfaction of the authority that the proposed road can be constructed to the authority's standards, consent should be granted.

Roads authorities tend to have standards for new roads in their area, which standards are usually approved by the Council prior to publication. Some standards list the documents to be submitted with an application for consent. Those documents may include a location plan and a layout plan showing specified technical detail.

## 5.3.2   NOTIFICATION OF APPLICATION FOR CONSTRUCTION CONSENT

The applicant must serve notice of the application on owners of all land, which would front, abut or be included in the new road or the extension of the existing road. The authority has the power to specify other persons who should be notified of the application by the applicant. The notice should invite written representations to be submitted to the authority within twenty-eight days of intimation. The authority must consider any written representations made within the twenty-eight day period by any person who was notified of the application. Having done so, the authority may either grant construction consent without conditions or subject to such conditions as it thinks fit, or refuse construction consent. If the authority intends either to grant consent subject to a condition or to refuse consent, it must allow the applicant an opportunity to be heard as regards their application. The right to a hearing only extends to the applicant. Third party objectors have no right to a hearing.

17   Strathclyde Regional Council v Persimmon Homes (Scotland) Ltd 1996 SLT 176.

### 5.3.3   COMPLETION OF CONSTRUCTION

All construction consents are subject to a condition that the construction be completed within a specified period being a period not less than three years from the date of the consent. This period must be specified by the local roads authority in the consent but the authority may subsequently extend the specified period by notice.[18] If security has been lodged with the authority in relation to private residential development associated with the road construction, the authority may impose a condition requiring additional security when extending the completion period.[19]

### 5.3.4   APPEAL TO THE SCOTTISH MINISTERS

The applicant has a right of appeal to the Scottish Ministers within twenty-eight days of the date of intimation of the decision of the local roads authority. The right of appeal is in respect of a decision to refuse consent or to grant consent subject to conditions. There is no right of appeal against the statutory condition that the construction be completed within three years of the date of consent.

The appeal procedure is set out in the Road Construction Consent (Appeals Procedure) (Scotland) Regulations 1986.[20] The appeal must be accompanied by a statement of the grounds of appeal, together with:

- A copy of the application
- The names and addresses of all those upon whom notice of the application was served in accordance with section 21 of the Roads (Scotland) Act 1984 ('section 21 parties').
- A copy of the local roads authority's notice of decision.

Having accepted the appeal as valid, the Scottish Ministers must notify the local roads authority in writing of the appeal. The authority will be asked to submit the following information by a specified date.

- A statement of the reasons for reaching their decision.
- A copy of each representation (if any) made by section 21 parties and any follow up correspondence.
- A copy of the record of any hearing.
- Any other information which appears to the Scottish Ministers to be relevant.

As well as notifying the local roads authority, the Scottish Ministers must also notify section 21 parties in writing of the appeal and give them the opportunity to make written representations by a specified date.

18   R(S)A 1984, s 21 (4).
19   See R(S)A 1984, s 17 and the Security for Private Road Works (Scotland) Regulations 1985, SI 1985/2080, reg 11, see also para 5.4.1 ff below.
20   SI 1986/509.

The Scottish Ministers have the power to delegate the decision to an appointed person. If so, they must advise the appellant, the local roads authority and all section 21 parties of the name of the appointed person. If the appeal is to be the subject of a hearing, the identity of the appointed person may not be known until the commencement of the hearing.

The Scottish Ministers may determine the appeal on the basis of the written information submitted to them but they may hold a hearing, if they consider it appropriate to do so. The Scottish Ministers, or the appointed person, must notify their decision, with the reasons for the decision, in writing to the appellant, the local roads authority and the section 21 parties. In the determination of the appeal, they may allow or dismiss the appeal and they may modify any part of the local roads authority's decision.

The decision on appeal is final. There is no right of appeal to the Court of Session. This does not however preclude the possibility of the common law remedy of judicial review of the decision of the Scottish Ministers on the basis that the decision is ultra vires.

## 5.3.5   POWERS OF ENTRY

During the construction period, a person authorised by the local roads authority has the right to enter any land at all reasonable hours to inspect any work being undertaken under a construction consent.[21] The officer must produce a duly authenticated document showing his authority to gain entry. Except in an emergency, entry should not be demanded as of right unless at least seven days notice is given to the occupier. The authority is entitled to recover expenses reasonably incurred by it in relation to its inspection procedures. Expenses are recoverable from the person to whom the consent has been granted. If more than one person is liable to meet the expenses, the authority may apportion the expense accordingly. Wilful obstruction of the officer is an offence. If the officer causes damage to land or property in exercising the power of entry, compensation may be claimed from the authority.

## 5.3.6   ENFORCEMENT POWERS

Any person, other than a roads authority, who constructs a new road or an extension of an existing road without construction consent, is guilty of an offence.[22] Likewise, any person who contravenes or fails to comply with a condition imposed by a construction consent is guilty of an offence. However, failure to comply with the statutory condition that construction be completed within three years of consent does not constitute an offence. If the local roads authority have evidence of an offence, the matter can be referred to the Procurator Fiscal who will decide whether or not to prosecute the alleged offender.

21    R(S)A 1984, s 140.
22    R(S)A 1984, s 22.

Apart from reporting an alleged offence to the procurator fiscal, the local roads authority can take other steps to remedy the situation.

If there is a breach of a condition imposed by a construction consent, the local roads authority may serve a notice on the person holding the consent.[23] The notice will require the recipient to bring the new road into conformity with the construction consent within a reasonable period, which will be specified in the notice. The decision to serve a notice is discretionary.

The local roads authority may also stop up or temporarily close any new road which has been constructed either without a construction consent, or, in contravention of or non-compliance with a condition imposed by a construction consent.[24] Stopping up or temporary closure may take place whether or nor court proceedings are pending in relation to the alleged offence. However, if, in any such proceedings, it is found that either construction consent existed or that there was no contravention of, or failure to comply with the conditions of a construction consent, the authority must end the stopping up or temporary closure.

A local roads authority is more likely to take direct action to stop up or close a road if road safety is compromised or if the developer has proceeded without consent. Otherwise, in the case of a breach of a condition, it may decide to allow the developer an opportunity to remedy the situation. If so, it will serve a notice requiring remedial action within a specified time. Failure to respond is likely to result in stopping up/closure and, perhaps, court proceedings. A decision to stop up or close a road, whether under construction or completed, may have serious commercial repercussions.

## 5.4   ROAD BONDS

In cases of residential development the Roads (Scotland) Act 1984 provides a financial mechanism to ensure that an adequate road system is constructed to service the development.[25] The roads must be constructed to a standard satisfactory to the local roads authority so that the roads can be added to the authority's list of public roads. This removes the potential maintenance liability from the purchasers of the houses in the development. This protection for the house owners is achieved by means of roads bonds, which must be provided by the developer. The procedure is set out in the Security for Private Road Works (Scotland) Regulations 1985.[26]

---

23  R(S)A 1984, s 21(5).
24  R(S)A 1984, s 23.
25  R(S)A 1984, s 17.
26  SI 1985/2080 (amended by the Security for Private Road Works (Scotland) (Amendment) Regulations 1998, SI 1998/3220).

## 5.4.1 THE SECURITY FOR PRIVATE ROAD WORKS (SCOTLAND) REGULATIONS 1985

The regulations apply to the construction of private dwelling houses and the conversion of existing buildings for that purpose if the development will front or abut a private road that has not yet been constructed. They do not apply where the development will front or abut an existing road not of a standard acceptable to the local roads authority.[27] The regulations do not apply to residential development by specified bodies which include local authorities, Scottish Homes and certain housing associations.[28]

The regulations provide that the relevant development cannot commence until any construction consent required for the private road has been obtained and the security in respect of that road has been provided in accordance with the regulations. In addition, at least two weeks' prior written notice of intention to commence work must be given to the local roads authority. The security may be in the form of a bond or the deposit of a sum of money. In the case of a bond, it must be made out in favour of and lodged with the local roads authority. It must remain in force until the road has been adopted to the list of public roads. In the other case, the sum of money must be lodged with the authority and retained by it until the road has been adopted. There is, however, provision for partial release of the deposited sum where the road construction is underway and the authority is satisfied that the remaining part of the security lodged is sufficient to meet the cost of completing construction. It is for the local roads authority to calculate the amount of security required and they will notify the construction consent applicant either when the consent is issued or at a later date.

There is provision for a scheme of apportionment of security where more than one person proposes to carry out the development in respect of the same private road.[29] Joint owners must lodge the security in joint names for the total amount required unless otherwise agreed by the authority.

The local roads authority must place any sum lodged with it on deposit in a bank or building society account in its name, earning interest at current rates until the deposit, or any part thereof, falls to be repaid. Interest is payable to the person who lodged the deposit with the authority who must make arrangements for payment of the interest at regular, agreed intervals during the period of retention.[30]

If there is a delay in carrying out the development following the grant of a construction consent and the lodging of the security, the person who lodged the security may withdraw it. However, it must be re-lodged before commencement of the development. Where the authority extends the period of time specified in the construction consent for completion of

27  SI 1985/2080, reg 3(1).
28  SI 1985/2080, reg 3(2) (substituted by SI 1998/3220).
29  SI 1985/2080, reg 7.
30  SI 1985/2080, reg 9.

the road, it may impose a condition requiring additional security to be provided to cover the increased cost of work to construct the road.[31]

Having lodged the security with the authority, the owner may wish to sell or transfer the land on which the development will take place. If the security is in the form of a deposit, then he and the new owner must serve a joint notice on the authority intimating the sale or disposal and stating the name and main residence of the new owner. The authority will retain the deposit but it will treat it as if it had been lodged by the new owner as from the date of intimation. If the security is in the form of a bond, the authority will retain the bond, which shall continue in force unless the new owner lodges a bond in similar terms. If the new owner lodges such a bond, the authority must return the original bond to the person who lodged it for cancellation.[32]

If, after commencement of the development, the road is not constructed within the specified period, the local roads authority shall construct the road in terms of the consent[33] whether or not a security in respect of the private road has been lodged. The specified period is whichever period last expires of either:

1.    The period stated in the construction consent or as subsequently extended by the authority.

2.    The period specified in an enforcement notice in terms of s 21(5) of the 1984 Act. (Notice requiring new road to be brought into conformity with construction consent.)

If, after completion of the private road in accordance with the construction consent, defects appear in it before it has been added to the list of public roads, the authority will serve a notice on the person who lodged the security. The notice must state that the authority is not satisfied with the condition of the private road and it must specify the defects and the work required to rectify them. The notice will require that person to carry out the remedial works within whatever reasonable period is specified by the authority. Failure to comply with the terms of this notice will entitle the authority to carry out the remedial works itself.

If the local roads authority either has to complete the private road or rectify defects in it, it may for that purpose call up any bonds lodged in respect of the road and apply the proceeds or it may use any deposit it has retained.

If the local roads authority consider that the amount of security lodged with it exceeds the amount required it must release the appropriate part of the security. It must do so either as soon as practicable after one of the specified stages has been reached or, where one of the specified stages has been reached and the person who lodged the security has applied for a partial release, within six weeks of their application.

31    SI 1985/2080, reg 10.
32    SI 1985/2080, reg 12.
33    SI 1985/2080, reg 13.

The specified stages[34] are:

1. Completion of the base course, the drainage and the kerb base in the carriageway (in accordance with the construction consent);

2. completion of construction, including traffic signs, gully connections, manholes and carriageway lighting (in accordance with the construction consent);

3. expiry of the maintenance period (or the date of completion of works necessary to rectify defects occurring during that period, if such completion is later than the expiry of that period) or the addition of the relevant private road to the list of public roads, whichever is the earlier.

Where construction of the road has reached one of these stages, the appropriate part of the security to be released is the amount originally lodged (or the amount remaining where part has previously been released) less a sum sufficient to meet the cost of completion of the road or ten per cent of the original security, whichever is greater. However, full release is made in relation to head 3 above.

The bond must be returned for cancellation or the deposited sum refunded by the authority in the following circumstances:

1. On notification from the person who proposed to undertake the development and who lodged the security, that the proposals have been abandoned. In this case, within six weeks of notification.

2. On consideration by the authority that the security is no longer required for any reason.

It is an offence for any person to carry out development in contravention of the Regulations.[35]

## 5.5 THE ENVIRONMENTAL IMPACT ASSESSMENT PROCESS

In the majority of cases, the planning permission process for a new road, or a road improvement project of significant size, will give rise to a requirement for an Environmental Impact Assessment ('EIA') which will involve the preparation of an environmental statement.

The principles of EIA are the same for any project that falls within certain parameters. Some projects of size always require a full EIA whilst others, subject to thresholds, may require EIA at the discretion of the decision-maker. Other projects may not require EIA.

34   SI 1985/2080, reg 15 (amended by SI 1998/3220).
35   SI 1985/2080, reg 16.

## 5.5.1   THE UNDERLYING PRINCIPLES

The legal requirement for EIA in UK law originated with the European Community. The EC introduced general principles for the assessment of environmental effects of development with a view to supplementing and co-ordinating development consent procedures governing public and private projects likely to have a major effect on the environment. There are five key directives:

1.  Directive 2001/42 EC on the assessment of the effects of certain plans and programmes on the environment (the SEA Directive)

2   Directive 2003/4/EC, which provides specifically for access to information on the environment;

3.  Directive 85/337/EEC on the assessment of the effects of certain public and private projects on the environment;

4.  Directive 97/11/EC, which significantly amended and strengthened EC Directive 85/337; and

5.  Directive 2003/35/EC, which amends EC Directive 85/337 to implement the public participation and access to justice requirements of the Århus Convention

All five Directives have been implemented by UK legislation. In any legal challenge, the courts can look behind the primary and secondary legislation to establish whether an individual's rights have been transgressed by a failure on the state's part to comply with the obligations contained in the Directives.[36] The general effect of the Directives is to establish the principle that the decision-maker may not proceed to a decision on a project unless he has ingathered, publicised and considered adequate accurate information on the projected impact on the environment.

The response of succeeding UK administrations has been to enhance the requirements of the planning system, or related public permission processes, to make certain projects subject to the Directive requirements.

The implementing legislation enacted by succeeding UK governments embodies the principle that, if the decision-maker has taken his decision in the light of significant accurate information on the environmental impact of the proposal, the decision will be valid. In those circumstances, the state's international obligations both to society and to individual citizens will be fulfilled, irrespective of the outcome of the decision-making process.

---

36   *R v North Yorkshire County Council, ex parte Brown* [1999] 1 PLR 116, HL; *R v Durham County Council ex parte, Huddleston* [2000] 1 WLR 1484, [2000] CMLR 313, [2000] 1 PLR 122, [2000] EGCS 39.

A parallel, but closely related, area of law derives from the European Convention on Human Rights. Human rights law recognises the right of the state to allow development and to arbitrate between opposing views in the public interest, even if the decision does impinge to some extent on an individual's rights. However, it also recognises that a failure to collect information on the environment, and a failure to make that information available to its citizens, is a key contravention of an individual's rights by the State.[37]

The 2003 Directive requires Member States to make provision for persons with sufficient interest to have access to a review procedure, before a court of law or other impartial and independent body, to challenge decisions, acts or omissions subject to the public participation requirements of the 1985 Directive (as amended).

Generally, therefore, a defensive attitude to the compilation of information on the environmental impact of a project, or to public participation in its consideration, may be counterproductive.

## 5.5.2 THE PURPOSE OF ENVIRONMENTAL IMPACT ASSESSMENT

EC Directive 97/11 states that:

'Community policy is based on the precautionary principle and on the principle that preventative action should be taken, that environmental damage should as a priority be rectified at source and that the polluter should pay'.

There are two main purposes for carrying out an EIA of a proposal:

1.  to inform the process of whether or not permission should be granted; and

2.  to assist the designer of the project and the decision-maker to identify where any adverse impacts on the environment can be mitigated either towards removal, or towards acceptable levels.

On this latter point, clearly the responsibility starts with the designer. As the process of EIA is carried out, the designer should respond to potential adverse effects on the environment and consider carefully what mechanisms and strategies can be used to mitigate those adverse effects.

---

37  *Geurra v Italy* 9 July 1999; The European Court of Human Rights held that local government's failure to give local people essential information that would have entitled them to assess the risks they and their families might run if they continued to live in Manfredonia, a town particularly exposed in the event of an accident at a factory, amounted to a breach of Article 8 of the European Convention on Human Rights (right to respect for private and family life).

## 5.5.3    THE ENVIRONMENTAL IMPACT ASSESSMENT (SCOTLAND) REGULATIONS 1999

### 5.5.3.1    *Introduction*

The Environmental Impact Assessment (Scotland) Regulations (the "Regulations")[38] replaced the first and second generation EIA Regulations. They implemented the 1997 Directive, which enhanced the thresholds, boundaries and thinking behind the selection of projects requiring formal EIA, and, very importantly, created a compulsory paper trail for the process of deciding whether, and how, an EIA should be done for a particular project. They were amended by the Environmental Impact Assessment (Scotland) Regulations 2006 (the "2006 Regulations"),[39] which transposed the requirement of the 2003 Directive.

The Regulations contain a general methodological approach directed at all projects within the scope of the statutory planning process. Part III applies to roads.[40]

### 5.5.3.2    *Regulation 3 Prohibition*

The Regulations are negatively framed. Regulation 3 prohibits the granting of planning permission for a Schedule 1 development or a Schedule 2 development that is likely to have significant environmental effects due to factors such as its nature, size or location, unless EIA procedures have been followed.

### 5.5.3.3    *Schedule 1 Development: Roads*

Schedule 1 of the Regulations applies to:

*   The 'construction of motorways, and express roads'[41]

*   The 'construction of a new road of four or more lanes, or realignment and/or widening of an existing road of two lanes or less, so as to provide four or more lanes, where such new road, or realigned and/or widened section of the road would be ten km or more in an continuous length'[42]

For all such developments, an EIA is compulsory and no permission can be granted for that road unless full EIA procedures have been followed.

38   SSI 1999/1, as amended.
39   SSI 2006/614.
40   SSI 1999/1, Pt III comprises regs 48–53 which amend ss 20A, 20B, 55A, 55B, 151 and Sch 1 of the Roads (Scotland) Act 1984. Note that these provisions of the 1984 Act are in turn further amended by SSI 2006/614.
41   SSI 1999/1, Sch 1, para 7(2). 'Express roads' means roads complying with the definition in the European Agreement on Main International Traffic Arteries of 15 November 1975.
42   SSI 1999/1, Sch 1, para 7(3).

### 5.5.3.5   Schedule 2 Development: Roads

The transport, or infrastructure, projects specified by Schedule 2 will usually only require an EIA if on sites in excess of 0.5 hectare. Such projects include:

1.   industrial estate development projects;

2.   urban development projects; and

3.   construction of intermodal trans-shipment facilities and of intermodal terminals unless included in Schedule 1.[43]

The construction of roads (unless included in Schedule 1) will usually only require an EIA if the area of the work exceeds one hectare.[44] Motorway service areas will normally only require an EIA if the area of the development exceeds 0.5 hectare.[45] The one exception to all these general rules is where the project is to be carried out in a sensitive area, for which see below.

If a new road is to form part of a development area, engineers constructing the road should ensure that roads aspects are taken into account in considering whether or not the development as a whole requires to be submitted to the EIA process.

### 5.5.3.4   Schedule 2 Development: General

A 'Schedule 2 Development' means development, other than exempt development,[46] as described in Column 1 of the Table in Schedule 2 where:

1.   any part of that development is to be carried out in a sensitive area; or

2.   any applicable threshold or criteria in the corresponding part of Column 2 of that table is respectively exceeded or met in relation to that development.

A 'sensitive area' comprises:

(i)    land notified, or in respect of which an order has been made, under the Nature Conservation (Scotland) Act 2004 (i.e. sites of special scientific interest and nature conservation areas);

(ii)   properties appearing on the World Heritage List under the 1972 UNESCO Convention for the Protection of the World Cultural and Natural Heritage;

43   SSI 1999/1, Sch 2, Table, head 10(a)–(c).
44   SSI 1999/1, Sch 2, Table, head 10(f).
45   SSI 1999/1, Sch 2, Table, head 10(p).
46   Exempt development is development in respect of which Scottish Ministers have made a direction under SSI 1999/1, reg 4(4).

    (iii)   Scheduled Monuments under the Ancient Monuments and Archaeological Areas Act 1979;

    (iv)   a European site under the Conservation (Natural Habitats etc) Regulations 1994; or

    (v)   an area designated as National Parks under the National Parks (Scotland) Act 2000 or as a National Scenic Area.

The relevant planning authority or the Scottish Ministers shall not grant planning permission for an EIA development unless they have first taken the environmental information into consideration, and they must state in their decision that they have done so.[47]

### 5.5.4    CONSTRUCTION BY THE SCOTTISH MINISTERS AS ROADS AUTHORITY

Regulation 49 of Part III of the Regulations substitutes section 20A of the Roads (Scotland) Act 1984 which deals with environmental assessment of certain road construction projects. Section 20A was further amended by the 2006 Regulations.[48] The Scottish Ministers, where they are considering the construction of a new road for which they are the roads authority, must determine whether or not it falls within a category requiring environmental assessment. If so, they must prepare an environmental statement and publish notice of it not later than the date when details of the project are published. They must also publish their determination regarding the need for environmental assessment of a project.[49]

The Scottish Ministers must publish notice of the environmental statement to ensure that members of the public who are likely to be concerned are given a reasonable opportunity to express an opinion before they decide whether to proceed with the project.[50] Before making a decision on whether to proceed, the Scottish Ministers must take into consideration any opinion expressed to them within a period of six weeks from the date of publication of notice of the environmental statement. In addition, the Scottish Ministers must ensure that consultation bodies are given an opportunity to express an opinion on the project and the environmental statement before they decide whether to proceed with the project. Consultation bodies are:

    1.    The appropriate planning authority where the proposed project is likely to affect land in their area;

47   SSI 1999/1, reg 3(2).
48   SSI 2006/614, reg 7 (see also s 20B).
49   Roads (Scotland) Act 1984, s 20A(3) (substituted by SSI 1999/1, reg 49 and further amended by SSI 2006/614, reg 6).
50   R(S)A 1984, s 20A(5) (as so substituted and amended). See s 20(5A–5D) of the 1984 Act (as inserted by SSI 2006/614) for the matters that the notice must cover and provision for making the environmental statement available for inspection.

2.    Scottish Natural Heritage;

3.    The Scottish Environment Protection Agency;

4.    Historic Scotland and

5.    Other bodies designated by statutory provision as having specific environmental responsibilities.[51]

### 5.5.4.1 Content of environmental statement published by the Scottish Ministers

The environmental statement must contain, among other things, the following information:

1.    a description of the project comprising information on the site, design and size of project;

2.    a description of the measures envisaged in order to avoid, reduce and, if possible, remedy significant adverse effects.

In addition, it may include the information referred to in Schedule 4 of the Regulations, if the Scottish Ministers consider that:

(a)    such information is relevant to the specific characteristics of the project and of the environmental features likely to be affected by it; and

(b)    having regard in particular to current knowledge and methods of assessment, the information may reasonably be gathered.[52]

Similar provisions apply to road improvement projects to be undertaken by the Scottish Ministers as roads authority.[53]

### 5.5.4.4 Procedural Requirements

When the Scottish Ministers have published an environmental statement, they must now take into consideration that statement and any opinions expressed by a member of the public, by any of the consultation bodies, by any EEA state consulted where the project is likely to have a significant impact upon the environment of that state, by members of the public in that state or by the EIA consultation bodies in that state.[54]

51    R(S)A 1984, s 151 (amended by SSI 1991/1, reg 49 and SSI 2006/614 reg 6).
52    R(S)A 1984, s 20A(7) (substituted by SSI 1999/1, reg 49).
53    R(S)A 1984, s 55A (substituted by SSI 1999/1, reg 50 and amended by SSI 2006/614 reg 6).
54    R(S)A 1984, Sch 1, paras 7(1A), 13(1A) (substituted by SSI 1999/1, reg 52 and amended by SSI 2006/614 reg 6). As to consultation with EEA states, see R(S)A 1984, s 20B (added by SSI 1991/1, reg 49 and amended by SSI 2006/614 reg 6).

When the Scottish Ministers have decided whether to proceed with the project in relation to which an environmental impact assessment has been made, they must publish their decision together with a statement confirming that they have complied with their obligations to take into consideration the statements and opinions expressed by the public and others. They must also notify the consultation bodies and make available to the public documents containing:

1.   the content of the decision and any conditions attached to it;

2.   the main reasons and considerations on which the decision is based including, if relevant, information about the participation of the public and details of how information, evidence and representations submitted were taken into account;

3.   information regarding the right to challenge the validity of the decision and the procedures for doing so; and

4.   where their decision is to proceed with the project, a description of the main measures which will be taken to avoid, reduce and, if possible, offset any major adverse effects of the project.

Any requirement for publication in connection with an environmental impact assessment will be met by publication in the *Edinburgh Gazette*, at least one local newspaper and, where the Scottish Ministers use a website for the purpose of giving information to the public about projects of a category into which the project in question falls, by publication on that website.[55]

## 5.5.5    CONSTRUCTION BY LOCAL ROADS AUTHORITY

A local roads authority requires planning permission to construct a new road[56] and must therefore comply with the general provisions of the Regulations. Its proposals will fall within the scope of the Regulation 3 prohibition outlined above.

### 5.5.5.1    National Policy Guidance

Government policy advice and technical advice to support applicants and planning authorities is contained within Circular 15/1999 *Environmental Impact Assessment (Scotland) Regulations 1999*. Planning Advice Note 58 also provides support and advice on how the process is best carried out.

---

55    R(S)A 1984, Sch 1, paras 1(1C) and 7(1C) added by SSI 1999/1, reg 52 and amended by SSI 2006/614 reg 6.
56    See pp [74] ff above.

*5.5.5.2   Screening Opinions*

A significant enhancement to the previous regime for EIA relates to the formal introduction of a screening process.[57] The decision on whether an EIA was necessary was rarely formalised at local authority level prior to the 1999 Regulations. It was often unclear whether the local authority had, in fact, considered whether an EIA was necessary. This practice appears to have been a European tendency, and it gave rise to the EC Directive 97/11 and its enhanced regime.

A 'screening opinion' means a written statement of the opinion of the relevant planning authority as to whether development is EIA development.[58] A formal determination to this effect by the planning authority is a necessity for all Schedule 2 development. Developers may apply to the planning authority for a screening opinion before making an application for planning permission.[59] In making the determination, the planning authority must have regard to the relevant 'selection criteria'.[60]

When requesting a screening opinion the applicant should submit a plan sufficient to identify the land, a brief description of the nature and purpose of the development and of its possible effects on the environment, and such other information or representations as the applicant may wish to provide or make. If the decision-maker is dissatisfied with the information provided, it must request further information in writing from the applicant.

The planning authority must adopt a screening opinion within three weeks of the request, or a longer period, as agreed. On adopting a screening opinion, the authority must copy it to the applicant. Where it fails to adopt a screening opinion within the relevant period, or if it adopts an opinion to the effect that the development requires an environmental statement,[61] the applicant may request the Scottish Ministers to make a screening direction. This applies even if the authority has not received the additional information which they have sought from the applicant.

A screening direction may be requested from the Scottish Ministers who also have power to seek more information.[62]

As there is a statutory recourse to the Scottish Ministers, an application for judicial review of a planning authority's decision on a screening opinion is unlikely to be received by the courts. However, as there is no provision for appeal from Scottish Ministers, a judicial review application on the terms of a screening opinion may be competent, on a point of

57   SSI 1999/1, regs 4–6.
58   SSI 1999/1, reg 2(1).
59   SSI 1999/1, reg 5.
60   SSI 1999/1, reg 4(5) and Sch 3.
61   As to 'environmental statement', see SSI 1999/1, reg 2(1).
62   SSI 1999/1, reg 6.

law, or on the basis of a contravention of the European Convention on Human Rights. As an exception to this, a third party aggrieved by the steps taken in relation to a screening opinion request could submit the decision of the planning authority to judicial review, since they have no right of appeal to the Scottish Ministers or otherwise.

### 5.5.6   THE PREPARATION OF AN ENVIRONMENTAL STATEMENT

*5.5.6.1   Scoping Opinions*

The extent of the information and the particular topics to be studied in any particular environmental statement is a matter to be agreed between the decision-maker and the developer within the context of the statutory framework. The decision-maker and, ultimately, the Scottish Ministers have the commanding opinion as to what work should actually be done. This process is known as 'scoping' and the Regulations provide for scoping opinions to be provided.

A person, who proposes to make an application which will require an environmental statement,[63] may ask the relevant planning authority to state in writing its opinion as to the information to be provided in the environmental statement.[64] Again, an authority can respond by asking for more information. An authority may not formulate a scoping opinion unless it has consulted the person who made the request, and various consultation bodies, but, in general terms, a scoping opinion must be formulated within five weeks of the date of the request. The consultation bodies include:

1.  any adjoining planning authority where the development is likely to affect land in their area;

2.  Scottish National Heritage;

3.  the water and sewerage authority for the areas in which the development is to take place;

4.  the Scottish Environmental Protection Society;

5.  the Health and Safety Executive;

6.  Scottish Ministers where the consulting authority is the planning authority.

---

63   As to 'environmental statement', see SSI 1999/1, reg 2(1).
64   SSI 1999/1, reg 10.

# PART THREE

# 6 Toll Roads and Road User Charging

## 6.1 INTRODUCTION

Both the New Roads and Street Works Act 1991 and the Transport (Scotland) Act 2001 enable charges to be levied on road users for the use of specific public roads. The 1991 Act enables tolls to be collected on new roads promoted by roads authorities and funded and built by the private sector, which would then recoup its investment through charging tolls. The 2001 Act provides enabling powers for local roads authorities to introduce road user charges to support the objectives of a local transport strategy, in particular to tackle congestion and environmental problems. The revenues must also be used to further the objectives of the local transport strategy.

Tolls and road user charging are controversial, and their use as a funding or policy tool is politically difficult. A proposal to introduce a charging scheme under the 2001 Act in Edinburgh was abandoned following rejection in a 'referendum' held by The City of Edinburgh Council. Public opposition to tolls resulted in the abolition of tolling on the Skye Bridge in December 2004, on the Erskine Bridge in 2006 and on the Forth Road Bridge in December 2007.

## 6.2 TOLL ORDERS

The 1991 Act allows for the creation of toll roads.[1] It also amends the procedures for making or confirming orders or schemes under the 1984 Act to include toll orders.[2] Toll roads created by the 1991 Act are also designated as 'special roads'.[3] They therefore require to fulfil both the statutory requirements for special roads and for toll roads.

The process involves either the roads authority or the Scottish Ministers making both a toll order for the proposed road and a special roads scheme.[4] If the order or scheme is made by the roads authority it has to be confirmed by the Scottish Ministers but not otherwise.[5] Information about the proposed order must be published in a local newspaper and in the *Edinburgh Gazette*. There must be an opportunity for anyone to inspect the draft order free of charge for a specified period of not less

1  NRSWA 1991, s 27.
2  See R(S)A 1984, Sch 1, paras 14A–14E (added by NRSWA 1991, Sch 8, Pt III, para 96).
3  See R(S)A 1984, ss 7 and 151(1). See also Ch 4, pp ff.
4  NRSWA 1991, s 27(1), (2), (4); R(S)A 1984, s 7, Sch 1.
5  NRSWA 1991, s 27(2).

than six weeks from publication. There must also be a statement that any person can object to the making or confirmation of the order within that period.[6] The Scottish Ministers have a discretion over whether or not to hold a public inquiry.[7] They may make or confirm the toll order with or without modification after considering any outstanding objections and the inquiry report if any.[8] They can make or confirm the order wholly or partly and, in the latter case, can defer a decision on the outstanding part.[9]

Reference is again made to the Roads (Scotland) Act 1984 for the validity and date of operation of the toll order.[10] So far as practicable, the special road scheme proceedings under the 1984 Act and the toll order must be carried out at the same time.[11] The Scottish Ministers cannot approve one without the other but can, of course, refuse them both.[12] The Ministers make or confirm the toll order by statutory instrument.[13]

### 6.2.1   TOLL PERIOD

The toll order must specify a period for tolls to be applied.[14] Tolls can either cease being charged on a specific date or at the end of a period specified in the order. The order can also be terminated by reference to the achievement of a financial objective or of the passage of a specified number of vehicles over the road or by other means specified in the toll order.[15] Where the right to charge and collect tolls has been assigned, it is still a matter for the special roads authority to decide when the tolls should stop.[16]

### 6.2.2   EXTENSIONS TO TOLL PERIOD

In certain circumstances the special roads authority can make a toll extension order.[17] This can happen in three situations. Firstly, where the authority is entitled to assign the right to charge and collect tolls by the order and does not do so. Secondly, where the assignation terminates or is terminated before the end of the original toll period and thirdly, where

---

6    R(S)A 1984, Sch 1, para 14A(1), (2) (added by NRSWA 1991, Sch 8, Pt III, para 98).
7    R(S)A 1984, Sch 1, para 14B (as so added).
8    R(S)A 1984, Sch 1, para 14C(1) (as so added).
9    R(S)A 1984, Sch 1, para 14C(2) (as so added).
10   See NRSWA 1991, s 27(3) and R(S)A 1984 Sch 2.
11   NRSWA 1991, s 27(4). See also Ch 4, pp ff.
12   NRSWA 1991, s 27(5).
13   NRSWA 1991, s 27(10).
14   NRSWA 1991, s 29(1).
15   NRSWA 1991, s 29(2).
16   NRSWA 1991, s 29(3). See paragraph [6.3.1] in relation to the assignation of the right to collect tolls.
17   NRSWA 1991 s 30.

the authority wants to charge and collect tolls beyond the toll period.[18] The extension toll order cannot authorise the assignation of the right to charge and collect tolls.[19] The extension order is made by the Scottish Ministers where they are the roads authority and by the local authority where it has that responsibility. In the latter case, the Scottish Ministers must confirm the order.[20] There are time limits on extension orders being made. Any such order must come into force on the earlier of the following two occurrences. Either not later than the end of the previous toll period or two years after the premature termination of an assignation.[21]

An extension order is governed by the same statutory provisions as a toll order itself in relation to the toll period, the amount of tolls, the application of fair trading laws, variation and revocation, collection of tolls, suspension and exemption from tolls, restrictions on access to toll roads and reporting requirements.[22] As with toll orders, extension orders are made or confirmed by statutory instrument.[23] However, the procedures under the Roads (Scotland) Act 1984 regarding the making or confirming of orders and regarding the validity and date of operation of orders do not apply to extension orders.[24]

### 6.2.3   VARIATION OR REVOCATION OF TOLL ORDER

A toll order can be varied or revoked in much the same way as it was created. Namely, by the Scottish Ministers if they made the original order and by the roads authority if it was responsible for making the original order, subject to confirmation by the Scottish Ministers.[25] The Scottish Ministers can confirm an order with or without modifications.[26] Again this is done by statutory instrument, and again the provisions of the Roads (Scotland) Act 1984 on making and confirming orders and regarding the validity and date of operation of orders also do not apply here.[27] The order can make such supplementary, incidental and transitional provisions as seem necessary or expedient to the roads authority.[28] It is not possible to vary a toll order to extend the toll period.[29] This should be done by an extension toll order which is only available in certain limited circumstances.[30] Nor can it extend the length of the road which is subject to a toll charge if the original order did not cover the

---

18   NRSWA 1991, s 30(1).
19   NRSWA 1991, s 30(2).
20   NRSWA 1991, s 30(3).
21   NRSWA 1991, s 30(4).
22   NRSWA 1991, s 30(5).
23   NRSWA 1991, s 30(6).
24   NRSWA 1991, s 30(6).
25   NRSWA 1991, s 34(1).
26   NRSWA 1991, s 34(4).
27   NRSWA 1991, s 34(7).
28   NRSWA 1991 s 34(6).
29   NRSWA 1991, s 34(2) but see paragraph 6.2.2..
30   See paragraph 6.2.2.

whole road.[31] If the right to charge and collect tolls has been assigned, the consent of the concessionaire is necessary before there can be any variation or revocation of the toll order.[32]

### 6.2.4   QUASHING A TOLL ORDER

The Court of Session can quash a toll order on the application of an aggrieved person.[33] If it does so, the related special road scheme also ceases to have effect.[34]

### 6.2.5   COMPENSATION PAYMENTS

If the roads authority has entered into a contract with another party for the design or construction of a toll road it must make provision for compensation to be paid for agreed expenses in the event of either the authority not going ahead with the special road scheme or the Scottish Ministers failing to make or confirm the toll order or the special road scheme.[35] If the person contracted to design or construct the road fails to complete it as agreed, then he must pay the authority compensation for costs its incurred in accordance with the contract. This includes administrative expenses taking into account staff costs and overheads.[36] This is without prejudice to any other liability, for example, for breach of contract.

## 6.3   COLLECTION OF TOLLS

The Scottish Ministers have a fairly wide power to make regulations by statutory instrument for the collection of tolls in the toll order.[37] The provisions can vary depending on the type of road and there can be different types of tolls. They can also make tolls for particular roads and impose specific tolls.[38] The regulations can require that a list of toll charges be displayed and can spell out the mechanism for changing toll charges. If the regulations do impose such conditions and they have not been complied with, then the toll cannot be lawfully charged.[39] Anyone demanding payment of a toll which is unauthorised commits an offence punishable on summary conviction by a fine up to level 3 on the standard scale.[40]

31   NRSWA 1991, s 34(3).
32   NRSWA 1991, s 34(5).
33   Roads (Scotland) Act 1984, Sch 2, paras 2, 3.
34   NRSWA 1991, s 27(6).
35   NRSWA 1991, s 27(7).
36   NRSWA 1991 s 27(8).
37   NRSWA 1991, s 37(1), (5).
38   NRSWA 1991, s 37(2).
39   NRSWA 1991, s 37(3).
40   NRSWA 1991, s 37(4). The maximum fine is currently £1,000: Criminal Procedure (Scotland) Act 1995 s 225. The level can be altered by statutory instrument.

## 6.3.1 ASSIGNATION OF RIGHT TO COLLECT TOLLS

The toll order can allow the special roads authority to assign its right to charge and collect tolls to someone else for such a period and on such terms and conditions as it sees fit.[41] This person is known as 'a concessionaire'.[42] The assignation can only be granted where the concessionaire agrees to comply with terms which may be specified in it as to design, construction, maintenance, operation or improvement of the road.[43] Included in any assignation is the right of the concessionaire to any income which the roads authority would have received (except to the extent that the authority has incurred expense) as a charge for occupation of the road, or as a charge for any services in relation to the road, except for those supplied by the roads authority itself.[44] The concessionaire is also entitled to recover any contribution by a third party towards the cost of maintenance or improvement of the road.[45] The concessionaire must be consulted about what sum is to be charged where the authority has a discretion as to the amount.[46]

## 6.3.2 TRANSFER AND TERMINATION OF ASSIGNATION

A concessionaire can voluntarily assign his right to charge and collect tolls to someone else with the consent of the special roads authority.[47] Where an assignation is terminated prematurely, the authority must take reasonable steps to find a new concessionaire. In the meantime the authority itself can charge and collect tolls for up to two years starting on the date of termination until a fresh assignation is granted, the toll period expires or an extension toll order commences which ever is the earlier.[48] The new assignation is treated in the same way as the original.[49] The original assignation can deal with the issue of whether any tolls collected by the authority or any payment made by the new concessionaire should be applied for the benefit of the first concessionaire or his creditors.[50] [The Transfer of Undertakings (Protection of Employment) Regulations 1981] (or any regulations which replace them) apply where an assignation is terminated and the authority either collects the tolls itself or grants a fresh assignation to a new concessionaire. This protects the rights of employees of the original concessionaire who might otherwise lose their jobs and associated benefits.[51]

41  NRSWA 1991, s 28(1).
42  NRSWA 1991, s 28(3).
43  NRSWA 1991, s 28(2).
44  NRSWA 1991 s 28(5).
45  NRSWA 1991, s 28(5)(c).
46  NRSWA 1991, s 28(6).
47  NRSWA 1991, s 35(1).
48  NRSWA 1991, s 35(2).
49  NRSWA 1991, s 35(3).
50  NRSWA 1991, s 35(4).
51  [Ie SI 1981/1794 (as amended). See NRSWA 1991, s 35(5). See further Craig and Miller *Employment Law in Scotland* (2nd edn) p 27.].

### 6.3.3    FACILITIES FOR TOLL COLLECTION

Clearly if tolls are to be collected, there must be some means of doing so. The person who is authorised to charge tolls can set up and maintain facilities for toll collection.[52] Where this is a concessionaire, the consent of the special roads authority is required.[53] A duty is placed on those responsible for the design and construction of toll collection facilities, as well as on those who are collecting tolls, to take account of the need to avoid delaying the emergency services.[54] The special roads authority has the power to acquire land for the purpose of or in connection with facilities for the collection of tolls.[55]

### 6.3.4    REFUSAL OR FAILURE TO PAY TOLLS

It is an offence to refuse or fail to pay a toll without reasonable excuse or to attempt to evade payment.[56] The offender is liable on summary conviction to a fine up to level 3 on the standard scale.[57] A toll collector can refuse or prevent the passage of someone where it appears they have not paid the toll without reasonable excuse[58] The collector can also require them to remove their vehicle and in the event of non-compliance can have it removed.[59] In doing either of these things, the collector can use such assistance as he thinks is necessary.[60] A charge is payable for removal of the vehicle in such circumstances.[61] Where any removal charge or toll is not paid this can be recovered along with a reasonable amount to cover administrative expenses.[62]

### 6.3.5    TOLL EXEMPTIONS AND SUSPENSION OF TOLLS

The toll order can exempt certain categories of traffic from payment and must exempt marked police cars, ambulances, fire engines, invalid carriages and vehicles being used by or to carry disabled persons.[63] The person authorised to collect tolls can also grant other exemptions as he

---

52    NRSWA 1991, s 39(1). 'Facilities' are defined in NRSWA 1991, s 39(4) as 'such buildings, structures, or other facilities within the boundary of the road, or on land adjoining the road, as are reasonably required for the purpose of or in connection with the collection of tolls in pursuance of a toll order.'
53    NRSWA 1991, s 39(1).
54    NRSWA 1991, s 39(2).
55    NRSWA 1991, s 39(3) and R(S)A 1984, s 104(3)(c).
56    NRSWA 1991, s 38(1).
57    NRSWA 1991, s 38(1). The maximum fine is currently £1,000: Criminal Procedure (Scotland) Act 1995 s 225. The level can be altered by statutory instrument.
58    NRSWA 1991, s 38(2)(a).
59    NRSWA 1991, s 38(2)(b).
60    NRSWA 1991, s 38(2).
61    NRSWA 1991 s 38(3); see also the regulations [to be added].
62    NRSWA 1991, s 38(4).
63    NRSWA 1991, s 36(1), (2).

thinks fit[64] as well as suspending collection altogether provided the toll order allows this.[65]

## 6.4 AMOUNT OF TOLLS

The maximum amount that can be charged as a toll must be specified by the special road authority, but only where the toll order does not allow for assignation of the right to collect to a concessionaire.[66] Where collection rights can be assigned the order cannot normally specify a maximum charge.[67] It can only do so where the toll order relates to a road which is or includes a major crossing, such as the Skye Bridge or the Forth Road Bridge, and where there is no reasonably convenient alternative.[68] Setting a maximum amount does not necessarily mean specifying a figure, it can be by reference to a formula.[69] The Scottish Ministers can determine by regulations what constitutes a 'major crossing' and 'a reasonably convenient alternative', although they have not actually done so.[70]

Where the maximum tolls are specified, different amounts can apply for different types of traffic and these can be varied according to a formula laid down in the order.[71] If the authority has the power to assign the right to collect but does not use it, then it cannot charge tolls at all unless an extension order is made.[72]

### 6.4.1 VARIABLE TOLL CHARGES

Different tolls may be charged depending on a number of factors including the distance travelled or the day, time, week, month or other period or on the type of traffic.[73] Where a concessionaire has been appointed these variations are subject to the provisions of the assignation. It is also possible to offer a discount where tolls are paid in advance.[74]

### 6.4.2 TOLLS FOR MAJOR CROSSINGS

As already noted above, there can be restrictions on the maximum amount of toll which can be charged for a major crossing.[75] The toll order

---

64 NRSWA 1991, s 36(1).
65 NRSWA 1991, s 36(3)(a). See also paragraph 6.4.2.
66 NRSWA 1991, s 31(1).
67 NRSWA 1991, s 31(3).
68 NRSWA 1991, s 31(3) and s 32(1).
69 *Robbie the Pict v Hingston (No 1)* 1998 SLT 1196.
70 See also para 6.4.2 below.
71 NRSWA 1991, s 31(2).
72 NRSWA 1991, s 31(4).
73 NRSWA 1991, s 36(3)(c), (d).
74 NRSWA 1991 s 36(3)(b).
75 See para 6.4 above.

must specify maxima where there is no reasonably convenient alternative crossing.[76] The Act defines a 'major crossing' as one of navigable waters more than 100 metres wide and a 'reasonably convenient alternative' as another crossing, excluding a ferry, which is toll free and within five miles of the crossing.[77]

## 6.5   RATING AND VALUATION

A toll road is exempt from rates and must not be included in the valuation roll. Nor should any buildings, structures, or other facilities reasonably required for the purpose of or in connection with toll collection where these are either within the boundary of the road or on land adjoining the road.[78] As a result of a European Court ruling, Value Added Tax is now payable on certain toll charges.[75]

## 6.6   RESTRICTED ACCESS TO TOLL ROADS

Where a toll road exists no one, except someone acting by or on behalf of a government department or Minister of the Crown where this is necessary for the discharge of their functions, is allowed to construct a road or private access which would allow access to it unless he has the consent of the special road authority and any concessionaire.[79]

## 6.7   TRAFFIC REGULATION ON TOLL ROADS

A concessionaire appointed to collect tolls must be consulted by the road traffic authority before any regulations or orders specifically affecting the road are made under the Road Traffic Regulation Act 1984.[80]

Traffic signs[81] can be placed on or near the road by the concessionaire, or by someone acting on his behalf, subject to any directions given by the traffic authority.[82] If the concessionaire does not comply with the traffic authority's direction on the placing of signs, the authority can do the work itself and recover its reasonable expenses from the concessionaire.[83]

The concessionaire is entitled to issued a notice temporarily prohibiting or restricting traffic[84] in the same way as a traffic authority.[85] Where this

76   NRSWA 1991, s 32(1).
77   NRSWA 1991, s 32(3). This can be altered by regulations.
78   NRSWA 1991, s 27(9).
79   NRSWA 1991, s 40(1), (2).
80   NRSWA 1991, s 43(2).
81   As defined in RTRA 1984, s 64(1).
82   NRSWA 1991, s 43(3).
83   NRSWA 1991, s 43(3).
84   Under RTRA 1984, s 14.
85   NRSWA 1991 s 43(4).

is due to road works, the concessionaire can recover the whole costs incurred in doing so from the undertaker[86] responsible.[87] This includes the cost of any notification of the public and the provision of traffic signs.[88] The Scottish Ministers have power to make regulations by statutory instrument[89] to govern the procedure for issuing a notice as well as for its maximum duration and for the requirement for alternative routes to be provided for traffic[90] [but have not done so]. Where the concessionaire issues a notice, this can be varied or revoked by the traffic authority. It also ceases to have effect if the authority makes provision[91] which is inconsistent with it.[92]

## 6.8   FAIR TRADE LAWS APPLY TO TOLLS

For the purposes of the Enterprise Act 2002, a person charging tolls is deemed to provide a service namely providing the facility to use the road in return for the toll charged.[93]

## 6.9   REPORT ON TOLL ROADS AND TOLL ORDERS

The Scottish Ministers are required to provide an annual report to Parliament[94] in the following circumstances:

1.   if they enter into a contract for the design and construction of a toll road;

2.   if a new toll road is opened for public use and the Scottish Ministers are the roads authority;

3.   if the Scottish Ministers make or confirm a toll order, or vary or revoke one.[95]

The report must be placed before the Parliament on or before 31 July of the following year[96] and contain such information on toll orders which are in force during that year, or part of it, regardless of when they were made as the Scottish Ministers consider appropriate.[97] This latter provision is somewhat confusing as it appears to extend the duty to report to include any toll orders which are in force when the report is

86   See paragraph 19.4.
87   NRSWA 1991, s 135(1).
88   NRSWA 1991, s 135(2).
89   See NRSWA 1991, s 43(6).
90   NRSWA 1991, s 43(4).
91   By order or notice under RTRA 1984, s 14.
92   NRSWA 1991, s 43(5).
93   NRSWA 1991, s 33.
94   Formerly Westminster and now the Scottish Parliament. NRSWA 1991, s 41(1).
95   NRSWA 1991, s 41(2).
96   NRSWA 1991, s 41(4).
97   NRSWA 1991, s 41(3).

made but only where one of the specified events occurs. Otherwise there appears to be no duty to report.

## 6.10   ENVIRONMENTAL ASSESSMENT

The provisions of the Road Traffic (Scotland) Act 1984 on environmental assessment of road projects also apply to toll roads.[98]

## 6.11   ROAD USER CHARGING

Part 3 of the 2001 Act allows local authorities and local traffic authorities to introduce a charging scheme by making a charging order individually or jointly.[99] A charging scheme is defined as meaning "a scheme for imposing charges in respect of the use of keeping of motor vehicles on roads".[100] The scheme can only be made in respect of roads for which the charging authority or authorities are the local traffic authority[101] and there can only be one charge on any road at any one time.[102]

The authority or authorities introducing the scheme must have in place a local transport strategy for their area[103] and in preparing their local transport strategy they must have had regard to any guidance issued by the Scottish Ministers in that regard.[104] The charging scheme must directly or indirectly help the charging authority achieve the policies in their local transport strategy.[105]

### 6.11.1 THE CHARGING ORDER

The charging scheme must be contained in an order made by the charging authority.[106] The charging scheme and thus the order must specific the following: –

(a)   the roads in respect of which charges are imposed;

(b)   the events in respect of which a charge will be imposed in respect of a motor vehicle being used or kept on a road;

98   NRSWA 1991, s 42(1), (2). See further Ch 5.
99   T(S)A 2001, s 49(1).
100  T(S)A 2001, s 49(5).
101  T(S)A 2001, s 49(2).
102  T(S)A 2001, s 54(1)(b).
103  T(S)A 2001, s 49(3)(a).
104  Scotland's Transport Future: Guidance on Local Transport Strategies February 2005.
105  T(S)A 2001, s 49(3)(b).
106  T(S)A 2001, s 50(1).

(c)   the classes of motor vehicles in respect of which charges are imposed;

(d)   the classes of motor vehicles which are exempt from charges or in respect of which reduced rates of charges are imposed;

(e)   the charges imposed;

(f)   the period during which it is to remain in force; and

(g)   make provision for or in connection with the collection, payment and recording of charges.[107]

Different charges may be specified for different locations, times of day, vehicle classes, distance travelled or other factors, allowing the charging authority to devise schemes to deal with particular issues in their area.[108]

## 6.11.2 MAKING THE CHARGING ORDER

Before making an order the charging authority must consult with those parties prescribed in regulations.[109] The consultees include the chief constable for any police force for the police area in which a road to which the charging scheme relates is situated; the chief officer of the Scottish Ambulance Service; the fire authority; the Road Haulage Association; the Freight Transport Association, the Automobile Association; the Royal Automobile Club and any other organisation or persons likely to be affected by the proposed charging schemes the charging authority thinks fit ("the statutory consultees"). If the charging scheme is likely to affect traffic on another authority's road, that authority must be consulted. Similarly if the scheme would affect traffic on a crown road, the appropriate crown authority must be consulted and if traffic would affect a road on which public passenger services are provided then the Public Transport Authority must be consulted.

At the start of the consultation, the charging authority must provide each consultee with the draft order; the relevant map; a statement of reasons and any other necessary or appropriate information. The statutory consultee must make repesentations, if any, within 3 months of the start of the consultation. At the end of this period the charging authority must prepare a consultation report detailing those persons consulted, their representation and the extent to which the charging authority will implement any proposals contained in the representation. This report must be sent to each of the consultees at the start of the objection period.

---

107  T(S)A 2001, s 53(1).
108  T(S)A 2001, s53(4).
109  The Road User Charging (Consultation and Publication) (Scotland) Regulations 2003 SSI 2003/292.

In addition to this obligation to consult imposed on the charging authority, the Scottish Ministers can at any time prior to confirming the order carry out further consultation or request that the charging authority carried out further consultation.[110]

Following the statutory consultation, the charging authority must publish a notice containing details of the charging scheme in a newspaper in the area in respect of which the charging scheme. In addition the charging authority should take such other appropriate steps to ensure adequate publicity about the charging scheme. Such steps may include displaying notices on the roads affected, publishing the order on the internet and publishing a notice in the Edinburgh Gazette. This triggers the start of an objection period which must last for no less than 28 days. All objections must be in writing and contain a statement of the grounds for objection. At the end of the objection period, the charging authority must prepare and publish a report detailing the number of objections received, a summary of the general nature of the objections, the charging authority's response and state whether an inquiry will be held.

On consideration of the objection report, the charging authority may decide to hold an inquiry.[111] It should be noted that the Scottish Ministers can also hold any inquiry at any point prior to confirmation of the order.[112] Although the 2001 Act provides that the charging authority may hold an inquiry if it thinks it appropriate, no procedure is set down. Nor are there any statutory requirements or policy guidance on the scope or format of the inquiry. However the Scottish Ministers may prescribe the circumstances in which an inquiry must be held.[113]

Following any inquiry, and having considered any outstanding objections and the inquiry report, the charging authority can make the order with or without changes.[114] Within 14 days of the order having been made, the charging authority must publish details of the charging order in a local newspaper. The order however must also be confirmed by the Scottish Ministers.[115] The order must be submitted to the Scottish Minsters for confirmation within seven days of it being made and the charging authority must provide the Scottish Ministers with any other information that they may require in order to confirm or to not confirm, as the case may be, the order. The Scottish Ministers can confirm the order with or without modifications.[116] Following confirmation, the order will come in to force on the date determined by the charging authority. Once the order has been confirmed, the charging authority must give notice of the scheme to the chief constable; give

---

110  T(S)A 2001, s52(2).
111  T(S)A 2001, s52(4).
112  T(S)A 2001, s52(3).
113  T(S)A 2001, s52(5).
114  T(S)A 2001, s50(1).
115  T(S)A 2001, s51(1).
116  T(S)A 2001, s51(3).

notice to those objectors who had outstanding objections giving reasons for making the order and make copies of the order, the relevant map, the consultation report, the objection report, the inquiry report, if an inquiry was held, and the order containing the confirmed scheme available for inspection in their offices.

## 6.11.3 VARYING OR REVOKING THE ORDER

Any variation to or revocation of a charging scheme or order must be made in the same way and the regulations apply to any such variation or revocation. Again any variation or revocation must be confirmed by the Scottish Ministers.[117]

## 6.11.4 EXEMPTIONS FROM THE CHARGE

Regulations[118] set out mandatory exemptions to any charging scheme and these include emergency service vehicles, and vehicles displaying a blue badge, and buses. A charging authority can create further exemptions as it sees fit. It can also reduce the rate of the charge payable for certain vehicles again as it sees fit. The order must contain provisions to allow persons to register to claim an exemption, whether mandatory or discretionary, or a reduced charge.

## 6.11.5 PAYING THE CHARGE

The registered owner of a vehicle is liable to pay the road user charge imposed by the charging order except if that vehicle is exempt. However there are exceptions to this. These provisions in the regulations are intended to deal with the situation where the previous registered owned has sold the car and notified the DVLA of this change in ownership or where the vehicle is a hire car.

## 6.11.6 PENALTIES

A penalty will be charge where the registered owner has failed to pay the charge within the time period and in the manner set out in the charging order. The order will specific the level of the penalty which will be reduced for early payment but which will increase if payment is not made on time. Again the registered owner is liable to pay the penalty.

117 T(S)A 2001, s50, 51 and 52.
118 The Road User Charging (Exemption from Charges) (Scotland) Regulations 2003 SSI 2204/509.

Different rates of penalty charges may be specified for

(a)    different classes of penalty charge;

(b)    different times;

(c)    different times of day;

(d)    different parts of a charging area;

(e)    different distances travelled;

(f)    different classes of vehicles; or

(g)    different circumstances in which penalty charges are imposed.

The regulations also give the charging authority the power to enter, seize and remove vehicles. They can also dispose of the vehicle either by selling it or dealing with it as scrap. In addition they can take possession of the vehicle and will only release it on payment of the penalty and all costs incurred for storing the vehicle.

### 6.11.7  APPLYING THE CHARGE

The net proceeds from a charging scheme must be used to facilitate whether directly or indirectly the achievement of the charging authority's local transport strategy.[119] This can be done by paying money to any other local traffic authority, local transport authority or other person.[120]

119  T(S)A 2001 Schedule 1 paragraph 5(1)(a).
120  T(S)A 2001 Schedule 1 paragraph 5(1)(b) as amended by the Transport (Scotland) Act 2005.

# 7 Roads and Planning

## 7.1 INTRODUCTION

The construction, operation and maintenance of the public road network is an important consideration in town and country planning. The national and local road infrastructure is necessary to facilitate development and the requirements and views of the local roads authority are taken into account at all levels in both development planning and development management. In recent years there has been a fundamental review of the planning system as well as important changes in the governance of our roads and transport systems. Much of this change stems from European Directives and policy as well as from government reviews such as the Stern Review.[1]

There is now a clear relationship between planning and transport, as evidenced from the following:

National Planning Framework     National Transport Strategy
Strategic Development Plan     Regional Transport Strategy
Local Development Plan     Local Transport Strategy
Planning Permission     Green Travel Plan

## 7.2 NATIONAL PLANNING FRAMEWORK

In 1999, agreement was reached between the European Commission and Member States on a European Spatial Development Perspective (ESDP).[2] The ESDP set common objectives and principles for balanced and sustainable development and economic and social cohesion across the European Union. The European Commission encouraged Member States to prepare spatial planning frameworks to provide a context for resource allocation in the enlarged European Union. The National Planning Framework for Scotland[3] was published in 2004. ('NPF')

The NPF provides a framework to guide the spatial development of Scotland to 2025 and it will be updated every 4 years. It identifies priorities for investment in strategic infrastructure "to enable Scotland to play to its strengths." The NPF was subjected to Strategic Environmental Assessment[4] and considers:

---

1    See Chapter 3.
2    Published January 1999.
3    See http://www.scottishexecutive.gov.uk/library5/planning/npf04–02.asp.
4    The Environmental Assessment (Scotland) Act 2005.

- People and homes;
- The economy;
- Scotland's cities;
- Transport

Infrastructure is a key issue and the NPF acknowledges that the competiveness of a place relies heavily on adequate investment in infrastructure, including transport. It states that the "common thread running through all economic scenarios is the importance of infrastructure, particularly transport infrastructure."[5]

On transport, the NPF states that a "key determinant of Scotland's environmental performance over the next 20 years will be the extent to which it is possible to shift to more sustainable modes of transport and more sustainable patterns of land use planning." Accordingly, one of the ten elements of the spatial strategy is "to highlight long term transport options and promote more sustainable patterns of transport and land use." Further comments on transport include the following:

- "To compete successfully in the world economy, Scotland requires a modern, flexible and well integrated transport system with high quality links to the rest of the UK, Europe and the world.";

- A clear long term vision is vital because transport infrastructure is capital intensive, takes a long time to deliver and has a lifespan measurable in decades. It also helps to give to developers and transport operators the certainty they need if they are to commit to major strategic investments.";

- Transport issues will have to be addressed at the outset in planning for future development. They cannot be left to be dealt with as an afterthought."; and

- "Development plans should identify the key locations where well planned, integrated development can benefit from and contribute to future development of public transport services."

The NPF was put on a statutory basis by the Planning Etc. (Scotland) Act 2006. It is currently under review by the Scottish Executive with a view to publication during 2008.[6]

## 7.3   SCOTTISH PLANNING POLICY

The Scottish Executive is gradually replacing the suite of National Planning Guidelines (NPG), National Planning Policy Guidance (NPPG) with statements of Scottish Planning Policy (SPP). These documents provide a national policy framework for the planning system and they

5    NPF2 2004.
6    NPF2 Consultative Draft was published in January 2008.

must be taken into account in the preparation of development plans and in development management. The former system of structure plans and local plans has been replaced by a system of Strategic Development Plans and Local Development Plans in terms of the Planning Etc. (Scotland) Act 2006.

In determining an application for planning permission, the legal requirement is to take into account the relevant terms of the development plan and all other material considerations.[7] The relevant terms of national planning policy are material considerations for this purpose. These national policy documents must therefore be taken into account in processing applications and related appeals by the planning authority and the Scottish Ministers.

## 7.4  SSP 17: PLANNING FOR TRANSPORT

In August 2005, the Scottish Executive issued Scottish Planning Policy 17: Planning for Transport. This document replaces NPPG 9: The Provision of Roadside Facilities on Motorways and Other Trunk Roads in Scotland; NPPG 17: Transport and Planning and SPP17: Transport and Planning Maximum Parking Standards Addendum to NPPF 17.

SPP 17 sets out five integration objectives and acknowledges that the planning system is a key mechanism for the integration of land use, economic development, environmental issues and transport planning. It states that regional transport strategies to be prepared by Regional Transport Partnerships will have to be co-ordinated with structure planning. Likewise, local plans and local transport strategies should co-ordinate land use and transport planning at a local level.[8]

SPP 17 covers a range of issues including major strategic projects; local plans and transport projects and assessing development proposals. The latter deals with maximum parking standards, Transport Assessment and Travel Plans.

## 7.5  TRANSPORT ASSESSMENTS

SPP 17 states that Transport Assessment methodology should focus on delivering an appropriate non-car mode share in respect of access to the proposed development.[9]

---

7    TCP(S)A 1997, s 37(2).
8    Paragraphs 9 and 10 of SPP 17.
9    See Transport assessment and Implementation: A Guide published with SSP 17.

## 7.6    TRAVEL PLANS

SPP 17 states that Travel Plans associated with a planning permission should be specified through a planning agreement, negotiated with the developer, in order that they may be adequately implemented and enforced. The Transport Assessment should include details of the proposed Travel Plan as part of the application for planning permission.

## 7.7    PLANNING OBLIGATIONS AND DEVELOPERS' CONTRIBUTIONS

In recent years, Travel Pans and other developers' contributions to roads and transport have been secured by means of a planning agreement in terms of section 75 of the Town and Country Planning Act (Scotland) 1997. However, the Planning Etc. (Scotland) Act 2006 replaces the bilateral planning agreement with a provision that enables a person to enter into a planning obligation, either by agreement with the planning authority or unilaterally. This provision for a unilateral obligation reflects the position in England and Wales.

The planning obligation will restrict or regulate the development or use of land, either permanently or during such period as may be specified in the 'relevant instrument', which contains the obligation(s). A planning obligation may be unconditional or subject to conditions and it may require payment of a specified amount or an amount determined in accordance with the relevant instrument. It may also require payment of periodical sums either indefinitely or for a specified period. There is a procedure to apply to the planning authority to have the planning obligation modified or discharged with a right of appeal to the Scottish Ministers against the decision of the planning authority.

It is generally accepted within the development industry that developers should contribute to the cost of provision of off-site roadworks and to other public benefits reasonably related to their development proposals. Planning authorities may secure a contribution to such roadworks in three ways:

1.    First, by the imposition of a suspensive planning condition, commonly referred to as a Grampian condition.[10] This involves a prohibition on the commencement of development or the use/occupation of the development until the roadworks have been completed. A suspensive condition is necessary if the works are to be undertaken on land which is either outwith the planning application boundary ('the red line') or outwith the control of the applicant. When granting planning permission, the planning authority has the power to impose conditions regulating the development or use of any land under the control of the applicant, whether or not it is

10   *Grampian Regional Council v Secretary of State for Scotland 1984* SC (HL) 58.

land in respect of which the application was made.[11] By imposing a Grampian condition, the authority is not requiring the applicant to undertake the off-site roadworks. It is prohibiting the development until those works are carried out by whomsoever. This approach was sanctioned by the House of Lords in the Grampian Regional Council case.

2. The second method of securing a contribution to off-site roadworks is by means of a planning obligation, the terms of which may require either the carrying out of the works or a financial contribution towards the funding of the works.

3. The third mechanism allows a developer to contribute to the cost of funding off-site road works by entering into an agreement with the local roads authority in terms of section 48 of the Roads (Scotland) Act 1984. The authority may have regard to the extent of the contribution, if any, in determining whether to undertake the construction or effect the improvement. This form of agreement constitutes a contract between the parties to the agreement. Unlike a section 75 agreement, it is not enforceable against successors in title. As the planning permission runs with the land, the planning authority may expect the agreement to do likewise. However a section 48 agreement may be appropriate in certain circumstances. The provision envisages joint funding of road construction projects. Both the Scottish Ministers and the local roads authority are entitled to enter into a section 48 agreement in respect of roads within their responsibility.

Commercial difficulties may arise if the developer is unaware of the extent of the contribution required until after he has concluded a contract with the landowner. In practice, most developers obtain a contractual position with the landowner before pursuing planning permission. Until they have a secure position, they may be reluctant to spend money on the proposal, which means that they will not commence pre-application discussions with the planning authority. As development costs affect the financial terms of the contract, it would be better if landowners and developers had advance notice of the expectations of the planning authority. This is most effectively achieved through the development plan process. Inclusion of the authorities expectations in the local plan has the double advantage of openness and permitting the public to make representations on the terms of the plan during its preparation.

## 7.8   DEVELOPMENT MANAGEMENT

The development and use of land is largely regulated by the Town and Country Planning (Scotland) Act 1997 as amended by the Planning Etc. (Scotland) Act 2006. The twin pillars of the planning system are the development plan and planning permission. There are two tiers of planning authority:

11   Town and County Planning (Scotland) Act 1997, s 41.

1.    Scottish Ministers.

2.    Local planning authorities.

The 2006 Act introduced strategic development plans and local development plans. The Scottish Ministers will designate the strategic development plan areas, which will centre on the four city regions. The development plan in a strategic development plan area will comprise the strategic development plan, the local development plan and any supplementary guidance issued in connection with those plans. The development plan outwith strategic development plan areas will consist of the local development plan and any supplementary guidance issued in connection with that plan.

The development management process centres on the definition of 'development' in terms of section 26 of the 1997 Act. If a particular proposal constitutes development, then planning permission is required. Development constitutes 'the carrying out of building, engineering, mining or other operations in, on, over or under land, or the making of any material change in the use of any buildings or other land'. Section 26 goes on to provide a list of operations or uses that are not to be taken as constituting development for the purposes of the Act. One of those exceptions is the carrying out by a local roads authority of any works required for the maintenance or improvement of a road, provided the works are carried out within the boundaries of the road. However, if such works are not exclusively for the maintenance of the road and if they would have a significant impact on the environment, then they would fall within the statutory definition of development.[12]

Applications for planning permission are made to the local planning authority. Applications will be processed in accordance with General Development Procedure Order.[13] The planning authority must consult specified categories of authorities/persons in certain cases.[14] The planning authority must give the consultees not less than fourteen days notice and they must not determine the application until the after the expiration of the period of notice.

## 7.8.1    CONSULTATION PROCEDURES IN RESPECT OF ROADS AUTHORITIES

### 7.8.1.1    *The Scottish Executive Development Department*

The Scottish Ministers must be consulted in the following circumstances:

1.    In the four undernoted categories of road or proposed road, where either the development involves development of land

---

12   See paragraph 5.2.2 above on Permitted Development.
13   Town and Country Planning (General Development Procedure) (Scotland) Order 1992, SI 1992/224.
14   SI 1992/224, art 15.

within sixty-seven metres of the middle of such a road or the development consists of or includes the formation, laying out or alteration of any means of access to such a road. The categories of road are:

a) a trunk road;

b) a proposed trunk road or a proposed special road, the route of which is shown in the development plan or in respect of which the Scottish Ministers have given written notice to the planning authority, together with maps/plans sufficient to identify the proposed route of the road;

c) any road which is part of the route of a special road to be provided by the Scottish Ministers under a special road scheme but which has not yet been transferred to them;

d) any road which has been or is to be provided by the Scottish Ministers in terms of a trunk road order or special road scheme but has not yet been transferred to any roads authority.

2. Where development is likely to result in a material increase in the volume or a material change in the character of traffic entering or leaving a trunk road.

3. Where development is for the purpose of creating a motorway service area or new development within the boundary of such an area.

4. Where there is development of land within 400 metres of the boundary of any motorway for the purpose of providing such services as refreshments, fuel or parking.

5. Where there is development of an area of land exceeding two hectares situated within one kilometre of a motorway junction for the purpose of providing fuel and refreshments.

### 7.8.1.2   *The local roads authority*

The consultation procedure under Article 15 of the Town and Country Planning (General Development Procedure) (Scotland) Order 1992 applies to roads, other than trunk roads, for which the planning authority are not also the roads authority. Since 1996 the planning authority is also the roads authority so there is no statutory requirement to consult the local roads authority with the exception of toll roads. There remains a requirement for the planning authority to consult the roads authority concerned where the development involves the formation, laying out or alteration of any means of access to land affording access to a toll road.

In practice however, planning officers will consult roads officers in relation to applications for planning permisison, This is important because the decision-maker should be advised of all material considerations in relation to the proposed development. The views of the roads authority will be a material consideration. Failure to report those views to the decision maker could render the decision open to challenge on the basis that the planning authority has acted unreasonably in the Wednesbury[15] sense by failing to take into account a material consideration.

The legal implications of the relationship between a planning authority and a statutory consultee were considered in the case of *Tayside Regional Council v Secretary of State for Scotland*.[16] This was an example of a planning authority taking a different view from that of the water and sewerage authority on two proposals for residential development. The issue was whether there was adequate sewerage capacity to serve the developments. At this stage the regional council was the statutory authority for water and sewerage. The planning authority granted planning permission despite an objection from the regional sewerage authority. The sewerage authority subsequently refused consent to connect the development to the main sewers on the basis of lack of capacity. The developer's appeal to the Secretary of State was upheld as the capacity could be provided at a reasonable cost. The regional council challenged the Secretary of State's decision but the court refused to intervene on the basis of the council's duties to provide sewerage facilities under the Sewerage (Scotland) Act 1968, and on the facts proved. However, there is a duty on the Sewerage Authority to provide such sewers and sewage treatment works as may be necessary for effectually draining their area of domestic sewage and surface water where this is practicable at reasonable cost. There is no corresponding duty on roads authorities but an analogy can be drawn, as demonstrated in the case of *R v Warwickshire County Council, ex parte Powergen*.[17]

Powergen received conditional outline planning permission on appeal to develop a former power station site for retail development. The proposed highway works were detailed and illustrated on drawings submitted with the application. A condition was imposed prohibiting use of the development until a bridge had been widened to facilitate the installation of traffic signals as part of the access arrangements. The appeal decision was not challenged by either the county council or the district council. In order to purify the planning condition, Powergen had to carry out the road works, which meant entering into an agreement with the highway authority under section 278 of the Highways Act 1980.[18] Its provisions are not dissimilar to those in section 48 of the Roads (Scotland) Act 1984 although there are notable differences. The English legislation is more restrictive as there is a test of public benefit, which is not present in section 48, and the cost must relate to the execution of works which the authority is or may be authorised to carry out. Unlike

15  *Associated Provincial Picture Houses Ltd v Wednesbury Corporation* [1984] 1 KB 223, HL. This case established the criteria for an unreasonable administrative decision.
16  1996 SLT 473.
17  [1998] JPL 131, CA.
18  As substituted by the New Roads and Streetworks Act 1991, s 23.

section 48, there is no express requirement to take the extent of the contribution into account when deciding whether to construct or improve a road. The public benefit test was significant in this decision. The court's interpretation of the test was that the highway authority had to be satisfied with the road safety implications of the development. If not satisfied, it had no discretion to enter into the agreement. The highway authority refused to enter into an agreement with Powergen because it was not satisfied with the road safety aspects. Its decision was based on the same grounds put forward and rejected in the planning appeal. Powergen attempted to negotiate with the authority to agree upon a solution acceptable to both sides. The authority rejected a further two schemes submitted by Powergen, who then sought judicial review. Powergen succeeded at first instance but the highways authority appealed to the Court of Appeal. The issue for the court was the proper relationship between the role of the planning authority and the role of the highways authority. The court dismissed the appeal by the highways authority. It stated that, following a successful appeal by the developer, the highway authority had no option but to co-operate in implementing the planning permission by entering into a section 278 agreement. In other words, the highway authority's discretion to enter into a section 278 agreement was limited by its interaction with the planning process. It had no right to veto or frustrate the planning permission. To determine otherwise 'would leave the highway authority able to override the planning process' according to the leading judgement of Lord Justice Simon Brown.[19] Notwithstanding this decision, his lordship acknowledged that road safety implications are clearly material to the determination of an application for planning permission. The court held that the highway authority had acted unreasonably in the Wednesbury sense and, therefore, their decision was ultra vires. However, his Lordship did not rule out the possibility of a different outcome if there had been a fresh objection by the highway authority, which was sufficiently different from its earlier one.[20] The comment in the *Journal of Planning Law* on the case observes that this effectively restricts the highway authority's statutory powers and that, once permission has been granted on appeal, the power to enter into a section 278 agreement became a duty.

It is asserted that it is not for the courts to determine whose was the better view and that it is unsatisfactory for both the highway authority to be able to veto planning permission and to be forced into entering into an agreement against its better judgement. This case reinforces the importance for effective co-ordination and consultation between the planning authority and the roads authority, even if both functions are the responsibility of one council. It also reinforces the distinction between a grant of planning permission, which involves a comprehensive assessment of all material considerations and a grant of a road construction consent, which involves a technical assessment to ensure that the road will be constructed to an appropriate standard. The issue of a road construction consent should not be used to frustrate the planning process.

19  [1998] JPL 131 at 136.
20  [1998] JPL 131 at 137.

No such pressure should be brought to bear on roads officers who are operating under a separate statutory framework.

### 7.8.2    TRANSPORT ASSESSMENT

The roads authority is likely to ask the applicant to provide a Transport Assessment in support of an application for planning permission. Any such request should be made formally through the planning authority, which has the power to make a direction requiring further information in order to enable it to deal with the application.[21]

### 7.8.3    PERMITTED DEVELOPMENT RIGHTS

Under the Town and Country Planning (Scotland) Act 1997, the Scottish Ministers are empowered to make a Development Order. The effect is to grant planning permission automatically for specified types of development without having to submit an application for planning permission to the planning authority. The most recent order is the Town and Country Planning (General Permitted Development) (Scotland) Order 1992.[22] The Order imposes standard conditions on all categories of permitted development. In particular, nothing in the Order permits development contrary to any condition imposed by any planning permission. Nor does the Order authorise any development, other than the categories listed below, which requires or involves the formation, laying out or material widening of a means of access to an existing road which is a trunk road or a classified road or creates an obstruction to the view of persons using any road used by vehicular traffic, so as to be likely to cause danger to such persons.[23] The foregoing restriction does not apply to development permitted by:

- Part 9. Repairs to private roads and private ways.

  Class 27 permits the carrying out on land within the boundaries of a private road or private way of works required for the maintenance or improvement of the road or way.

- Part 11. Development under Local or Private Acts or Orders

  Class 29 permits development authorised by a local or private Act of Parliament but it does not permit development if it consists of or includes:

  1. the erection, construction, alteration or extension of any building, bridge, aqueduct, pier or dam; or

  2. the formation, laying out or alteration of a means of access to any road used by vehicular traffic; unless the prior approval of the

21   SI 1992/224, art 13.
22   SI 1992/223 (as amended).
23   SI 1992/223, art 5.

planning authority in respect of detailed plans and specification is first obtained

- Part 12. Development by Local Authorities

  Class 31 permits the carrying out by a roads authority on land outwith but adjoining the boundary of an existing road of works required for or incidental to the maintenance or improvement of the road.

- Part 24. Toll Road Facilities

  Class 71 permits development consisting of:

  1. the setting up and the maintenance, improvement or other alteration of facilities for the collection of tolls;

  2. the creation of a hard surface to be used for the parking of vehicles in connection with the use of such facilities.

  Class 71 imposes specific conditions relating to the proximity of the development to the toll road and other restrictions relating to the overall floorspace and the height of the structure.

- Part 26. Development by the Scottish Ministers as roads authority

  Class 73 Permits the carrying out by the Scottish Ministers of Development in connection with a project for (1) the construction of a new road for which the Scottish ministers are roads authority, (2) the improvement of a road authorised by an order such as is mentioned in paragraph 1 of schedule 1 to the 1984 Act and (3) the improvement of a road without such an order.

  Class 74 Permits the carrying out by the Scottish Ministers of Development (other than development falling within class 73) in exercise of their functions under the 1984 Act, or development in connection with, or incidental to, the exercise of those functions.

Other relevant classes of permitted development include:

1. Class 8: Sundry Minor Operations, including the formation, laying out and construction of a means of access to a road, which is not a trunk road or a classified road, where that access is required in connection with development permitted by any class other than Class 7. (Erection, construction, maintenance, improvement or alteration of a gate, fence or wall or other means of enclosure).

2. Class 28: Repairs to Services. The carrying out of any works for the purposes of inspecting, repairing or renewing any sewer, main, pipe, cable or other apparatus, including breaking open any land for that purpose. This class is subject to the condition that on completion of the works, or nine months after commencement of the works, whichever is earlier, the land shall be restored to either its former condition or a condition that is acceptable to the planning authority.

3.    Class 30: Development by Local Authorities. Class 30 permits the erection or construction and the maintenance, improvement or other alteration by a local authority of (a) any building, works or equipment not exceeding four metres in height or 200 cubic metres in capacity on land belonging to or maintained by them, being building works or equipment required for the purposes of any function exercised by them on that land otherwise than as statutory undertakers, or (b) lamp standards, refuse bins, public shelters and similar structures or works required in connection with the operation of any public service administered by them.

### 7.8.4    ARTICLE 4 DIRECTIONS

It is open to both the Scottish Ministers and the planning authority to make a direction under Article 4 of the Order to withdraw the permitted development rights in relation to a particular area. The developer should confirm the position with the planning authority before undertaking development on the basis of its authorisation in terms of the order. Article 4 directions are usually made in respect of conservation areas.

# 8 Ownership of Roads

## 8.1 THE SCOTTISH MINISTERS AS ROADS AUTHORITY

### 8.1.1 GENERAL POWERS

The Scottish Ministers may acquire land, compulsorily or by agreement, for the construction or carrying out of works authorised by a trunk road order.[1] They may also acquire land for the purposes of constructing, improving, maintaining or servicing a trunk road other than a special road.[2] A special roads authority has the same powers in relation to special roads.[3] Section 111 of the 1984 Act enables proceedings required in respect of the compulsory acquisition of land for purposes connected with a special road or a trunk road to be taken concurrently with proceedings relating to a special road scheme or trunk road order. Further advice on compulsory purchase procedures is set out in SDD Circular 42/1976: Compulsory Purchase Procedures.[4]

If land forming common or open space is required for road purposes, the Scottish Ministers are entitled to acquire other land for replacement purposes. If such land is to be acquired compulsorily, it is not subject to the distance limits imposed by virtue of the Roads (Scotland) Act 1984.[5] The Scottish Ministers are entitled to acquire land for the provision of picnic sites.[6]

## 8.2 THE LOCAL ROADS AUTHORITY

### 8.2.1 GENERAL POWERS

A roads authority may acquire land, compulsorily or by agreement, for the following purposes:

1  R(S)A 1984, s 104(2).
2  R(S)A 1984, s 104(2).
3  R(S)A 1984, s 104(3).
4  See also SOEnD Circular 39/1992: Disposal of Surplus Government Land – The Crichel Down Rules and SEDD Circular 4/2003: Title Conditions (Scotland) Act 2003: Consequential Amendments to Planning and Compulsory Purchase Legislation.
5  ie by virtue of the Roads (Scotland) Act 1984, s 109, Sch 5, Pt I. The current limits are 200 metres or 800 metres from the middle of the road depending upon the power being exercised.
6  R(S)A 1984, s 108.

1.   The construction, improvement or protection of a public road.

2.   The provision or improvement of a road to be provided or improved in terms of a stopping up order under the Planning Acts.

3.   The provision of a public right of way, which is to be provided as an alternative to a right of way to be extinguished under the Planning Acts.

4.   Any other purpose for which land is required in connection with an order, as mentioned in head 2 above.[7]

The roads authority may also acquire land for the provision of any buildings or facilities needed for the purpose of constructing, improving, maintaining or servicing a public road.[8] Any power to acquire land compulsorily includes the power to acquire a servitude or other right in or over the land by the creation of a new right. In addition to compulsory purchase powers contained within the 1984 Act or other Public Acts, the local authority may have powers of compulsory acquisition under private Acts of Parliament.

The courts have held that the acquisition by an authority of land in connection with the construction of a road was not the equivalent of declaration of that land in its entirety to public passage and, in the circumstances of this case, the roads authority was justified in law in seeking to obtain financial consideration in exchange for granting any rights of access over the land.[9]

### 8.2.2   COMMON GOOD LAND

A roads authority is also entitled to acquire replacement land for land forming part of a common or open space, which is required for the above listed purposes.[10] This provision is of particular importance if the roads authority intend to acquire land which has the status of 'common good land'. Land may acquire the character and quality of common good property either by the terms of the relevant title or by proof of immemorial possession and use by inhabitants.[11] Common good land is inalienable in the absence of authority from the court. If land forms part of the common good, the local authority may have to apply to the Court of Session or to the sheriff to authorise disposal of the land. The court may authorise disposal of the land subject to conditions.[12] The courts may impose a condition requiring replacement land to be made available for the purposes of fulfilling the former function of the common good land. This provision is therefore important to enable the roads authority to acquire replacement land.

7   R(S)A 1984, s 104(1).
8   R(S)A 1984, s 105(3).
9   Elmford Ltd v City of Glasgow Council 2001 S.C. 267.
10  R(S)A 1984, s 104(3).
11  *Murray v Forfar Magistrates* (1893) 20 R 908, (1893) 1 SLT 105.
12  Local Government (Scotland) Act 1973, s 75.

## 8.2.3 AMENITY LAND

The roads authority is empowered to acquire land, which, in its view, is desirable to preserve or to improve the amenity of a public road or a proposed public road.[13] However, it cannot exercise powers of compulsory purchase to acquire land for this purpose.

## 8.2.4 BLIGHT

It is possible that the existence or use of a road, either constructed or improved by the authority or planned to be constructed or improved by it, could have an adverse effect on surrounding land. In such circumstances, the roads authority may acquire land for the purpose of mitigating those adverse effects.[14] It may do so by agreement or by compulsory acquisition. This power to acquire land can only be exercised if the acquisition is begun before the date on which the road or the improved road is opened to public traffic. If such land is acquired compulsorily, it shall be treated as if it were acquired for the construction or improvement of the road for compensation purposes.[15]

Moreover, the roads authority may acquire land blighted by either road works or the use of a road. In the first situation, it may acquire land, the enjoyment of which is seriously affected by the carrying out of *road construction or improvement works*. The second situation relates to land, the enjoyment of which is seriously affected by *the use* of the constructed or improved road. There are statutory constraints in relation to this power. First of all, it may only be exercised if the seller can establish an interest that qualifies for protection under the blight provisions contained in the Planning Acts.[16] Secondly, the roads authority may only acquire by agreement. It cannot resort to compulsory powers of purchase. Finally, the power is only exercisable if, in the case of road works,[17] acquisition is begun before the date on which the relevant road is open to public traffic or, in the case of use of the road, acquisition is begun before the end of one year after the date on which the relevant road is open to public traffic.

## 8.2.5 CATTLE GRIDS

A roads authority may acquire land for the purpose of providing, altering or improving a cattle-grid (or a by-pass in relation to a cattle-grid).[18] Such land may be acquired by agreement or under compulsory powers of purchase. If the acquisition is by agreement, the authority may acquire by purchase, lease or otherwise.

13  R(S)A 1984, s 105.
14  R(S)A 1984, s 106(1).
15  R(S)A 1984, s 106(5). As to cattle grids generally, see p 149 ff.
16  Town and Country Planning (Scotland) Act 1997, s 100(2), (3).
17  R(S)A 1984, s 106(2)(a).
18  R(S)A 1984, s 107. As to cattle grids generally, see p 149 ff.

## 8.2.6　COMPENSATION ON COMPULSORY PURCHASE

The compensation provisions applicable for compulsory acquisition of land are complex and outwith the scope of this text. In general terms, any dispute will be settled by the Lands Tribunal for Scotland. Section 110 of the Roads (Scotland) Act 1984 sets out certain assumptions that have to be taken into account by the Lands Tribunal in determining a claim for compensation. These are:

1. To have regard to the extent to which the remaining contiguous land belonging to the same person may benefit from the road construction/improvement.

2. In the case of land authorised to be acquired for widening a public road, to set off against the value of the land to be acquired, any increase in the value of other land belonging to the same person which will accrue to him by reason of the creation of a frontage to the road as widened. This provision is without prejudice to the generality of head 1.

3. To take into account, and embody in its award, any undertaking given by the authority as to the use to which the land, or any part of it, will be put.

## 8.2.7　COMPULSORY ACQUISITION ON BEHALF OF A THIRD PARTY

National planning policy is supportive of directing new investment into existing town centres to achieve the government's objectives on sustainable development. It is possible that roads authorities will become under pressure to exercise their powers of compulsory acquisition to assist in site assembly, particularly for off-site road works. If a roads authority agrees to co-operate in this way, it should ensure that it is properly indemnified by the developer for all costs and compensation payments arising from processing and implementation of the order.

In *Wards Construction (Medway) v Barclays Bank plc*[19] Kent County Council had agreed to undertake road improvements to assist with implementation of planning permission for residential development. The council acquired two parcels of land, one under a compulsory purchase order. The Lands Tribunal initially awarded £500,000 for the order land. However, following an appeal to the court, the compensation claim was remitted back to the tribunal, who revised the award to £2.15m.[20]

19　[1994] 2 EGLR, CA.
20　See also *Ozanne v Hertfordshire County Council [1988]* RUR 133.

## 8.3   VESTING OF PUBLIC ROADS

Every road that is entered in the list of public roads vests in the roads authority for the purposes of its functions under the 1984 Act.[21] However, such vesting does not confer any heritable right in relation to the road.

## 8.4   BRIDGES

Any bridge, which carries a public road, does not vest in the roads authority unless the bridge has been acquired by the roads authority, whether compulsorily or by agreement. Until such acquisition, the roads authority has no duty or power to manage or maintain the bridge, as distinct from the public road carried by it. Any entry in its list of public roads must contain a statement to the effect that the road does not comprise the bridge carrying the road. However, the roads authority may enter into an agreement with the bridge owner.[22] The agreement may provide for:

1.   The roads authority to make a payment to contribute towards the cost of maintenance, improvement or reconstruction of the bridge, or the road carried by the bridge or the approaches thereto.

2.   The transfer to the roads authority of the responsibility for the maintenance and improvement of the road carried by the bridge or the approaches thereto.

3.   The bridge, or the road carried thereby, or the approaches to the bridge to heritably vest in the roads authority.

The bridge owner is entitled to enter into such an agreement even if the bridge was constructed under statutory powers. This provision allows the roads authority to make financial contributions to the upkeep of a bridge or the road carried by the bridge but it can only take on responsibility for the bridge if it acquires title to it. The bridge must heritably vest in the roads authority before it can become responsible for it. This contrasts with roads, which vest in the roads authority on being entered in the list of public roads, notwithstanding the authority's lack of heritable interest in the road. Of course, the roads authority will have a heritable interest in the road if it was constructed on their land.

In the case of Transco plc v Glasgow City Council 2005 SLT 958, a utilities company, which had carried out work on a bridge carrying two gas pipelines, sought recompense from the roads authority on the basis that the authority had been 'unjustifiably enriched' by the work undertaken of the company. The company had a statutory duty in relation to the provision and maintenance of the gas mains, which were carried by a bridge. This bridge ceased to be used by vehicular traffic

21   R(S)A 1984, s 1(9).
22   R(S)A 1984, s 79.

following construction of a new bridge in 1987. The old bridge had been a source of concern following structural engineering reports and a flood that had occurred in 1994. The company argued that so long as the bridge was a road, the authority had a duty to maintain it so any maintenance works carried out by the company resulted in unjustifiable enrichment. The authority argued that they could not have been compelled to carry out works on the bridge; they could have decided to stop it up and remove it from their list of public roads. Although the action was dismissed as irrelevant based on the law of unjustified enrichment and recompense, the court held that while it was possible that when challenged to maintain the bridge, the authority could have initiated the stopping up procedure which would have led to the delisting of the bridge, as a matter of relevancy, it could not be said that so long as the bridge was a road, they could not be compelled to maintain it. The case report states that bridge was entered on the authority's list of public roads. However, it is not clear if that entry in the list of public roads followed acquisition of the bridge in terms of Section 1(10) of the 1984 Act. If the authority had not acquired the bridge in terms of Section 1(10) (b) then the bridge entry in the public list would have been ultra vires. Furthermore, it would have been open to the authority to delist a road without processing a stopping up order.

When a road has been stopped up by virtue of an order made under the 1984 Act or under the Planning Acts, the solum of the road vests in the owner or owners of land which adjoins the road, subject to any prior claim by any person by reason of title.[23]

## 8.5   OWNERSHIP OF SUBSOIL

In undertaking road works or disposing of road arisings, consideration should be given to the ownership of the subsoil. However, there is limited statutory or judicial guidance on the extent of that interest or on how much of the solum of the road is within the control of the roads authority by virtue of vesting under the 1984 Act.

The Highways Act 1980 provides that 'every highway maintainable at the public expense, together with the materials and scrapings thereof, vests in the authority who is for the time being the highway authority for the highway'. There is no such provision in the 1984 Act. This point was considered in the English case of *Schweder v Worthing Gas Light and Coke Co Ltd* in which Mr Justice Eve said:

'How much of the subsoil is necessarily dedicated for this purpose is a matter of evidence in each case. It maybe the subsoil is of such a nature that only a very shallow stratum is required for the maintenance of the surface of the road; on the other hand it may be that the character of the subsoil renders a much thicker stratum necessary'[24]

---

23   R(S)A 1984, s 115. See Chapter 9.
24   1912 1 CH 83; 1913 1 CH 118.

The subsoil of a road belongs to adjoining landowners in the absence of any prior claim by title. In a significant English case, owners of adjoining land were held to be treated as occupiers of the subsoil notwithstanding that it was impossible, without major works, to gain access to the subsoil and still protect the highway.[25] Their blight notice in respect of the proposed construction of a bypass was upheld. This case may have implications in commercial situations requiring works to the public road if owners of the subsoil compensation in respect of their interest.

25   *Norman v Department of Transport* [1996] 24 EG 150.

# 9 Stopping Up and Diversion of Roads

## 9.1 INTRODUCTION

Situations may arise in which an existing road requires either to be stopped up or modified in some way. The initiative may come from the roads authority as a result of its improvements to the local road network. The authority may have decided to close a road, which is no longer necessary or is considered to have become unsafe. Stopping up may also be necessary to allow a development to proceed in terms of a planning permission. A decision to make a statutory order raises several practical and legal considerations:

1. Should the order be made under planning or roads legislation?

2. Is there a procedural advantage in adopting one or the other statutory process in the particular circumstances?

3. If the order is to accommodate a development, what are the implications for land control?

4. Is stopping up necessary? Is there a more appropriate procedure to achieve the objective?

5. What are the cost and time implications of pursuing an order to confirmation and implementation?

6. What scope is there for flexibility once the procedure is underway?

## 9.2 THE STATUTORY PROVISIONS

The roads authority and the planning authority each have separate powers to stop up a road. The roads authority's powers are contained within sections 12, 68, 69, 70 and 152(2) of the Roads (Scotland) Act 1984. The planning authority's power is contained within section 207 of the Town and Country Planning (Scotland) Act 1997. The Scottish Ministers have power under both Acts to make a stopping up order.[1]

In general terms, the roads authority will act in cases involving road safety or road management whereas the planning authority will take responsibility if the stopping up is related to a development proposal. However, it is for the local authority to decide which is the relevant power in the circumstances of the case.

1 Roads (Scotland) Act 1984, s 68; TCP(S)A 1997, s 202.

## 9.3   THE ROADS (SCOTLAND) ACT 1984

### 9.3.1   SECTION 12 ORDERS

Section 12 relates to roads that cross or join public roads other than special roads.[2] The roads authority may make an order in relation to a public road or a proposed public road known for the purposes of the section as the 'main road'. The order may authorise the roads authority for the main road to stop up, divert, improve or otherwise alter a side road which either crosses or otherwise enters the route of the main road or will be affected by the construction or improvement of the main road. This section also authorises the authority to construct a temporary road to facilitate the operations involved in the construction or improvement of the main road. It is therefore a provision that allows the roads authority to manage and implement improvements or additions to the public road network.

The order may also authorise the roads authority to stop up any private means of access to land adjoining or adjacent to land which forms either part of the route of the main road or the site of any works authorised by the order. The authority may provide a new means of access to any such land.[3] Before stopping up a private means of access the roads authority must be satisfied that:

1.   No access to the land is reasonably required; or

2.   Another reasonably convenient means of access to the land is available or will be provided by virtue of the order.[4]

Although the roads authority may stop up the means of access in any way which seems to it to be appropriate, it must not obstruct any public right of way on foot.[5] It is an offence for any person to use a means of access, which has been stopped up under this provision, unless he is exercising a public right of way on foot.[6]

Any person suffering damage as a result of the stopping up of an access to any land under this provision is entitled to recover compensation from the roads authority. The damage must be by depreciation of any interest in the land or by being disturbed in his enjoyment of the land. In assessing compensation, any new means of access provided by the roads authority must be taken into account.[7] The Lands Tribunal for Scotland can determine any question of disputed compensation.[8]

2   See Chapter 4.
3   R(S)A 1984, s 70.
4   R(S)A 1984, s 71(3).
5   R(S)A 1984, s 71(4).
6   R(S)A 1984, s 71(5).
7   R(S)A 1984, s 71(6).
8   R(S)A 1984, s 117.

## 9.3.2   PROCEDURE FOR SECTION 12 ORDERS

The procedure for making and confirming orders under section 12 is contained within Parts I and III of Schedule 1 to the 1984 Act. It is the same procedure for making trunk road orders.[9] The procedure for a section 12 order differs from the procedure for stopping up orders made under sections 68 and 69, which is contained in regulations.[10]

## 9.3.3   SECTION 68 ORDERS

Under section 68 of the 1984 Act, the roads authority has the power to make a stopping up order either on its own initiative or at the request of any person. The order may be made in relation to public or private roads. The authority may make the order in two situations:

1.    If, in its opinion, the road has become dangerous to the public; or

2.    if, in its opinion, the road is or will become unnecessary.

If the road has become dangerous because it enters or crosses the route of another public road or it has become affected by the construction or improvement of such other road, the order cannot be made under section 68 but rather should be made under section 12 of the 1984 Act.[11]

Before making an order under section 68, the roads authority must satisfy itself that a suitable alternative road exists or that no alternative road is necessary. If the order is made only on the ground that the road will become unnecessary, it will not come into operation until the road has become unnecessary and a suitable alternative road exists.

The order may provide for the stopping up of a road, subject to the reservation of a means of passage along the road for pedestrians, cyclists or both. It is possible that a road has or will become unnecessary for vehicular traffic but it may still be useful for pedestrians or cyclists. If the road is to be stopped up because it has become dangerous to the public, it may not be safe to reserve a means of passage for pedestrians or cyclists. The roads authority will decide whether or not any such reservation is appropriate in the circumstances of the case, taking into account its implied duty to promote road safety.

Any rights of statutory undertakers in respect of any of their apparatus, which on the relevant date, is in, on, over, along or across the road must be preserved in the order. The relevant date is the date immediately before the date of the order.

9    See Chapter 4, p 67.
10   See p 131 below.
11   See p 128 above.

### 9.3.4   SECTION 69 ORDERS

The power contained within section 69 of the 1984 Act allows a roads authority to regulate potentially dangerous situations involving private accesses from a road onto other land. The roads authority may by order stop up a private access from a road, public or private, if it considers that it is likely to cause danger to, or to interfere unreasonably with traffic on the road. The roads authority may provide a new means of access to the land to replace the one stopped up. However, a private means of access cannot be stopped up under this section in advance of:

1.    Resolution of all objections to the making of the order;

2.    the expiry of six weeks from the date of first notification of the proposal to make the order; and

3.    in cases where the roads authority have to provide a new means of access, its provision by the authority.

The roads authority cannot stop up an access under section 69 unless it is satisfied that:

a.    No access to the land is reasonably required; or,

b.    another reasonably convenient means of access to the land is available or will be provided in terms of the order.

Likewise, although the roads authority can decide how to stop up the access, it cannot obstruct any public right of way on foot. Use of the stopped up access is an offence unless the person is exercising a public right of way on foot and the same compensation provisions apply to section 69 orders as apply to section 12 orders.[12]

### 9.3.5   SECTION 152(2) ORDERS TO REDETERMINE PUBLIC RIGHTS OF PASSAGE

A section 68 order is restricted to situations in which a road, public or private, has become dangerous to the public, or has or will become unnecessary, as outlined above. There may be situations which do not fall within the scope of section 68 but nevertheless, the roads authority may wish to re-determine the means of exercise of the public right of passage along a public road. For example, the roads authority may wish to prohibit passage by vehicular traffic but retain or introduce a right of passage for pedestrians or cyclists.

Section 1 of the 1984 Act empowers the roads authority to determine the means of exercise of a public right of passage over a public road, or any part of it. This power does not extend to private roads. Section 152(2) extends the section 1 power to include the power to redetermine, by order, the means of exercise of a public right of passage. In relation to

12    R(S)A 1984, s 71 and p 128 above.

public roads, therefore, the roads authority may make a section 152(2) order to redetermine the means of exercise of the public right of passage. For example, it may authorise a change from a carriageway to a cycle track, or from a cycle track to a footpath.

### 9.3.6   PROCEDURE

The procedure for making orders under sections 68, 69 and 152(2) of the 1984 Act is contained in the Stopping Up of Roads and Private Accesses and the Redetermination of Public Rights of Passage (Procedure) (Scotland) Regulations 1986.[13] The procedure involves publication of a statutory notice in the local newspaper and in the *Edinburgh Gazette* and service of the order and the accompanying plan, the statutory notice and a statement of reasons for making the order on:

1.   Where the roads authority is not the local roads authority, the local roads authority.

2.   The planning authority and any other roads authority affected by the proposal.

3.   Where the order relates to a private means of access, the owner and occupier of any land to which the order relates and the owner and occupier of any land which it is proposed to acquire for the provision of a new means of access.

4.   Any statutory undertakers having apparatus under, in, on, over, along or across that road.

A statutory notice must also be displayed in a prominent position at or near the ends of the road to be stopped up or over which the public right of passage is to be redetermined. The authority must take all reasonable steps to keep the notice exhibited in that position and in a legible condition for at least twenty-eight days.

The order documents must be available for public inspection at the main office of the roads authority and at other venues chosen by the authority having regard to the convenience of members of the public.

### 9.3.7   OBJECTIONS TO A STOPPING UP ORDER

Any person may object to a stopping up order.[14] They must make their objection to the relevant roads authority within a twenty-eight day period from notification to the address given on the statutory notice. In response, the roads authority must send an explanation of the purpose of and the need for the order, together with any comments on the terms of the objection, which it wishes to make.

13   SI 1986/252.
14   R(S)A 1984, s 71(2).

If the objection is withdrawn and there are no outstanding objections to the order, the authority may proceed to confirm the order. If the objection is maintained and not withdrawn:

1.    Scottish Ministers, if they are the roads authority, must consider the objection and, thereafter, they may make the order.

2.    If the local roads authority is the roads authority, it must remit the matter to the Scottish Ministers for determination. They may confirm the order with or without modification or they may refuse to confirm it. They must notify their decision in writing to the local roads authority and to each person who did not withdraw their objection.

The regulations do not make provision for a hearing or public inquiry into outstanding objections. Immediately after an order has been made or confirmed, the roads authority must publish the decision in statutory form. It must also publicise the decision of the Scottish Ministers to refuse to confirm an order. There is no right of appeal to the Court of Session in relation to decisions to confirm orders under sections 68, 69 or 152(2). However, the decision of the Scottish Ministers would be open to challenge by means of judicial review.


### 9.3.8   POWER OF LOCAL ROADS AUTHORITY TO MODIFY AN ORDER PRIOR TO CONFIRMATION

The statutory provisions empower the Scottish Ministers to confirm an order with or without modification.[15] They can also empower a local roads authority to confirm an order in circumstances in which there are no objections or objections made have been withdrawn. However, the statutory provisions do not expressly prohibit modification by the local roads authority prior to confirmation of the order.

This contrasts with the provisions of the Town and Country Planning (Scotland) Act 1997 under which the planning authority can confirm an order *unmodified* in circumstances in which there have been no objections or objections made have been withdrawn.[16] This restriction may create significant practical difficulties for the planning authority. It may be that an objector is willing to withdraw his objection if the order is modified to take account of his concerns. The planning authority may find itself in a situation in which there are no outstanding objections, subject to modification of the order. As it is only entitled to confirm an order unmodified, it would have to refer the order to the Scottish Ministers for confirmation as a modified order. The other option would be to start again with a fresh order taking account of the agreed modification. Both options could create delay in confirmation of the order. If the authority

15    R(S)A 1984, s 71(2)(a).
16    TCP(S)A 1997, Sch 16.

starts the process afresh, there may be new objections. Such delay or uncertainty could be problematic if the order is necessary to allow implementation of a development.

A local roads authority may decide to modify its order to resolve an outstanding objection. It is arguable that it is not entitled to do so and that it should start again by making a fresh order taking account of the modifications. It has no express power to confirm with or without modification. Moreover, it has no way of knowing whether or not another party would object to the modification. The statutory intention is to publicise the proposal and to allow a period for submission of objections. Failure to undertake public consultation in respect of the modification could render the confirmed order open to legal challenge.

### 9.3.9   STOPPING UP PRIVATE ACCESS TO LAND BY AGREEMENT

Section 72 of the 1984 Act allows the roads authority to enter into an agreement with the occupier of land and with any other person having an interest in the land to stop up a private means of access to that land from a public road or a proposed public road. The agreement may provide for payment of compensation by the roads authority to that person in respect of any damage suffered as a result of the stopping up.

The stopping up may be implemented in any way considered appropriate by the roads authority but it must not obstruct any public right of way on foot. It is an offence for any person to use a means of access stopped up under this provision unless the person is exercising a public right of way on foot.

Section 72 provides for such agreements to be registered in the Land Register of Scotland or recorded in the Register of Sasines, making the terms of the agreement enforceable against singular successors. However the agreement is not binding on parties who in good faith and for value acquired rights to the land affected prior to registration or recording of the agreement.

### 9.3.10   VESTING OF THE SOLUM OF A STOPPED UP ROAD

Where a road is stopped up under the 1984 Act or any other enactment, and the road has ceased to be used as a road, the solum of the road vests in the owner or owners of the land which adjoins the road, subject to any prior claim of any person by reason of title.[17] This means that there are two pre-conditions to the vesting of the solum of a stopped up road:

17   R(S)A 1984, s 115.

1.    The road must have been stopped up under a competent
      statutory provision; and

2.    the road must have ceased to be used as a road.

If those pre-conditions are met, then the solum will vest in any party
with a prior claim by title. If there is no such prior claim, the solum will
vest in the owner or owners of land, which adjoins the road.

Any dispute arising from this provision may be referred on summary
application by any interested party to the sheriff whose decision on the
matter shall be final.

## 9.4   THE TOWN AND COUNTRY PLANNING (SCOTLAND) ACT 1997

### 9.4.1   SECTION 207 ORDERS: STOPPING UP/DIVERSION BY LOCAL PLANNING AUTHORITY

If a road, other than a trunk road or a special road, has to be stopped up
or diverted to facilitate or accommodate a development proposal, the
order is usually promoted by the planning authority under section 207 of
the 1997 Act. Before making an order, the planning authority should be
satisfied that the stopping up or diversion is necessary to enable the
development to be carried out in accordance with a planning permission
or by a government department. For instance, the development may
involve construction of a building on the road. In those circumstances, it
would be necessary to stop up at least part of the road, if the
development is to proceed. It is possible that some traffic management
measures, including stopping up, may be desirable but not necessary to
enable a development to be carried out in accordance with a planning
permission. The planning authority should be satisfied that the stopping
up is necessary, not merely desirable before proceeding to make an
order.

A section 207 order may provide for the construction or improvement of
any other road and it may direct that this newly constructed or improved
road should be added to the list of public roads. The order may contain
incidental or consequential provisions considered necessary or expedient
by the planning authority. This general power enables the authority to
make a financial contribution, or to require a third party to make a
payment or a contribution towards the cost of doing any work provided
by the order. The order may also provide for the preservation of any
rights of statutory undertakers in respect of apparatus located within the
road and affected by the order.

A section 207 order may be made in respect of a road, which is
temporarily stopped up or diverted under any other enactment.[18] There

18   TCP(S)A 1997, s 207(3).

is a requirement for the planning authority to consult the local roads authority, where they are separate authorities. The planning authority may also make an order to stop up or to divert a footpath or bridleway affected by development.[19] In such cases, it must also be satisfied that the stopping up or diversion is necessary to enable development to be carried out in terms of a planning permission or by a government department.

The planning authority has the power to make an order to change a road to a footpath or bridleway as part of an adopted proposal to improve the amenity of part of its area.[20] This power does not extend to trunk roads or principal roads for the purposes of advances under section 3 of the 1984 Act. Such an order may provide for the extinguishment of any right which persons may have to use vehicles on that road, although it may provide for certain categories of vehicle to use the road notwithstanding the extinguishment of the general right.[21]

### 9.4.2   SECTION 202 ORDERS: STOPPING UP/DIVERSION BY THE SCOTTISH MINISTERS

The Scottish Ministers have a similar power to stop up or divert any road if they are satisfied that it is necessary to do so in order to enable development to be carried out in accordance with a planning permission or by a government department. However, the Ministers' powers include the power to stop up or divert a trunk road or a special road and are wider than those of the planning authorities.

### 9.4.3   PROCEDURE FOR ORDERS UNDER THE TOWN AND COUNTRY PLANNING (SCOTLAND) ACT 1997

The procedure for making and confirming stopping up orders is contained in Schedule 16 to the 1997 Act.

Part I of Schedule 16 deals with the making of orders by the Scottish Ministers. If an objection to the order is made and maintained by a local authority or statutory undertaker, they must hold a public inquiry to consider the objection(s). If the objection is made and maintained by a party other than a local authority or statutory undertaker, the Scottish Ministers may dispense with an inquiry if they are satisfied that it is unnecessary.

Part II of Schedule 16 deals with the procedure for confirmation of orders made by the planning authority. The planning authority must advertise the fact that it has made an order by publication of a notice in prescribed form. The notice shall state:

19   TCP(S)A 1997, s 208.
20   TCP(S)A 1997, s 203.
21   As to the procedure for orders under s 203, see TCP(S)A 1997, Sch 16, Pt II.

- The general effect of the order.

- That the order has been made and is about to be confirmed.

- The place where the order may be inspected.

- The time and manner for submission of representations/objections (not less than twenty-eight days from the date of first publication of the statutory notice).

The notice must be published in the *Edinburgh Gazette* and in at least one local newspaper and it must be served on:

- Every owner, occupier, lessee of any land to which the order relates.

- Every local authority whose area includes any of that land.

- Statutory undertakers.

If there are no objections or if any objections made are subsequently withdrawn, the planning authority may confirm the order but without any modification. If an objection is duly made and not withdrawn, the order must be referred to the Scottish Ministers for confirmation. Before deciding whether or not to confirm the order, they must afford to any objector an opportunity of being heard by a person appointed by them. This means that objectors will be offered the opportunity of a public inquiry.

Both the Scottish Ministers and the planning authority have limited powers to promote draft orders in anticipation of planning permission.[22] This enables the planning authority to publish a notice of the draft of an order if:

1.  The planning authority would, if planning permission for any development had been granted, have the power to make an order under section 207; and

2.  the development is the subject of an application for planning permission.

This allows the planning authority to publish the draft order and invite objections as it is dealing with the planning application. However, it must be satisfied that, if planning permission were granted, the stopping up order would be necessary.

## 9.5   PUBLIC PATH DIVERSION ORDERS

The Countryside (Scotland) Act 1967 enables a planning authority to make a public path diversion order.[23] For the purposes of this power, a

22   TCP(S)A 1997, Sch 16, paras 2(1), 3(1).
23   Countryside (Scotland) Act 1967, s 35.

public path is a way over which the public have the following but no other rights of way; a right of way on foot with or without a right of way on pedal cycles. The onus is on the owner, tenant or occupier of land crossed by a public path to satisfy the planning authority that it is expedient to divert the line of the path in order to secure the efficient use of land or to provide a shorter or more convenient path across their land. The order must be submitted to the Scottish Ministers for confirmation.

The order may:

1.  Create a new public path if it appears to the planning authority to be requisite for effecting the diversion; and

2.  extinguish from a specified date the right of way over so much of the path as appears to the planning authority to be requisite for effecting the diversion.

The specified date should be such as to allow any works required in relation to the new path to be carried out. Before deciding to make a public path diversion order, the authority may require the owner, tenant or occupier to enter into an agreement regarding compensation and expenses.

The Scottish Ministers will not confirm the order unless:

a.  They are satisfied that it is expedient to divert the line of the path either in the interests of the efficient use of land or to secure a more convenient or shorter route.

b.  They are satisfied that the new line of the path will not be substantially less convenient to the public in consequence of the diversion.

c.  They have had regard to the effect that the diversion would have on public enjoyment of the path as a whole.

d.  They have had regard to the effect that the order would have in relation to other land served by the existing right of way.

e.  They have had regard to the effect that the new right of way would have in relation to land over which the right is created.

## 9.6   PUBLIC PATH EXTINGUISHMENT ORDERS

The planning authority also has the right to close public paths under section 34 of the 1967 Act. It must consider it expedient to close the path on the ground that it is not needed for public use. The order must be submitted to the Scottish Ministers for confirmation. The Scottish Ministers will not confirm an extinguishment order unless they are satisfied that it is expedient to do so, having regard to:

1.  The extent to which it appears to them that the path would be likely to be used by the public.

2.    The effect which the extinguishment of the right of way would have in respect of the land served by the path.

## 9.7   PROCEDURE FOR PUBLIC PATH ORDERS

The procedure is set out in Schedule III to the 1967 Act. The planning authority must publish a notice in the prescribed form stating:

1.    The general effect of the order, that it has been made and is about to be submitted for confirmation.

2.    Naming a place where the order may be inspected.

3.    Specifying the time for submission of objections, being not less than twenty-eight days from first publication.

The notice must be published in at least one local newspaper and displayed in a prominent position at the end of the relevant section of path to be closed or diverted. If there are no objections or if objections are made and subsequently withdrawn, the Scottish Ministers may confirm the order with or without modifications or conditions. If an objection is maintained, the Scottish Ministers must afford the opportunity of being heard by a person appointed by them, which means a public inquiry.

## 9.8   LAND REFORM (SCOTLAND) ACT 2003

The Land Reform (Scotland) Act 2003 imposed a duty on local authorities to assert, protect, keep open and free from obstruction any route, waterway or other means where access can be reasonably exercised. Local authorities must draw up a plan for a system of core paths sufficient to provide reasonable public access throughout their area.[24] The authorities have the power to acquire land and to maintain and manage the core paths. They are empowered to do any-thing which they consider appropriate for the purposes of maintaining a core path and keeping it free from obstruction or encroachment.[25]

24   Section 17 of the 2003 Act.
25   Section 19 of the 2003 Act.

# PART FOUR

# 10 Road Maintenance and Improvement

## 10.1 INTRODUCTION

Roads authorities are under a duty to manage and maintain public roads[1] in their areas. This includes a power to reconstruct, alter, widen, improve or renew and decide how the public right of passage can be exercised over these roads.[2] The Scottish Ministers are responsible for the management and maintenance of trunk roads, special roads provided by them and any other road which is not the responsibility of the local roads authority and have the same range of functions.[3] Within these broad parameters roads authorities, both local and national, have many more specific power and duties and it is these that will be considered in this chapter. The Scottish Ministers can reach agreement with the local roads authority for it to act as their agent and carry out their roads management and maintenance functions.[4] They can also decide to contract out the majority of these functions, though not all, to the private sector.[5]

## 10.2 LEVELS OF PUBLIC ROADS

The roads authority has the power to raise, lower or alter the level of a public road as it thinks fit.[6] However, this is subject to any order which may have been made in relation to a special road[7] or in respect of a road which crosses or joins a public road, or proposed public road, which is not a special road.[8]

## 10.3 ROAD SAFETY

There are a number of provisions which deal with various aspects of road safety for pedestrians and other road users.

1    ie roads which are on the list of public roads. See also Chapter 2.
2    R(S)A 1984, s 1(1). See also Chapter 9.
3    R(S)A 1984, s 2(1).
4    R(S)A 1984, s 4. See also Chapter 2.
5    See the Deregulation and Contracting Out Act 1994, s 69 and the Secretary of State's Trunk Road Functions (Contracting Out) (Scotland) Order 1996, SI 1996/878, reg 2.
6    R(S)A 1984, s 24.
7    Under R(S)A 1984, s 9.
8    ie under R(S)A 1984, s 12. See also Chapter 4.

## 10.3.1   FOOTWAYS, SUBWAYS AND FOOTBRIDGES

The roads authority has a duty to provide 'proper and sufficient' footways for public roads which appear to be necessary or desirable for the safety or convenience of pedestrians.[9] A 'footway' is associated with a carriageway and allows passage over a road on foot.[10] In effect this is a pavement beside a road but this is not a term used in the legislation.

There is a power to construct, light and maintain pedestrian subways under the road or footbridges over it.[11] The authority can provide subways or footbridges to make it less dangerous for pedestrians to cross a public road or to protect traffic from danger.[12] The authority can also construct and maintain works in the carriageway of a public road in the following three situations:

1.    To separate traffic either on one side from that on the other carriageway, or, where traffic going in both directions is using the same carriageway, for example, while road works are carried out, on a dual carriageway.[13]

2.    At junctions to regulate the movement of traffic.[14] This would normally be a roundabout.

3.    To provide refuges for pedestrians crossing the road.[15] For example traffic islands.

## 10.3.2   FENCES OR BARRIERS

Fences or barriers, walls, pillars, rails and raised paving can be provided and maintained by the roads authority to safeguard people using a public road.[16] These can be used to segregate footways, footpaths, cycle tracks and carriageways, classes of users of cycle tracks, where a footpath gives direct access to a road and along the sides of bridges, embankments and other dangerous parts of the road.[17]

Fences or posts can be erected and maintained to prevent access to a road, or proposed road, or to delimit the road, or proposed road. In the latter case, stones or other markers can also be used.[18] In doing any of these things the roads authority must not interfere with an agricultural

9    R(S)A 1984, s 25.
10   R(S)A 1984, s 151(1), (2).
11   R(S)A 1984, s 26.
12   R(S)A 1984, s 26.
13   R(S)A 1984, s 27(a).
14   R(S)A 1984, s 27(b).
15   R(S)A 1984, s 27(c).
16   R(S)A 1984, s 28.
17   R(S)A 1984, s 28(a)–(d). A 'footpath' allows passage on foot and is not associated with a carriageway. A 'cycle track' permits passage by pedal cycle and may include passage on foot: s 151(1), (2).
18   R(S)A 1984, s 29(1).

fence or gate,[19] obstruct a public right of way[20] or means of access which has been granted planning permission,[21] or obstruct an access created before 1 July 1948.[22]

### 10.3.3 HAZARDS OF NATURE

The roads authority can provide and maintain any necessary barriers or other works to protect a public road, or proposed public road, against snow, flood, landslide or other hazards of nature.[23] This is in addition to the power to provide such things as fencing and is subject to the provisions on road drainage.[24]

### 10.3.4 ROAD DRAINAGE

The roads authority has a range of powers which allow it to carry out works to drain a public road, or proposed public road, or to take steps to prevent surface water from flowing onto it.[25] A 'drain' includes a ditch, gutter, watercourse, bridge, culvert, tunnel, pipe or holding pond and any associated pumping machinery.[26] The authority can construct or lay drains as necessary in the road or in land adjoining it or near to it.[27] It can erect and maintain barriers to divert surface water into or through a drain.[28] It also has powers to scour, cleanse and keep road drains open and can discharge the surface water from them into any inland or tidal waters.[29] If the roads authority constructs or lays a drain it has a duty to scour, cleanse and keep it open.[30] Before carrying out any works in connection with road drainage the authority must notify the owner and the occupier of affected land of its intentions. It must describe the proposed works and inform them of their right to object within twenty-eight days of service of the notice.[31] Where the owner or occupier maintains an objection then the consent of the Scottish Ministers is required if it is a local roads authority proposing to do the work. The Scottish Ministers may grant consent unconditionally or may impose such terms and conditions as they think fit. Their decision on the matter

19   R(S)A 1984, s 29(2)(a).
20   R(S)A 1984, s 29(2)(b).
21   R(S)A 1984, s 29(2)(c) and Part III of the Town and Country Planning (Scotland) Act 1997. See also Chapter 7.
22   Unless it contravened ss 1 or 2 of the Restriction of Ribbon Development Act 1935. R(S)A 1984, s 29(2)(d).
23   R(S)A 1984, s 30.
24   R(S)A 1984, ss 28, 31.
25   R(S)A 1984, s 31.
26   R(S)A 1984, s 31(6).
27   R(S)A 1984, s 31(1)(a).
28   R(S)A 1984, s 31(1)(b).
29   R(S)A 1984, s 31(1)(c), (d).
30   R(S)A 1984, s 31(2).
31   R(S)A 1984, s 31(3).

is final.[32] Where the Scottish Ministers are carrying out the works they must consider the objection before proceeding.[33]

It is an offence for anyone to alter, obstruct or interfere with any drain or barrier provided by the authority or under its control without its consent. In such circumstances, the authority can repair or reinstate any damage and recover the cost of doing so from the person responsible.[34]

The roads authority can also contribute towards the cost of execution and maintenance of drainage works or flood prevention operations which are desirable for the protection or enjoyment of a public road, or proposed public road.[35]

## 10.3.5   SNOW AND ICE

A roads authority must take reasonable steps to stop snow and ice endangering the safe passage of pedestrians and vehicles over public roads.[36] In the case of *Grant v Lothian Regional Council* [37] a pedestrian fell on an ice covered pavement and fractured both elbows. She sued the council at common law and under section 34 of the Roads (Scotland) Act 1984[38]. The Outer House of the Court of Session held that the council's system for clearing roads and pavements was reasonable and that leaving the pavement of a minor road untreated for two days did not establish fault at common law or under the Act.

The council operated a winter weather emergency service and established priorities for dealing with snow and ice. Carriageways were given higher priority than footways and footpaths. The icy conditions had developed on a Saturday evening and Ms Grant fell on Monday morning. At weekends (and this was also the New Year holiday weekend) there were less staff available and they concentrated on roads as footways required salt and grit to be spread by hand which was more time consuming and required more manpower. The court found that deciding on the priorities for salting and gritting was within the discretion of the roads authority and, in the absence of any fault in the exercise of that discretion, the pursuer's case failed.

32   R(S)A 1984, s 31(4)(b).
33   R(S)A 1984, s 31(4)(a).
34   R(S)A 1984, s 31(5).
35   Ie drainage works under the Land Drainage (Scotland) Act 1958 (as amended by the Flood Prevention and Land Drainage (Scotland) Act 1997) and flood prevention operations under the Flood Prevention (Scotland) Act 1961 (as so amended): R(S)A 1984, s 32.
36   R(S)A 1984, s 34.
37   1988 SLT 533.
38   See note 37 above.

## 10.3.6 ROAD LIGHTING

Local roads authorities must provide and maintain lighting for roads, or proposed roads, which in their opinion should be lit.[39] This duty only covers roads which they are or will be responsible for maintaining, namely public roads.[40] Three categories of road are specifically excluded from the duty to light:

1.  An existing road which is a prospective public road in terms of Part IV of the New Roads and Street Works Act 1991.[41]

2.  A new road which is being constructed or is about to be other than by or on behalf of the authority.[42]

3.  A private road which the authority is obliged to adopt and place on the list of public roads.[43]

The authority may choose to provide and maintain lighting within its area where it is not obliged to do so if it considers that any road, or proposed road, should be lit.[44]

The Scottish Ministers are not under a duty to provide lighting at all but may do so for the roads, including proposed roads, which they are responsible for.[45]

To facilitate the provision of lighting, whether under a duty or power, roads authorities, both local and national, can fix lamps and related structures as they consider necessary to rails, walls, or buildings fronting or abutting the road or proposed road.[46] Before doing so they must give twenty-eight days notice to the owner or occupier of affected land.[47] The owner or occupier can refer the matter to a sheriff within twenty-eight days of service of the notice and his decision is final.[48] No compensation is payable to the owner or occupier for fixing lamps and related structures as above or where maintenance is carried out by the roads authority.[49]

---

39  R(S)A 1984, s 35(1).
40  R(S)A 1984, s 35(1).
41  R(S)A 1984, s 35(2)(a) (amended by the New Roads and Street Works Act 1991). A road is a prospective public road where the local roads authority is satisfied that it is likely to become a public road and makes a declaration to that effect: NRSWA 1991, s 146(1).
42  R(S)A 1984, s 35(2)(b).
43  Ie under R(S)A 1984, s 16(1); R(S)A 1984, s 35(2)(c). See also Ch 4.
44  R(S)A 1984, s 35(4).
45  R(S)A 1984, s 35(3).
46  R(S)A 1984, s 35(5).
47  R(S)A 1984, s 35(5).
48  R(S)A 1984, s 35(7).
49  R(S)A 1984, s 35(6).

## 10.4    ROAD HUMPS

Originally a roads authority could only construct road humps in roads maintainable by it where the road had a speed limit of 30 mph or less[50] and it had been authorised by the Scottish Ministers to do so.[51] Now it can also install road humps whether or not the road is subject to a speed limit.[52] A 'road hump' is 'an artificial hump which is in, or on the surface of, a road and which is designed to control the speed of vehicles; and references to a road hump include references to any other works in connection with such a hump.'[53]

### 10.4.1    CONSULTATION AND LOCAL INQUIRIES ON ROAD HUMPS

Where a roads authority intends to install road humps it must consult the chief police officer for the area, the fire authority, the local council, the ambulance service and people or organisations who are likely to be affected or who represent road users. Where the authority is the Scottish Ministers the local council must also be consulted.[54] The authority must also publish notice in one or more newspapers circulating in the local area and post notices at appropriate points on the road.[55] The notice should state the nature, dimensions and location of the proposed road hump, the address for objections and the time limit for these to be made which must be not less than twenty-eight days from publication in the newspaper.[56] The authority is obliged to consider any such objections and if it thinks fit hold a local inquiry.[57] If a local inquiry is held this is subject to the provisions of s 210 of the Local Government (Scotland) Act 1973 which the Scottish Ministers may modify by regulation.[58]

### 10.4.2    CONSTRUCTION AND MAINTENANCE OF ROAD HUMPS

The Scottish Ministers can make regulations which govern the construction and maintenance of road humps in the interests of safety and the free movement of traffic.[59] The regulations do not apply where

---

50   Except where this is a temporary or variable limit under s 84(1)(b) or (c) of the Road Traffic Regulation Act 1984.
51   R(S)A 1984, ss 36, 40.
52   R(S)A 1984, s 36 as amended by the Road Traffic Act 1991, Schedule 4.
53   R(S)A 1984, s 40.
54   R(S)A 1984, s 37(1) and the Road Humps (Scotland) Regulations 1998, SI 1998/1448, reg 3.
55   R(S)A 1984, s 37(2).
56   R(S)A 1984, s 37(2), (3).
57   R(S)A 1984, s 37(4).
58   Ie the Local Government (Scotland) Act 1973, s 210(2)–(6): R(S)A 1984, s 37(5).
59   R(S)A 1984, s 38(1).

## 10.3.1  FOOTWAYS, SUBWAYS AND FOOTBRIDGES

The roads authority has a duty to provide 'proper and sufficient' footways for public roads which appear to be necessary or desirable for the safety or convenience of pedestrians.[9] A 'footway' is associated with a carriageway and allows passage over a road on foot.[10] In effect this is a pavement beside a road but this is not a term used in the legislation.

There is a power to construct, light and maintain pedestrian subways under the road or footbridges over it.[11] The authority can provide subways or footbridges to make it less dangerous for pedestrians to cross a public road or to protect traffic from danger.[12] The authority can also construct and maintain works in the carriageway of a public road in the following three situations:

1.   To separate traffic either on one side from that on the other carriageway, or, where traffic going in both directions is using the same carriageway, for example, while road works are carried out, on a dual carriageway.[13]

2.   At junctions to regulate the movement of traffic.[14] This would normally be a roundabout.

3.   To provide refuges for pedestrians crossing the road.[15] For example traffic islands.

## 10.3.2  FENCES OR BARRIERS

Fences or barriers, walls, pillars, rails and raised paving can be provided and maintained by the roads authority to safeguard people using a public road.[16] These can be used to segregate footways, footpaths, cycle tracks and carriageways, classes of users of cycle tracks, where a footpath gives direct access to a road and along the sides of bridges, embankments and other dangerous parts of the road.[17]

Fences or posts can be erected and maintained to prevent access to a road, or proposed road, or to delimit the road, or proposed road. In the latter case, stones or other markers can also be used.[18] In doing any of these things the roads authority must not interfere with an agricultural

9    R(S)A 1984, s 25.
10   R(S)A 1984, s 151(1), (2).
11   R(S)A 1984, s 26.
12   R(S)A 1984, s 26.
13   R(S)A 1984, s 27(a).
14   R(S)A 1984, s 27(b).
15   R(S)A 1984, s 27(c).
16   R(S)A 1984, s 28.
17   R(S)A 1984, s 28(a)–(d). A 'footpath' allows passage on foot and is not associated with a carriageway. A 'cycle track' permits passage by pedal cycle and may include passage on foot: s 151(1), (2).
18   R(S)A 1984, s 29(1).

# 10 Road Maintenance and Improvement

## 10.1 INTRODUCTION

Roads authorities are under a duty to manage and maintain public roads[1] in their areas. This includes a power to reconstruct, alter, widen, improve or renew and decide how the public right of passage can be exercised over these roads.[2] The Scottish Ministers are responsible for the management and maintenance of trunk roads, special roads provided by them and any other road which is not the responsibility of the local roads authority and have the same range of functions.[3] Within these broad parameters roads authorities, both local and national, have many more specific power and duties and it is these that will be considered in this chapter. The Scottish Ministers can reach agreement with the local roads authority for it to act as their agent and carry out their roads management and maintenance functions.[4] They can also decide to contract out the majority of these functions, though not all, to the private sector.[5]

## 10.2 LEVELS OF PUBLIC ROADS

The roads authority has the power to raise, lower or alter the level of a public road as it thinks fit.[6] However, this is subject to any order which may have been made in relation to a special road[7] or in respect of a road which crosses or joins a public road, or proposed public road, which is not a special road.[8]

## 10.3 ROAD SAFETY

There are a number of provisions which deal with various aspects of road safety for pedestrians and other road users.

1    ie roads which are on the list of public roads. See also Chapter 2.
2    R(S)A 1984, s 1(1). See also Chapter 9.
3    R(S)A 1984, s 2(1).
4    R(S)A 1984, s 4. See also Chapter 2.
5    See the Deregulation and Contracting Out Act 1994, s 69 and the Secretary of State's Trunk Road Functions (Contracting Out) (Scotland) Order 1996, SI 1996/878, reg 2.
6    R(S)A 1984, s 24.
7    Under R(S)A 1984, s 9.
8    ie under R(S)A 1984, s 12. See also Chapter 4.

the road hump has been authorised but conditions attached to the authorisation by the Scottish Ministers may relate to any of the matters covered by the regulations.[60] The Road Humps (Scotland) Regulations 1998[61] specify which roads humps can be installed in, their dimensions and siting and the requirement for warning signs to be erected. The regulations are not retrospective and do not apply to road humps which were constructed before 16 July 1998, that is under the 1990 regulations.[62]

Before road humps can be installed the road must have lighting which either complies with the British Standard BS5489 or equivalent or which comprises at least three electric lamps not more than thirty-eight metres apart or where lighting has been specially provided.[63]

The road hump must not be more than 100 millimetres at its highest point, no vertical face must exceed six millimetres and it must be at right angles to an imaginary line along the centre of the carriageway. A road hump cannot be installed on a railway level crossing or within twenty metres of one at its closest point or within two metres of any rail in the carriageway for vehicles carried on flanged wheels.[64] A road hump can be installed in the centre line of a pedestrian crossing but not in a Zebra crossing, a Pelican or Puffin controlled area or crossing or within 30 metres of the centre line of any of these crossings.[65]

Where a road hump is installed in a road, the authority must erect and maintain such appropriate traffic warning signs[66] as it considers necessary.[67]

The regulations are less onerous where there is a road hump in a road with a speed limit of twenty mph or less. Then it is only subject to the requirements on dimensions and on its position in relation to level crossings and rails in the carriageway and on its proximity to pedestrian and other crossings. There is no requirement for lighting or warning signs or for the hump to be at right angles to the centre of the carriageway.[68]

---

60  R(S)A 1984, s 38(3).
61  SI 1998/1448. These supersede previous road hump regulations 1990/2623 and 1989/1095 which were more restrictive for roads authorities.
62  SI 1998/1448, reg 8. There is no mention of the previous regulations in either the 1998 or 1990 regulations which is probably an oversight. The 1998 regulations came in to force on 16 July 1998.
63  SI 1998/1448, reg 4.
64  SI 1998/1448, reg 5(1).
65  SI 1998/1448, reg 5(2), (3). A 'pedestrian crossing' is the same as a 'crossing' in s 25(6) of the Road Traffic Regulation Act 1984, 'Zebra controlled area/ crossing,' 'Pelican controlled area/crossing,' 'Puffin controlled area/ crossing,' are defined in reg 3(1) of the Zebra, Pelican and Puffin Pedestrian Crossing Regulations and General Directions 1997, SI 1997/2400.
66  As prescribed in the Traffic Signs Regulations 1994, SI 1994/1519.
67  SI 1998/1448, reg 6.
68  SI 1998/1448, reg 7.

### 10.4.3　STATUS OF ROAD HUMPS

Where a road hump complies with the regulations, or with conditions attached to an authorisation, and the road has a speed limit of thirty mph or less,[69] or it is authorised, it is treated as part of the road rather than as an obstruction.[70] In addition, an obligation to maintain or reinstate the road includes the road hump.[71] The provisions of the New Roads and Street Works Act 1991[72] which restrict road works following substantial works for roads purposes apply to the construction, maintenance or removal of a road hump.[73]

## 10.5　TRAFFIC CALMING WORKS

In 1992 roads authorities were given powers to construct, and remove, traffic calming works on or from roads which they maintain.[74] These works should be as authorised by the Roads (Scotland) Act 1984 or the Roads (Traffic Calming) (Scotland) Regulations 1994. However, these powers do not prejudice an authority's right to construct or remove works which do not meet the requirements of either.[75] Such works cannot be installed if this would prevent the passage of any vehicle unless access is prohibited in terms of other provisions.[76] 'Traffic calming works' are those which affect the movement of vehicular and other traffic on a road for the purpose of promoting safety or preserving or improving the environment.[77] Traffic calming works comprise 'build outs', 'chicanes', 'islands', 'overrun areas', 'pinch points', 'rumble devices' and any combination of these which are methods of slowing down the flow of traffic.[78] Various associated ancillary works are permitted such as lighting, paving, providing grass or other covering, pillars, bollards, planters, walls, rails or fences, objects or structures spanning the road (or any combination of these)[79] where these promote road safety, preserve or improve the environment, make the calming works conspicuous or enhance their effect.[80]

Provided the regulations or authorisation under the 1984 Act are complied with the traffic calming works are not treated as an obstruction

---

69　Except where this is temporary or variable under s 84(1)(b) or (c) of the Road Traffic Regulation Act 1984.
70　R(S)A 1984, s 39(1)–(3).
71　R(S)A 1984, s 39(1).
72　NRSWA 1991, s 117.
73　R(S)A 1984, s 39(4). See Ch 14 below.
74　R(S)A 1984, ss 39A–39C (added by the Traffic Calming Act 1992, s 2, Sch 2).
75　See R(S)A 1984, ss 39B (as so added) and the Roads (Traffic Calming) (Scotland) Regulations 1994, SI 1994/2488. See also R(S)A 1984, s 39A(4).
76　SI 1994/2488, reg 8.
77　R(S)A 1984, s 40 (amended by the Traffic Calming Act 1992, s 2).
78　SI 1994/2488, reg 2, 3(1)(a).
79　SI 1994/2488, reg 3(1)(b).
80　SI 1994/2488, reg 3(2).

to the road, which they would otherwise be, but as part of the road itself. Any obligation to maintain or reinstate the road extends to such works.[81]

## 10.5.1    CONSULTATION ON TRAFFIC CALMING

A roads authority must consult the chief police officer, the fire authority, the local authority, the ambulance service and people or organisations who use the road and are likely to be affected, where it intends to introduce traffic calming measures.[82]

## 10.5.2    RESTRICTIONS ON TRAFFIC CALMING

Overrun areas and rumble devices must conform to the specifications laid down in the regulations although there is provision for a small margin of error where the size is slightly more than envisaged but not where it is less.[83]

## 10.5.3    TRAFFIC SIGNS

Where there are traffic calming works in a road, the authority must place and maintain such traffic signs as are necessary for the purpose of providing adequate warning for road users.[84] This does not apply to an overrun area which is an area of carriageway textured or coloured to look narrow. A sign alerting road users to this would defeat its purpose. Signs are also unnecessary if the works themselves provide adequate visual warning or if the road has a speed limit of twenty miles per hour or less.[85]

## 10.6    CATTLE-GRIDS

A roads authority can install and maintain cattle-grids in a road or proposed road and, if necessary, in adjoining land to control the passage of animals.[86] It can do so on its own initiative or at the behest of owners or occupiers of agricultural land. It need only consult with such owners and occupiers as it considers necessary.[87] It must also provide and maintain a gate or by-pass or other works to allow the passage of properly controlled animals and other lawful traffic which is unable to cross the grid.[88] A 'cattle-grid' is defined as a device designed to prevent

81    R(S)A 1984, s 39C (as so added).
82    SI 1994/2488, reg 4.
83    SI 1994/2488, regs 5, 6.
84    SI 1994/2488, reg 7.
85    SI 1994/2488, reg 7.
86    R(S)A 1984, s 41(1).
87    R(S)A 1984, s 41(1).
88    R(S)A 1984, s 41(2).

the passage of animals but which allows the passage of some or all other traffic. It includes any fence or other works necessary for the efficient operation of the cattle-grid.[89] A 'by-pass' in relation to a cattle-grid means a way over land which is not within the limits of the road, or proposed road, for traffic for which the by-pass is provided, or if any part of the by-pass is along an existing road for that traffic and other traffic entitled to use the road prior to its installation.[90] The authority cannot provide a cattle-grid (or a by-pass) on land which is not part of the road, or proposed road, and which does not belong to the authority unless it has reached agreement with those who have an interest in the land[91] or, where it is common or waste land adjoining or adjacent to the road, it has followed the required procedure laid down in Schedule 4 of the Act.[92]

## 10.6.1    SCHEDULE 4 PROCEDURE

The authority must publish a notice for two successive weeks in one or more newspapers circulating in the area stating the question for determination, indicating where any plans and related material can be inspected free of charge and at reasonable times and specifying a period of not less than twenty-eight days for representations and also the manner in which these should be made.[93] In addition, it must display a prominent notice at the site.[94] It can erect posts or boards or affix the notice to any building or structure in the road or on adjoining land although if the latter is occupied the occupier's consent is required.[95] If there are no representations, or any made are withdrawn, the authority can determine the issue.[96] Otherwise, where it is a local roads authority, the matter is referred to the Scottish Ministers. They can either hold a local inquiry[97] or allow the objector and the authority to appear before and be heard by a person appointed by them for the purpose.[98] The Scottish Ministers then consider a report from either the inquiry or hearing.[99] Where the Scottish Ministers are not the roads authority, the decision to proceed can be made by the local authority but only with the consent of the Scottish Ministers and subject to any conditions they may impose.[100] Where the Scottish Ministers are the roads authority they can decide the issue themselves following consideration of the report from the inquiry or hearing.[101] The Scottish Ministers can decide, in any event,

89   R(S)A 1984, s 41(6).
90   R(S)A 1984, s 41(6).
91   R(S)A 1984, s 46.
92   R(S)A 1984, s 41(3), (4).
93   R(S)A 1984, Sch 4, para 1(2)(a).
94   R(S)A 1984, Sch 4, para 1(2)(b).
95   R(S)A 1984, Sch 4, para 4.
96   R(S)A 1984, Sch 4, para 2.
97   The Local Government (Scotland) Act 1973 s 210 specifies the inquiry procedure.
98   R(S)A 1984, Sch 4, para 3(3), (7).
99   R(S)A 1984, Sch 4, para 3(4).
100  R(S)A 1984, Sch 4, para 3(4).
101  R(S)A 1984, Sch 4, para 3(3), (4).

that an inquiry or hearing is unnecessary if there are special circumstances, unless there is a representation from a roads authority other
than themselves when one or the other must be held.[102] Once the matter
has been decided, the Scottish Ministers must send notice of the outcome
to anyone who made a representation.[103] Where the Scottish Ministers
have delegated their roads functions to the local roads authority under
section 4 of the 1984 Act, it is treated as the roads authority in connection
with the above.[104] After complying with Schedule 4, the roads authority
can place part of a cattle-grid or provide a by-pass in any common or
waste land adjoining or adjacent to the road, or proposed road, if it
considers it expedient to do so, even though the land is not part of the
road and does not belong to the authority.[105] An authority can also only
provide a by-pass on a road, or proposed road, other than the one in
which the cattle-grid is being installed, if it has decided it is expedient to
do so and has complied with Schedule 4.[106]

Where it is necessary to properly control traffic and to allow the cattle-
grid to operate efficiently on a by-pass, the authority can provide and
maintain a gate or any other works.[107]

## 10.6.2 ALTERATION OR IMPROVEMENT OF CATTLE-GRIDS

The roads authority has power to alter or improve cattle-grids, by-
passes, gates or other works. It must ensure however that this does not
prevent traffic which was able to use the road before the alteration or
improvement from doing so afterwards by crossing the cattle-grid, going
through a gate or using any by-pass.[108]

## 10.6.3 REMOVAL OF CATTLE-GRIDS AND BY-PASSES

If it appears to the authority, after such consultation with owners and
occupiers of agricultural land as it considers necessary, that a cattle-grid
is no longer required, it can be removed along with any gate or other
works on the road associated with it. The authority is then required to
make good the site.[109] Where a cattle grid is removed, the authority can
direct that the use of any associated by-pass be discontinued and specify
that the public right of passage over it is extinguished from a particular
date.[110] If the by-pass was along a pre-existing road then it cannot

102  R(S)A 1984, Sch 4, para 3(5).
103  R(S)A 1984, Sch 4, para 3(6).
104  R(S)A 1984, Sch 4, para 6.
105  R(S)A 1984, s 41(4).
106  R(S)A 1984, s 41(5).
107  R(S)A 1984, s 41(7).
108  R(S)A 1984, s 41(8).
109  R(S)A 1984, s 42(1).
110  R(S)A 1984, s 42(2), (3).

extinguish any prior right of passage and if the cattle-grid is removed, it must ensure that any gates or other works connected with the by-pass which would obstruct the right of passage are also removed.[111] In any event, the authority has a general power to remove gates or other works related to the by-pass.[112]

### 10.6.4   MAINTENANCE AND MANAGEMENT OF CATTLE-GRIDS AND BY-PASSES

Responsibility for the maintenance and management of cattle-grids, by-passes and associated works are deemed to vest in the roads authority.[113] This includes any liability for loss, injury or damage.

### 10.6.5   AGREEMENT BETWEEN NEIGHBOURING AUTHORITIES ON CATTLE-GRIDS

Neighbouring authorities can agree that one of them will provide and remove cattle-grids for both in certain circumstances. The agreement can deal with the payment of all or part of the expense incurred as a result of its terms.[114] This power can be used where a public road is intersected, joined or continued by a road which is the responsibility of another roads authority.[115] An authority cannot unreasonably refuse to enter such an agreement and if there is a dispute about entering the contract, or about its terms, including payment, this is settled by arbitration.[116] If arbitration is necessary a single arbiter is to be appointed, if the parties cannot agree, by a sheriff or by the Court of Session on the application of either party.[117]

### 10.6.6   CATTLE-GRIDS AND GATES

A cattle-grid takes precedence over a gate provided by someone other than the authority. If a roads authority intends to provide a cattle-grid and complies with the requirements of Schedule 4 of the 1984 Act, then any right of another person to provide a gate is suspended if the cattle-grid will adequately achieve the same purpose in the authority's opinion.[118] This applies so long as the cattle-grid remains in place. The authority can require the removal of any existing gate or it can remove it.[119] On demand, the authority must reimburse any expenses reasonably

111  R(S)A 1984, s 42(4).
112  R(S)A 1984, s 42(2).
113  R(S)A 1984, s 43.
114  R(S)A 1984, s 44(2).
115  R(S)A 1984, s 44(1).
116  R(S)A 1984, s 44(3).
117  R(S)A 1984, s 44(4).
118  R(S)A 1984, s 45(1).
119  R(S)A 1984, s 45(1).

incurred in removing a gate in such circumstances.[120] It must also repay the expenses reasonably incurred where a gate is reinstalled within twelve months of the removal of a cattle-grid which it was originally set aside for.[121] A gate can still be erected with the approval of the authority where a cattle-grid is in place.[122]

There can be no objection to the exercise of the roads authority's powers on the basis that there was no right to install the gate in the first place. In addition, the exercise of these powers does not affect any question of whether there was such a right or prejudice the authority or anyone else from taking action to protect public rights of way or to prevent or remove obstructions.[123]

## 10.6.7  AGREEMENTS ON CATTLE-GRIDS AND BY-PASSES

In providing, altering or improving cattle-grids or by-passes the authority can enter agreements with persons having an interest in land to use it for these purposes.[124] The authority and the public can then exercise the rights specified in the agreement.[125] The agreement can include terms for payment for the use of land or for entering the agreement.[126] However, the agreement cannot prejudice the rights of, or grant rights against, anyone who is not a party to it.[127]

## 10.6.8  CONTRIBUTIONS TO THE COST OF CATTLE-GRIDS

A roads authority can reach agreement on payment of a financial contribution towards the cost of a cattle-grid with anyone who has sought its provision, or with anyone else willing to contribute towards the expenses. Payment can be by a one-off lump sum or by instalments of an amount specified in the agreement and can meet all or some of the costs.[128] The agreement can deal with related matters which the parties consider expedient for its purposes. In particular, it can include terms as to repayment of contributions to the extent specified if the cattle-grid is removed.[129] The authority can take account of the willingness of those who will derive special benefit, in the authority's opinion, from the provision of a cattle-grid in deciding whether or not to provide one.[130]

120  R(S)A 1984, s 45(2).
121  R(S)A 1984, s 45(3).
122  R(S)A 1984, s 45(1).
123  R(S)A 1984, s 45(4).
124  As to the enforcement of agreements and the classes of persons who may enter into them, see R(S)A 1984, s 46(3).
125  R(S)A 1984, s 46(1).
126  R(S)A 1984, s 46(2)(a).
127  R(S)A 1984, s 46(2)(b).
128  R(S)A 1984, s 47(1).
129  R(S)A 1984, s 47(2).
130  R(S)A 1984, s 47(3).

## 10.7   CONTRIBUTIONS FOR ROAD CONSTRUCTION OR IMPROVEMENT ('SECTION 48 AGREEMENTS')

Roads authorities also have the power to enter into agreements with anyone willing to contribute to the cost of construction or improvement of a road.[131] These are known as section 48 agreements. The authority can take the contributions into account in deciding whether to proceed with the road construction or improvement. These agreements may be considered where a proposed development means that a new road or improvements to an existing road are required as a result. The contribution can be in cash or in kind, for example, in the form of materials, professional services or labour. However, roads authorities do not regularly use section 48 agreements as they are perceived as having significant disadvantages when compared to planning agreements entered into under section 75 of the Town and Country Planning (Scotland) Act 1997 as amended.[132]

## 10.8   BUS SHELTERS

Local roads authorities have powers to provide and maintain bus shelters and queue barriers on public service vehicle routes.[133] They can enter agreements in connection with this and these can deal with financial contributions towards the cost of providing shelters and barriers.[134]

## 10.9   ROADSIDE PLANTING

Roads authorities can plant trees, shrubs, grass or other plants within or partly within the boundary of a public road, or proposed public road, which is being constructed.[135] They can also erect and maintain guards or fences or do what is expedient to maintain and protect planting whether or not it was carried out by them.[136] Any planting or fence or guard must not hinder the reasonable use of the road, or proposed road, by those entitled to use it.[137] Nor must they be a nuisance or injurious to the owner or occupier of land fronting or abutting the road, or proposed road.[138]

---

131  R(S)A 1984, s 48.
132  See further Chapter 7, p 110.
133  Local Government (Omnibus Shelters and Queue Barriers) (Scotland) Act 1958, s 1 as amended by R(S)A 1984, s 49. In some cases this is subject to the consent of landowners, which cannot be unreasonably withheld. Ie, consent is required where the shelter or barrier would obstruct or interfere with an existing access to land or premises abutting the road.
134  LG (OSQB) (S)A 1958, s 2 (as so amended).
135  R(S)A 1984, s 50(1).
136  R(S)A 1984, s 50(1).
137  R(S)A 1984, s 50(2).
138  R(S)A 1984, s 50(2).

The roads authority can authorise planting by an owner or occupier of land adjoining a public road or by any other person.[139] This should be in writing and the authority can grant the authorisation subject to conditions. For example, the authority can insist on a written undertaking, if it considers it necessary, from the person authorised to plant, to ensure the safety and convenience of road users or to protect the apparatus of statutory undertakers.[140]

The authority can withdraw an authorisation at any time by giving twenty-eight days notice and this may require the removal within that period of all or any of the planting and the reinstatement of the road.[141]

## 10.10   MITIGATING THE ADVERSE EFFECTS OF CONSTRUCTION

A roads authority can carry out works to mitigate the adverse effects of the construction, improvement, existence or use which any road has or will have on the surrounding area.[142] The works can include planting trees, shrubs or any other plants and laying out an area as grassland.[143] The authority can develop land acquired by it or redevelop land belonging to it to improve the surroundings of a road or proposed road.[144]

## 10.11   AGREEMENT ON USE OF LAND NEAR ROADS ('SECTION 53 AGREEMENTS')

The roads authority can enter agreements with anyone having an interest in land to restrict or regulate its use permanently or temporarily (for the period specified in the agreement) to mitigate the adverse effects of the construction, improvement, existence or use of a road or proposed road. The agreement can provide for planting and maintenance of trees, shrubs or plants and can restrict lopping or removing them.[145] It can include incidental and consequential provisions including those of a financial nature which appear necessary or expedient to the authority.[146] The agreement runs with the land unless a third party has acquired the right to it in good faith and for value before the agreement has been registered in the Land Register or Register of Sasines.[147]

---

139  R(S)A 1984, s 51(1).
140  R(S)A 1984, s 51(2). As to statutory undertakers see pp 217 ff.
141  R(S)A 1984, s 51(3).
142  R(S)A 1984, s 52(1).
143  R(S)A 1984, s 52(2).
144  R(S)A 1984, s 52(3).
145  R(S)A 1984, s 53(1).
146  R(S)A 1984, s 53(2).
147  R(S)A 1984, s 53(3), (4). The exception also applies to someone deriving title from the third party.

Section 53 Agreements are without prejudice to planning agreements made under section 75 of the Town and Country Planning (Scotland) Act 1997, which regulate the development or use of land.[148]

## 10.12   ROAD REFUSE OR STORAGE BINS

The roads authority can provide and maintain in or under a road (or proposed road) bins or other containers for a various purposes.[149] These can be used to collect and temporarily store road refuse and waste paper, to store sand, grit or other materials. They can be of a size and in a position determined by the authority.

---

148  R(S)A 1984, s 53(5). See also Chapter 7.
149  R(S)A 1984, s 54.

# 11 Road Management and Administration

## 11.1 INTRODUCTION

It has already been noted in Chapter 10 that roads authorities (local and national) have a duty to manage public roads in their areas.[1] This management function covers a variety of areas including temporary control of traffic, prevention of obstruction, control of animals, removal and prevention of danger and control of trading on or near certain roads. The Roads (Scotland) Act 1984 creates a number of offences related to road management and prescribes the penalties and the modes of trial for these. In addition, there are various administrative provisions dealing with matters such as the content and service of notices, the holding of inquiries, recovery of expenses and interest which are also considered in this chapter.

## 11.2 TRAFFIC CONTROL

A roads authority can make an order temporarily (for a period not exceeding seven days) restricting or prohibiting traffic or foot passage (in general or for particular classes of vehicle or person) on a road in the interests of public safety or convenience.[2] It can only do so where it is not possible for an order to be made under either section 14 or section 16A of the Road Traffic Regulation Act 1984.[3] Where practicable, the authority should specify an alternative route or routes.[4] The order cannot prevent access on foot to premises on or adjacent to the road or to premises which can only be reached on foot from the road.[5] The order can have such conditions, or exceptions, as the authority considers necessary attached.[6] Notice of the order must be advertised in a newspaper circulating in the area and it cannot take effect before the date of the advertisement.[7] It is an offence to contravene a restriction or prohibition.[8]

1 Roads (Scotland) Act 1984, s 1(1).
2 R(S)A 1984, s 62(1), (2)(b), (3) as amended by the Road Traffic Regulation (Special Events) Act 1994.
3 These sections also deal with temporary prohibition or restriction of traffic or foot passage in certain circumstances and in connection with certain events. See also Chapter 22
4 R(S)A 1984, s 62(1), (2)(b), (3).
5 R(S)A 1984, s 62(2)(a).
6 R(S)A 1984, s 62(2)(c).
7 R(S)A 1984, s 62(4).
8 R(S)A 1984, s 62(5).

## 11.3　ACCESS OVER VERGES AND FOOTWAYS

The roads authority can deal with owners or occupiers of premises who habitually take their vehicles over a verge or footway without having a satisfactory vehicular crossing.[9] The authority can serve a notice specifying what is required for the construction of a crossing. This also gives dates for commencement and completion of the work.[9] On completion, the crossing becomes part of the road.[10] There is a right of appeal to a sheriff within twenty-eight days of service of the notice.[11]

## 11.4　USE OF APPLIANCES ON FOOTWAYS, FOOTPATHS AND CYCLE TRACKS

Certain appliances or vehicles can be used on footways, footpaths and cycle tracks even although the use of other vehicles is restricted.[12] These are appliances or vehicles for the construction, maintenance, improvement or cleansing of a road,[13] for example street sweeping vehicles. Statutory undertakers[14] are also allowed to use appliances and vehicles for works in connection with their apparatus on footways, footpaths or cycle tracks which are maintainable by the roads authority.[15] This is with the proviso that they first obtain the consent (which can include reasonable conditions) of the authority.[16]

## 11.5　ANIMALS ON THE ROAD

It is not in anyone's interests for animals to be running free on a road as this represents a danger to road users and to the animals themselves. There are provisions which deal with different aspects of this, some perhaps more relevant than others nowadays.

### 11.5.1　REGULATION OF HORSEDRAWN CARTS

It is an offence for a driver of a vehicle pulled by one or more draught animals (normally horses) to convey anything on it which is not adequately secured and which would endanger other road users if it fell off.[17] It is also an offence to allow a child under fourteen years to drive

9　R(S)A 1984, s 63(1).
10　R(S)A 1984, s 63(2).
11　R(S)A 1984, s 63(3).
12　R(S)A 1984, s 64(1). For details of the restrictions, see para 11.11 below.
13　R(S)A 1984, s 64(1)(a).
14　As defined in R(S)A 1984, s 151 and by reference to s 214 of the Town and Country Planning (Scotland) Act 1997. 'Statutory undertakers' includes a sewerage authority: R(S)A 1984, s 64(3).
15　R(S)A 1984, s 64(1)(b).
16　R(S)A 1984, s 64(2).
17　R(S)A 1984, s 65(1), (3).

the vehicle on a road or to allow a child aged between fourteen and sixteen years to do so unless under the immediate supervision of a person aged eighteen years or over.[18]

## 11.5.2   CONTROL OF STRAY AND OTHER ANIMALS

It is an offence to leave an animal on a road or to allow it to stray onto a road unless the road runs through unenclosed land. Such animals can be seized and detained by the roads authority or by a police constable.[19] The person responsible has a defence if he took all reasonable steps to prevent the animal from straying onto a road.[20]

This does not make the roads authority responsible for the animals but gives it powers to deal with the situation. The outcome in the recent case of *Bennett v J Lamont & Sons*[21] is therefore not surprising. Bennett was seriously injured when his car collided with cows which had strayed onto a road. They had escaped through a hole in a farm wall. Bennett tried to recover damages from the farmers and from the roads authority. The case against the roads authority was based on breach of the common law duty of reasonable care as a result of its statutory duty under the 1984 Act s 1(1) to manage and maintain roads in its area. It was averred that this included a duty to take reasonable care to avoid dangers to road users from reasonably foreseeable hazards and to carry out annual inspections to meet this duty. The Outer House of the Court of Session rejected this argument and the case against the roads authority was dismissed. The court held that the pursuer had not pled a relevant case. It was not reasonable to expect the authority to have foreseen that the farmer would allow the cows to escape. Imposing a duty of care on the authority in these circumstances would not be fair, just or reasonable given the miles of unfenced road in Scotland where animals might roam.

The owner of an animal which has been seized or detained can recover it on payment of the reasonable expenses of the roads authority or the police.[22] He does not need to pay if he took all reasonable steps to ensure that the animal was not left on the road or did not stray.[23] The roads authority or the police can sell or dispose of the animal if the expenses are not paid within three days of an advertisement in a newspaper circulating in the area intimating the seizure, detention and prospective sale.[24] The proceeds of sale or disposal must be used to meet any expenses and any surplus given to the owner if he can be traced. Otherwise the authority or the police can retain the money.[25]

18   R(S)A 1984, s 65(2).
19   R(S)A 1984, s 98(1).
20   R(S)A 1984, s 98(5).
21   2000 SLT 17, 2000 Rep LR 2, 1999 GWD 31–1501.
22   R(S)A 1984, s 98(2).
23   R(S)A 1984, s 98(2).
24   R(S)A 1984, s 98(3).
25   R(S)A 1984, s 98(4).

### 11.5.3   RIDING OR DRIVING ANIMALS IN A ROAD

It is an offence to ride or drive a horse or other animal furiously, recklessly or carelessly in a road, whether or not it is attached to a cart or carriage.[26]

## 11.6   REMOVAL AND PREVENTION OF OBSTRUCTIONS

Obstructions on a road present an avoidable hazard for road users. Roads authorities have a range of powers to deal with situations to prevent both the view being obstructed and physical obstacles from impeding vehicular and other passage.

### 11.6.1   OBSTRUCTION OF VIEW

Restrictions can be imposed by the roads authority at or near a corner, bend or junction in a road where it is of the opinion that it is necessary to prevent danger arising from obstruction of the view.[27] This is achieved by serving an 'obstruction notice' on the owner or occupier giving him not less than twenty-eight days to alter the height or character of a wall, fence, advertising hoarding, hedge, tree or shrub.[28] Notice can also be served on the owner, occupier and anyone leasing the land restraining him (absolutely or subject to conditions) from allowing any building, wall, fence or advertising hoarding to be erected or hedge, shrub or tree to be planted.[29] The obstruction notice cannot prevent reconstruction or repair which does not create any new obstruction of view.[30] There is a right to object in writing to an obstruction notice within twenty-eight days of receipt stating the grounds of objection. The issue of whether the notice should be withdrawn or modified is decided in accordance with the procedure laid down in section 84 of the 1984 Act.[31] This provides for arbitration by a single arbiter where the parties agree to this, and where they do not, the matter is decided by the sheriff.[32] The arbiter or sheriff can order that any notice requirement or restriction will have effect with or without modification.[33] Any restrictions imposed come into force on service of the notice and remain in force until withdrawn by the authority. They are binding on any subsequent owner of the land unless he can prove that he had no cause to suspect there were any restrictions

---

26   R(S)A 1984, s 129(7).
27   R(S)A 1984, s 83(1).
28   R(S)A 1984, s 83(1)(a).
29   R(S)A 1984, s 83(1)(b).
30   R(S)A 1984, s 83(1).
31   R(S)A 1984, s 83(4).
32   R(S)A 1984, s 84(1).
33   R(S)A 1984, s 84(2). This procedure is also used to settle any disputes over the reasonableness of expenses but in this case neither the arbiter nor the sheriff have the power to order that payment shall be made.

after making due inquiries.[34] It is an offence not to comply with an obstruction notice.[35] Notwithstanding the terms of any conveyance, lease or other agreement, the person served with an obstruction notice has power to do what is necessary to comply with it.[36] He may also consent to the roads authority carrying out work on his behalf to comply with the notice.[37] A major qualification on the use of obstruction notices is the entitlement of the person served with one to recover his reasonable expenses incurred in complying with it from the roads authority. In addition, where a person suffers loss as a direct consequence of a notice requirement, or can prove his property is injuriously affected by restrictions in a notice, he can seek compensation from the authority provided he does so within six months of service of the notice.[38]

The roads authority cannot serve an obstruction notice for any wall forming part of an ancient monument or other object of archaeological interest unless the Scottish Ministers consent in writing. Nor can it do so for a wall forming part of or necessary for maintenance of a railway, canal, inland waterway, dock or harbour or for a protected tree[39] or for a listed building.[40]

## 11.6.2    OBSTRUCTIONS ON ROADS

Where an object has fallen onto a road and is causing an obstruction, the roads authority must, where practicable, notify the owner to remove it forthwith. If the owner cannot be traced or fails to remove the object within a reasonable time, or if it is an emergency, the authority must remove it.[41] Pending removal, the authority can take all reasonable steps to warn road users of the obstruction including placing lights, signs and fences on the road.[42] The roads authority's reasonable expenses can be recovered from the owner but not if he can prove that he took reasonable care to ensure the object did not cause or contribute to an obstruction.[43] Where practicable, the authority must notify the owner it has have removed an object. If he cannot be traced or has not recovered it after a reasonable time, the authority can dispose of it.[44] Any proceeds are used to meet the authority's expenses with any surplus returned to the owner

34    R(S)A 1984, s 83(3).
35    R(S)A 1984, s 83(7).
36    R(S)A 1984, s 83(5).
37    R(S)A 1984, s 83(6). This is without prejudice to the authority's general right to act in default in terms of s 141. See para 11.16 below.
38    R(S)A 1984, s 83(8).
39    ie one subject to a tree preservation order under s 160(1) the Town and Country Planning (Scotland) Act 1997.
40    As defined by s 1 of the Planning (Listed Buildings and Conservation Areas) (Scotland) Act 1997: R(S)A 1984, s 83(10).
41    R(S)A 1984, s 89(1). As to the removal of structures and projections, see ss 55, 87, 88.
42    R(S)A 1984, s 89(2).
43    R(S)A 1984, s 89(3).
44    R(S)A 1984, s 89(4).

if he can be traced. If not this can be kept by the authority.[45] It is also an offence to place or deposit anything in the road which obstructs the passage of road users or endangers them without lawful authority or reasonable excuse.[46] The Crown must decide which section of the 1984 Act to proceed under, as a person cannot be charged in respect of the same actings under this subsection and under various other provisions of the Act, namely section 129(9) or section 59(2),[47] sections 90, 95, 100(a) or 101.[48]

### 11.6.3    RESTRICTION ON OVERHEAD BRIDGES AND BEAMS

It is an offence to fix or place over, along or across a road an overhead bridge, beam, rail, pipe, cable, wire or other similar apparatus without the consent of the roads authority.[49] This does not apply to any works or apparatus of statutory undertakers.[50] The consent may have reasonable terms and conditions attached and breach of these is also an offence.[51] A person aggrieved by refusal of consent or by the terms and conditions attached to it can refer the matter to the sheriff within twenty-eight days.[52]

### 11.6.4    VEGETATION, FENCES AND WALLS

Vegetation, fences and walls can be dangerous to road users where they interfere or threaten the movement of vehicles and pedestrians. If a hedge, tree or shrub is overhanging a road this could prevent safe passage or obstruct or interfere with the road users' view or with lighting or with a traffic sign. It could also increase the likelihood of an obstruction being caused by drifting snow.[53] In such circumstances, the roads authority may serve notice on the owner of the vegetation, or on the occupier of the land it is growing in, giving him a maximum of twenty-eight days to remove the danger.[54] An owner or an occupier may refer the matter to the sheriff within the twenty-eight day period.[55]

Similarly, if a hedge, tree, shrub, fence or wall (or part of any of these) on or near a road is in poor condition and likely to cause danger by falling

---

45    R(S)A 1984, s 89(5).
46    R(S)A 1984, s 129(2).
47    See Chapter 12.
48    See below for details.
49    R(S)A 1984, s 90(1), (2).
50    R(S)A 1984, s 90(3). 'Statutory undertakers' are defined in s 151 and by reference to s 214 of the Town and Country Planning (Scotland) Act 1997.
51    R(S)A 1984, s 92(1), (2).
52    R(S)A 1984, s 92(4).
53    R(S)A 1984, s 91(1).
54    R(S)A 1984, s 91(1). The authority does not have power to act in default of the owner in this situation.
55    R(S)A 1984, s 91(9).

onto it, or if a retaining wall is a danger to the road or road users. Again, the authority can serve notice on the owner of the dangerous thing or on the occupier of the land it is situated in giving a maximum of twenty-eight days to remove the danger,[56] with the same right to refer the matter to the sheriff as above.[57] The authority does not need to notify if, in its opinion, the danger is imminent. If this is the case, it can carry out the work and recover its reasonable expenses from the owner or occupier.[58]

In both of these situations the authority can contribute as it sees fit to the reasonable expenses of the owner or occupier in removing the danger.[59]

The authority cannot use its power to act in default of the owner or occupier if the wall or retaining wall is part of an ancient monument or other object of archaeological interest. It can, however, serve a notice, but only with the consent of the Scottish Ministers. In granting consent, they can authorise the use of the authority's default power subject to any modifications as they may specify.[60] However, if the authority considers that danger is imminent, it can do what is necessary to safeguard road users before the Scottish Ministers' consent is obtained and without first serving notice.[61]

If work is required on a protected tree[62] or on a wall or retaining wall forming part of a listed building,[63] the planning authority must be notified.[64] There is no need to notify if the roads authority thinks that there is imminent danger.[65]

The Act states that these provision do not impose any liability on the roads authority for personal injury or damage to property.[66]

56 R(S)A 1984, s 91(3).
57 R(S)A 1984, s 91(9).
58 R(S)A 1984, s 91(3).
59 R(S)A 1984, s 91(5).
60 R(S)A 1984, s 91(4).
61 R(S)A 1984, s 91(4).
62 A 'protected tree' is one subject to a tree preservation order under s 160(1) the Town and Country Planning (Scotland) Act 1997.
63 As defined by s 1 of the Planning (Listed Buildings and Conservation Areas) (Scotland) Act 1997.
64 R(S)A 1984, s 91(6). This provision does not appear to have been amended despite the Local Government etc. (Scotland) Act 1994 creating unitary authorities with responsibility for both roads and planning.
65 R(S)A 1984, s 91(6).
66 R(S)A 1984, s 91(7).

## 11.6.5　RESTRICTION ON PLANTING TREES AND SHRUBS

There is a restriction on planting trees and shrubs[67] within five metres of a made-up carriageway unless the roads authority has consented.[68] This must not be unreasonably withheld.[69] The authority can serve notice on the owner or occupier of the land requiring the removal of any tree or shrub planted in contravention of this section within twenty-eight days.[70] Failure to comply is an offence.[71]

## 11.6.6　OTHER OFFENCES IN RELATION TO OBSTRUCTIONS

It is an offence to drive, lead or propel a vehicle or animal if any load being carried projects beyond the vehicle or animal and obstructs or endangers other road users.[72]

Anyone pitching a tent or camping in a road commits an offence.[73] Placing a shade, awning or other projection over or along a footway is an offence if it is less than 2.25 metres above it and/or less than fifty centimetres inwards from a carriageway.[74]

## 11.7　REMOVAL AND PREVENTION OF DANGER

There are a number of situations where the roads authority has powers to act to remove and prevent danger which could affect a road.

## 11.7.1　MAINTENANCE OF VAULTS AND CELLARS

Owners and occupiers have a duty to keep vaults, arches, cellars and tunnels under the road, openings into it, as well as doors or covers, pavement lights and walls or other supporting structures in good condition and repair.[75] If they fail to do so the authority can serve notice requiring replacement, repair or restoration to good condition within twenty-eight days of service.[76] There is a right to refer the matter to the sheriff within that period.[77] The authority can, if it wishes, pay the whole

---

67　In accordance with R(S)A 1984, s 51. See para 10.9 above.
68　R(S)A 1984, s 91(4) defines a 'made-up carriageway' as a carriageway or part of one which has been metalled or provided with a surface suitable for vehicular passage.
69　R(S)A 1984, s 92(1).
70　R(S)A 1984, s 92(2).
71　R(S)A 1984, s 92(3).
72　R(S)A 1984, s 129(3).
73　R(S)A 1984, s 129(4).
74　R(S)A 1984, s 129(8).
75　R(S)A 1984, s 66(1).
76　R(S)A 1984, s 66(2).
77　R(S)A 1984, s 66(3).

or part of the cost incurred by an owner or occupier in complying with their duties.[78] Anyone who leaves an opening into a vault or cellar uncovered and unfenced or insufficiently covered or fenced commits an offence.[79]

## 11.7.2 OPENING OF DOORS, GATES AND WINDOWS

The authority can also insist that a door, gate, window or shutter or bar which opens outwards into a road is made safe or more convenient for road users. The owner or occupier is notified of what he must do and of the timescale for compliance.[80]

## 11.7.3 DANGEROUS DITCHES

If a ditch (including a gutter or watercourse or part of a ditch) on land adjoining or near a public road (or proposed public road) is a danger to road users the authority can either fill it in or put pipes (including culverts, tunnels and other works) in its place. The ditch can only be filled in if the authority considers it unnecessary for drainage and the owner and all occupiers of the land agree to this in writing.[81] Otherwise pipes can be installed in the ditch or in land adjoining or near to it and then the ditch can be filled in.[82]

It is an offence for anyone to re-open the ditch or keep it open after it has been filled in without roads authority consent. In addition, the authority can reinstate or repair any work which is necessary as a result and recover the reasonable expense of doing so from the person responsible.[83]

## 11.7.4 MUD AND OTHER DEPOSITS FROM VEHICLES

It is an offence for a person in charge of a vehicle to allow mud, clay, farmyard manure or any other material to be dropped onto or deposited on the road and to fail to remove it as soon as reasonably practicable.[84] Note that the deposit must create or be likely to create a danger or

78  R(S)A 1984, s 66(4).
79  R(S)A 1984, s 129(1). The foregoing does not apply in relation to the duty under s 56(5) to first provide a door or cover as specified by the authority if an opening is left in a road after works or excavations are completed. This is itself an offence under s 56(6)(b). See para 12.1 ff.
80  R(S)A 1984, s 67.
81  R(S)A 1984, s 94(1), (3).
82  R(S)A 1984, s 94(1), (3).
83  R(S)A 1984, s 94(2).
84  R(S)A 1984, s 95(1). The person in charge of a vehicle is the owner or other person with immediate charge or control or someone who is present and entitled to give orders to the person in control: s 95(3). 'Vehicle' includes anything towed or pushed by a vehicle or any appliance: s 95(4).

substantial inconvenience to road users.[85] The roads authority can recover reasonable expenses as a result of any contravention from the person responsible.[86] These provisions can be difficult for the roads authority to enforce because of the number of qualifications they contain and because of the difficulty of proving who was responsible for any deposit.

### 11.7.5   PROTECTION OF ROAD USERS

The roads authority has a general power to take appropriate steps to protect road users from danger on land beside or near a road. This applies to anything which is a danger where there are no other provisions of the 1984 Act which would allow the authority to deal with it. If it is a building that is dangerous, the authority can enclose or screen it. The authority's reasonable expenses in connection with any of the above can be recovered from the landowner.[87] Where the danger to people or animals lawfully using the road involves barbed wire, an electric fence or a wall or a window-sill with spikes, broken glass, barbed wire or similar device, on land adjoining the road, the authority can serve a notice on the occupier requiring specific steps to be taken to remove the risk of injury within the period indicated.[88] There is a right to refer a dispute on the steps required by the notice, within twenty-eight days of service, or over the expenses, within twenty-eight days of intimation in writing of the intention to recover them, in either case to the sheriff.[89]

Where the roads authority is the occupier, then notice may be served on it requiring the removal of the risk, by a ratepayer or person liable to pay council tax within the area if it is a local authority, and by any person, if the Scottish Ministers are the occupiers.[90] While there is no timescale for compliance in this situation, the 1984 Act states that if the period expires without action being taken by the authority, then the person who served the notice can apply to the sheriff who can order the authority to comply if he is satisfied that the steps specified in the notice are necessary.[91]

## 11.8   HEAVY VEHICLE DAMAGE

If heavy vehicles or traffic cause damage to a public road resulting in extraordinary maintenance expenses for the roads authority, it can recover the cost from the vehicle operator. This is the person on whose orders the vehicles are on the road.[92] The cost is based on the difference

85   R(S)A 1984, s 95(1).
86   R(S)A 1984, s 95(2).
87   R(S)A 1984, s 93(1).
88   R(S)A 1984, s 93(2).
89   R(S)A 1984, s 93(6).
90   R(S)A 1984, s 93(3).
91   R(S)A 1984, s 93(4).
92   R(S)A 1984, s 96(1).

between the average expense in maintaining the road or other similar roads and the additional extraordinary expense as certified by the proper officer of the authority where it is a local roads authority. The costs can include those associated with the maintenance of a cattle grid on the road.[93] The traffic must be excessively heavy or extraordinary.[94]

The operator can reach agreement on a contribution towards making good any damage in advance with the authority.[95] Either party can seek a determination of the amount to be paid by arbitration. The operator is then liable to pay the sum to the authority which then loses its right to use the above procedure.[96] There is normally a twelve month time limit on taking action in the sheriff court to recover any sums due (whether agreed or enforced) to meet the cost of such damage.[97] Where the damage is the result of a particular building contract or of work extending over a long period, the time limit is within six months of its completion.[98]

## 11.9   TRADING ON OR NEAR TRUNK OR PRINCIPAL ROADS

It is an offence to use a stall or similar structure or any container or vehicle on any part of a trunk or principal road[99] or on unenclosed land within fifteen metres of any part of the road for the purpose of selling anything (including supplying or offering to supply a service for profit) unless the roads authority has consented in writing.[100] The consent can be subject to reasonable conditions. This is without prejudice to any other restriction, prohibition or requirement for consent, statutory or otherwise , which may apply to these activities[101] and also to section 129(9) of the 1984 Act which makes it an offence to display goods (in certain circumstances) for sale in a footway or footpath or to hang them over it.[102] However, these provisions do not apply in a number of situations. Namely where the sale is from or on a vehicle which is used for itinerant trading (and other purposes) with occupiers of premises, where the sale is of newspapers, where the sale is part of a relevant public market[103] or a private market with an operator's licence[104] or licensed street trading[105] or

93  R(S)A 1984, s 96(1), (2).
94  R(S)A 1984, s 96(1).
95  R(S)A 1984, s 96(3).
96  R(S)A 1984, s 96(3).
97  R(S)A 1984, s 96(4), (5).
98  R(S)A 1984, s 96(5).
99  Defined as a road classified as such by the Scottish Ministers under R(S)A 1984, s 11(1).
100 R(S)A 1984, s 97(1)–(3).
101 R(S)A 1984, s 97(5).
102 See below.
103 ie a market or fair held by virtue of a grant from the Crown or by virtue of prescription or held under statutory authority, or established or having its place fixed by a local authority.
104 In terms of s 40 of the Civic Government (Scotland) Act 1982.
105 Within the meaning of s 39 of the Civic Government (Scotland) Act 1982.

where it involves any activity granted a certificate under the Pedlars Act 1871.[106]

In addition, it is an offence to display goods for sale by placing them in or hanging them over a footway or a footpath unless this is in connection with the sale of newspapers, street trading, a private market or a certificated activity under the Pedlars Act 1871.[106]

## 11.10    PREVENTION OF FLOW OF WATER ONTO ROADS

It is an offence for a landowner and for an occupier to allow any flow of water, filth, dirt or other offensive matter from their land onto the road or to permit any percolation of water through the land onto the road.[107] To prevent this, a person can carry out necessary works in and excavate under the road. This requires the consent of the roads authority which may impose reasonable conditions.[108] Where there is a failure to comply, (in addition to being an offence) the authority can serve notice on the owner or occupier giving twenty-eight days (or a longer period) to carry out works to remedy the situation.[109] There is a right to refer the matter to the sheriff within twenty-eight days.[110]

Where works are carried out (whether voluntarily or to comply with a notice) these must be reinstated as soon as reasonably practicable. The authority must be notified when this has been done and the works must be maintained for twelve months from the authority certifying that they are satisfactory. Certification cannot be unreasonably withheld. Where there is a failure to reinstate or maintain, the authority can do so and recover its reasonable expenses.[111]

## 11.11    OFFENCES

A number of offences connected with roads have already been considered. The 1984 Act creates further offences, some of a general nature such as those dealing with damage to roads, and others which are more specific, such as taking or displacing construction materials, tools, machinery or equipment without reasonable excuse.

---

106  R(S)A 1984, s 129(9). Public markets are not excepted.
107  R(S)A 1984, s 99(1), (6). Land includes a structure over or across the road.
108  R(S)A 1984, s 99(2).
109  R(S)A 1984, s 99(4).
110  R(S)A 1984, s 99(4).
111  R(S)A 1984, s 99(5) applies s 56(4) and (10).

## 11.11.1 DAMAGE TO ROADS, SIGNS OR WORKS

It is an offence without lawful authority or reasonable excuse to deposit anything on a road which damages it;[112] to paint, inscribe or affix a picture, letter, sign or other mark to the road surface or to a tree, traffic sign, milestone, structure or works in or on a road;[113] or to light a fire (or allow it to spread) within thirty metres of a road thereby damaging the road or endangering traffic on it.[114]

## 11.11.2 PLACING ROPE, WIRE OR OTHER APPARATUS IN A ROAD

Placing rope, wire or other apparatus in a road (or allowing it to be placed) in a way which endangers road users without taking all necessary steps to give adequate warning is an offence.[115]

## 11.11.3 PLOUGHING UNENCLOSED LAND

It is an offence to plough unenclosed land adjoining a public road without making side ridges at least three metres broad along the sides of the road.[116]

## 11.11.4 CONSTRUCTION MATERIALS

Where materials, tools, machinery or other equipment have been deposited for use by the roads authority for construction or maintenance of a road, it is an offence for anyone to take them away or move them without reasonable excuse.[117] The same is the case if the equipment or materials are in a quarry which has been opened by the authority to obtain materials for road construction or maintenance.[118]

## 11.11.5 RESTRICTIONS ON VEHICLES IN A FOOTWAY, FOOTPATH OR CYCLE TRACK

Apart from the permitted use of certain appliances and vehicles,[119] it is an offence to drive, ride, lead or propel a vehicle or a horse or any swine or cattle in a footway, footpath or cycle track unless there is a specific

---

112  R(S)A 1984, s 100(a).
113  R(S)A 1984, s 100(b).
114  R(S)A 1984, s 100(c).
115  R(S)A 1984, s 101.
116  R(S)A 1984, s 102.
117  R(S)A 1984, s 129(10).
118  R(S)A 1984, s 129(10).
119  See para 11.4 above.

right to do so.[120] Allowance is made for vehicles and animals to be taken across the footway, footpath or cycle track, (as opposed to along it) and on a cycle track, for pedal cycles to be ridden or pushed and for prams, pushchairs and such like, and for wheelchairs, including those with electric motors, to be used, unless there is no public right of passage on foot.[121]

It is an offence to park a motor vehicle (as defined in the Road Traffic Act 1972) wholly or partly on a cycle track.[122]

## 11.11.6    OFFENCES BY CORPORATE BODIES

Where an offence has been committed by a corporate body, a director, manager, company secretary or other similar officer (or someone purporting to act in such a capacity) can also be charged, convicted and punished if they consented or connived in its commission or were guilty of neglect.[123] Where a corporate body is managed by its members this applies in relation to the acts and defaults of a member with management functions as if he was a director.[124]

## 11.11.7    PENALTIES AND MODES OF TRIAL

Offences under the 1984 Act are tried using summary court procedure[125] unless there is express provision to the contrary.[126] For example, a failure to obtain or a contravention of a construction consent[127] can be tried on indictment or summarily. The penalty on indictment is a fine and, on summary conviction, is the statutory maximum.[128] So far as other offences are concerned, Schedule 8 specifies the section of the 1984 Act which creates the offence and the maximum penalty which can be imposed. This is done by reference to a level on the standard scale.[129] A total of 40 offences are listed and the penalties range from a Level 1 fine for failure to remove an obstruction or for planting trees near a carriageway without consent, to Level 4 for depositing building materials in a

---

120  R(S)A 1984, s 129(5).
121  R(S)A 1984, s 129(5).
122  R(S)A 1984, s 129(6).
123  R(S)A 1984, s 130(1).
124  R(S)A 1984, s 130(2).
125  ie without a jury.
126  R(S)A 1984, s 131(1).
127  R(S)A 1984, s 22.
128  R(S)A 1984, s 131(2)(a) and Sch 8.
129  R(S)A 1984, s 131(2)(b) and Sch 8 (as amended by the Statute Law (Repeals) Act 1993 s 1(1), Sch 1). The levels are set out in s 225 of the Criminal Procedure (Scotland) Act 1995. The amounts can be altered by statutory instrument.

road without permission, for conveying an insecure load on a drawn vehicle or for failing to prevent the flow of water etc. onto the road.[130]

## 11.12   CONTENT AND SERVICE OF NOTICES

Unless there is express provision to the contrary, a notice issued or served by a roads authority under the 1984 Act which deals with action to be taken in relation to land must so far as necessary and reasonably practicable:

1.  give details including the location of the land;

2.  specify the nature of any works to be carried out and any requirements which have to be met;

3.  specify any period for compliance with the notice;

4.  state any power of the authority to enter land, carry out the works and recover their expenses in the event of non-compliance; and

5.  intimate any right of appeal under the act against the notice.[131]

The provisions which deal with actual service of notices are those in section 192 of the Local Government (Scotland) Act 1973 which relate to premises.[132] Where there is a right of appeal against a notice, it cannot be acted upon until either the time limit for doing so has expired or the appeal has been disposed of or abandoned unless there is express provision to the contrary.[133] Therefore lodging an appeal usually suspends the notice.

## 11.13   HOLDING OF INQUIRIES

The Scottish Ministers have the discretion to hold an inquiry in connection with any matters where they are authorised to act or make a determination under the 1984 Act.[134]

## 11.14   EXPENSES AND INTEREST

A roads authority can claim interest (from the date a demand for expenses is served until payment) where it is entitled to recover expenses

---

130  R(S)A 1984, s 131(2) and Sch 8.
131  R(S)A 1984, s 136.
132  R(S)A 1984, s 137.
133  R(S)A 1984, s 138.
134  R(S)A 1984, s 139(1). The provisions of s 210(2)–(8) of the Local Government (Scotland) Act 1973 apply to such inquires: R(S)A 1984, s 139(2), as does the Tribunals and Inquiries Act 1992: s 139(3).

under any provision of the Act.[135] It can also remit any sum (or part of it) payable as interest as it thinks fit.


## 11.15   POWERS OF ENTRY

Someone authorised by a roads authority has powers of entry to land at all reasonable hours in connection with various aspects of the 1984 Act such as carrying out inspections, surveying land, including searching or boring, or ascertaining whether work has been carried out.[136] On request he must produce proof of his authority. Normally at least seven days notice should be given to the occupier of the land.[137] If the authority proposes (1) laying and leaving or removing apparatus in connection with a survey or (2) searching or boring to ascertain the nature of the subsoil or whether minerals are present or to determine the nature of any mining or other activity which might affect the stability of a public road, the owner and occupier must be given at least seven days notice. If affected, the Coal Authority, any licensed operator (within the meaning of the Coal Industry Act 1994) and any other proprietor of underground mineral workings must also be given seven days notice.[138] Statutory undertakers can object in any of these circumstances and also where the authority is proposing taking other action or executing any work (authorised or required under the Act) if this would be seriously detrimental to their undertaking. In this event, the works cannot go ahead without the authority of the Scottish Ministers after consultation with the Minister responsible for the under-taking.[139] It is an offence to contravene either of these provisions.[140]

If entry is refused or prevented, or the land is unoccupied, or the occupier is temporarily absent, or the situation is urgent, then a sheriff, magistrate or justice of the peace can authorise entry by warrant if there are reasonable grounds for doing so.[141] It is an offence to wilfully obstruct authorised entry.[142] If land or other property is damaged or the enjoyment of the property is disturbed, anyone with an interest can seek compensation from the roads authority.[143]

135 R(S)A 1984, s 149. This is at the rate prescribed under s 40 of the Land Compensation (Scotland) Act 1963.
136 R(S)A 1984, s 140(1). As to liability for expenses incurred by a roads authority in this connection, see s 140(6), (7).
137 R(S)A 1984, s 140(2).
138 R(S)A 1984, s 140(3), as amended by the Coal Industry Act 1994, Sch 9.
139 R(S)A 1984, s 140(4).
140 R(S)A 1984, s 140(5)
141 R(S)A 1984, s 140(8).
142 R(S)A 1984, s 140(9).
143 R(S)A 1984, s 140(10).

## 11.16 DEFAULT POWER TO EXECUTE WORKS

Where the roads authority serves notice requiring works[144] or excavations to be carried out within a timescale and this is not done, it can do the work itself.[145] The authority can recover its expenses from the person responsible and can remit any amount or part of it as it sees fit. If more than one person is responsible, it can apportion the cost.[146] It may also grant a written extension to the time limit.[147]

## 11.17 POWER TO ORDER OCCUPIER TO ALLOW WORK

If the occupier of land is preventing the owner from carrying out work which he is required to do under the 1984 Act, a sheriff can order the occupier to allow it to proceed. The owner makes the application to the sheriff.[148]

## 11.18 APPLICATION TO THE CROWN

In general the 1984 Act does not apply to Crown land.[149] However, the Crown authority and the roads authority can agree that any of its provisions will apply subject to the terms of the agreement.[150] This can include such consequential and incidental provisions, including those of a financial character, as the Crown authority considers necessary or equitable.[151] 'The Crown authority' in relation to land belonging to the Queen is the Crown Estates Commissioners or other government department or person who manages the land; in relation to land belonging to a government department or held in trust for the Queen, it is the department.[152]

---

144 Defined in R(S)A 1984, s 151(1) with the addition of removal or reinstatement, taking steps, replacement, repair or putting into good condition, alteration, work and removal as mentioned respectively in ss 51(3) or 87(1), 57(1), 67 or 93(2), 66(2), 83(1), 91(1) or (2) and 92(2).
145 R(S)A 1984, s 141(1). This section does not apply where the Act already makes express analogous provision.
146 R(S)A 1984, s 141(2) applies s 140(6), (7).
147 R(S)A 1984, s 141(3).
148 R(S)A 1984, s 142.
149 R(S)A 1984, s 146(1).
150 R(S)A 1984, s 146(2).
151 R(S)A 1984, s 146(3).
152 R(S)A 1984, s 146(4).

# 12  Control over Works Affecting Roads

## 12.1  INTRODUCTION

The principal control over road works, as that term is normally understood, is to be found in the New Roads and Street Works Act 1991 and this is dealt with in detail in Chapters 14 to 21 of this book. However, the Roads (Scotland) Act 1984 also imposes duties on and gives powers to roads authorities to deal with situations involving work in roads or which can affect roads where this could jeopardise public safety.[1] For example, there are controls on works and excavations not covered by the 1991 Act and over dangerous works. In connection with building operations, permission is necessary before materials can be placed in a road or for staging or scaffolding to project into the road. There are also provisions which deal with obstructions in a road, the need to fence and light them, as well as separate regulation governing builders' skips. Permission is also required to put apparatus in a public road, where this is not dealt with by the 1991 Act and such works are not considered road works. Finally, there are provisions which allow the roads authority to charge for occupation of the road where certain time limits are exceeded in carrying out works. However, the regulations necessary to implement these have not been made.

## 12.2  CONTROL OF WORKS AND EXCAVATIONS

The roads authority has control over works and excavations in public roads where these are not already covered by the provisions of the 1991 Act or any other legislation.[2] The authority's written consent is required before works can be executed or excavations carried out. The consent can be subject to such reasonable conditions as the authority thinks fit.[3] The application must be in writing and, on receipt of it, the authority must notify the applicant of all statutory undertakers[4] whose apparatus is

---

1  The Crown, however, is not bound by the provisions of the Roads (Scotland) Act 1984: see *Lord Advocate v Dumbarton District Council and Strathclyde Regional Council* [1989] 3 WLR 1346, HL.
2  The provisions on the control of works and excavations contained in R(S)A 1984 do not apply to works or excavations covered by NRSWA 1991, Pt IV: R(S)A 1984, s 56(3) (amended by NRSWA 1991, s 168(1), Sch 8). As to works covered by NRSWA 1991, see Chapters 14 ff.
3  R(S)A 1984, s 56(1).
4  See pp 216–217 for definition of 'statutory undertaker in relation to road works.'

likely to be affected. The applicant must then notify the undertakers of the application in writing.[5]

Anyone carrying out works or excavations must make good any damage caused to the road as a result and notify the authority that this has been done. They are also responsible for the maintenance of the reinstatement for twelve months from the authority certifying that it is satisfied with it and certification must not be unreasonably withheld.[6]

If an opening is left in the road after the works or excavations are completed this must be covered as specified by the roads authority. For example a door or other cover may be used and must be constructed in a way and in materials specified by the authority.[7] It is an offence to carry out works or excavations without consent or to fail to cover any opening left in the road as specified by the roads authority.[8]

The roads authority can remove works or fill in excavations carried out without consent. It can carry out reinstatement and cover any opening in default of the person responsible.[9] It can also recover its reasonable expenses for doing so as well as those related to maintaining the excavation afterwards.[10] Where practicable, the authority must notify the person responsible for the works where anything has been removed. If they cannot be traced or do not recover the material within a reasonable time then it can be disposed of.[11] The proceeds of any disposal are offset against any expenses due to the authority and any surplus is returned if the person responsible can be traced. If not it can be kept by the authority.[12]

## 12.3   DANGEROUS WORKS

The roads authority has powers to deal with danger or potential danger as a result of works or excavations. It can serve notice on the person responsible requiring him to take steps to ensure that the danger is removed or does not actually develop into a danger in the first place.[13] There is a right to refer the matter to a sheriff within twenty-eight days of service of the notice and his decision is final.[14] Even where consent has been granted for works or excavations under the 1984 Act,[15] the notice may specify removal of the works or the filling in of excavations to deal

5    R(S)A 1984, s 56(2).
6    R(S)A 1984, s 56(4).
7    R(S)A 1984, s 56(5).
8    R(S)A 1984, s 56(6).
9    R(S)A 1984, s 56(7), (10).
10   R(S)A 1984, s 56(7), (10).
11   R(S)A 1984, s 56(8).
12   R(S)A 1984, s 56(9).
13   R(S)A 1984, s 57(1).
14   R(S)A 1984, s 57(6).
15   R(S)A 1984, s 56 or s 61.

with any actual or threatened danger.[16] The notice and removal of danger provisions do not apply where there is no consent,[17] which is itself an offence, and where there is no permission to place and maintain apparatus under a road.[18] In any case, anyone carrying out works or excavations which are a danger or become dangerous commits an offence.[19]

Once again the provisions on dangerous works do not apply to works or excavations which are already dealt with by Part IV of the 1991 Act.[20]

## 12.4 MATERIALS OR SCAFFOLDING

It is an offence to use a public or a private road,[21] or part of a road, for the storage of materials or otherwise without the written permission of the roads authority when involved in construction, repair, maintenance or demolition of any building.[22] This does not include placing a builders' skip in a road which is dealt with separately.[23] It is also an offence to erect staging or scaffolding which projects over part of a road without permission.[24] Even if consent has been obtained, its terms must be complied with otherwise an offence is committed.[25] Furthermore, it is an offence for any other person connected with the operations to deposit materials on the road either personally or through his employees or agents.[26]

Any permission granted can have conditions attached. The example given in the Act relates to the duration of the permission which can be time limited.[27] Compliance with the permission and any conditions is a defence to a charge of occupying the road or erecting staging or scaffolding but not to any alleged breach of the Health and Safety at Work Act 1974 or of any regulations or notices served under it.[28] There is a further defence if the person responsible for the material, staging or scaffolding being in the road or part of it can prove that he took all reasonable precautions and exercised all due diligence to avoid committing an offence.[29] It is difficult to envisage how this defence could be established where no permission was sought in the first place. However, it may be more readily used where there has been non-

---

16  R(S)A 1984, s 57(2).
17  Ie under R(S)A 1984, s 56(1).
18  In terms of R(S)A 1984, s 61(1).
19  R(S)A 1984, s 57(4).
20  R(S)A 1984, s 57(5) (amended by NRSWA 1991, s 168(1) Sch 8. See Chapters 14 ff for works covered by NRSWA 1991.
21  See Chapter 4.
22  R(S)A 1984, s 58(1).
23  R(S)A 1984, s 58(7) and s 85 and see 12.6 below.
24  R(S)A 1984, ss 58(1).
25  R(S)A 1984, ss 58(1), (2).
26  R(S)A 1984, s 58(3).
27  R(S)A 1984, s 58(2).
28  R(S)A 1984, s 58(2) and s 128(1).
29  R(S)A 1984, s 58(4).

compliance with a condition attached to a permission. Employees and workers have a defence if they thought they were acting in compliance with a permission and were acting on the instructions of, or under the authority of, either their employer or the person conducting the operations. They also have a defence where what happened was due to a mistake or to reliance on information supplied.[30] If an accused is claiming that he was acting under instruction or on authority or in reliance on information from another person he must notify the prosecution at least seven days before the court hearing and give any information he has which would identify or assist in identifying that person. Otherwise he cannot rely on the defence except with leave of the court.[31]

## 12.5   OBSTRUCTIONS

It is an offence to put anything in a road which causes an obstruction unless the roads authority has consented in writing.[32] The authority may attach reasonable conditions to the consent.[33] Where there is no consent, the person responsible for the obstruction can be asked to remove it by the authority or by a uniformed police constable. It is an offence not to do so.[34] In default, the roads authority or constable can remove it or have it removed if the person responsible cannot be traced or in an emergency.[35] Any expenses reasonably incurred can then be recovered from the person responsible[36] though it is difficult to envisage how that could be done if they cannot be traced!

As with works and excavations, if practicable, the person responsible must be notified if anything has been removed. If they cannot be traced or do not recover it within a reasonable time, the authority can dispose of it with the proceeds being used to offset any expenses. Any surplus must be given to the person responsible unless he cannot be traced.[37] The provisions dealing with obstructions do not apply where there are materials or scaffolding in a road,[38] in relation to builders' skips,[39] where the Refuse Disposal (Amenity) Act 1978 applies,[40] or where the road works provisions of the 1991 Act apply.[41]

30   R(S)A 1984, s 58(5).
31   R(S)A 1984, s 58(6).
32   R(S)A 1984, s 59(1), (2).
33   R(S)A 1984, s 59(1).
34   R(S)A 1984, s 59(3).
35   R(S)A 1984, s 59(4).
36   R(S)A 1984, s 59(4).
37   R(S)A 1984, s 59(5). Where a police constable is involved, it is the police authority and not the roads authority which has these duties.
38   See 12.4 above.
39   See 12.4 and 12.6 above.
40   RD(A)A 1978, s 2 deals with the penalty for unauthorised dumping of motor vehicles etc.
41   R(S)A 1984, s 59(6) (amended by NRSWA 1991, s 168(1), Sch 8.

## 12.5.1   FENCING AND LIGHTING OF OBSTRUCTIONS

There is a duty to fence and light obstructions or works on or in a road regardless of whether roads authority consent has been granted.[42] Failure to do so is an offence.[43] Breach of this duty may also give rise to civil liability even though this is not specifically provided for in the 1984 Act. In the case of *McArthur v Strathclyde Regional Council*[44] in the Outer House of the Court of Session, the action was dismissed as time barred. It was raised against the council when it should have been against the contractor responsible for the road works. McArthur averred that he was injured when his car struck an obstruction on the road associated with roadworks which were not visible or marked by any warning sign. He was too late in raising the action against the contractor as the three-year time limit for doing so had expired. As well as making a case for time bar, the contractor has argued that the pleadings were not specific enough in using the words 'associated with' and that the obligation to fence and light obstructions and excavations under the 1984 Act, section 60(1) could not give rise to civil liability.

On both counts the court disagreed. The words 'associated with' did give the contractor fair notice of the case against him, which was that the accident was caused by a danger as a result of his negligence. Although the 1984 Act made it an offence to breach section 60(1) and conferred powers of control on the roads authority, it was also intended for the protection of road users and entitled them to sue if the duty had been breached.

It is apparently not an offence for the roads authority itself to fail to fence and light obstructions despite the legislation stating that it applies to 'any person'. In *MacPhail v Tayside Regional Council*[45] the High Court upheld (by a majority of two to one) the decision of a justice of the peace that section 60 of the 1984 Act did not apply to a roads authority. There was strong dissent from one of the judges. The issue of the civil liability of the roads authority in such circumstances has not been litigated but such a situation would appear to come into the category of carrying out an operational task which could result in a successful claim.[46]

Any obstruction or works must be marked as specified in regulations so as to be immediately visible to oncoming traffic.[47] Only regulations relating to builders' skips have been made.[47]

---

42   R(S)A 1984, s 60(1).
43   R(S)A 1984, s 60(3).
44   (1994) Times, 20 May.
45   1992 SLT 182.
46   See Chapter 13 on Roads Authority Liability.
47   R(S)A 1984, s 60(1)(a) and 60(5). The Builders' Skips (Markings) (Scotland) Regulations 1986, SI 1986/642. R(S)A 1984, ss 85 and 86 deal specifically with the control of builders' skips and their removal where they are causing an obstruction or are a danger. All of the provisions relating to builders' skips are dealt with at 12.6 below.

If the obstruction or works mean that a building adjoining the road needs to be shored up or protected this must also be done.[48] Lighting is required during the hours of darkness (half an hour after sunset and before sunrise) to prevent danger to traffic and to warn of danger.[49] Fences, barriers and traffic signs as are necessary for preventing danger, for regulating traffic and for warning of danger must be erected and removed when they are no longer required.[50] The authority can step in and attend to these matters if the person responsible does not and can then recover its reasonable expenses from him.[51]

It is an offence for anyone to take down, alter or remove any fence, barrier, shoring or other support or protection, or any traffic sign or to remove or interfere with any light.[52]

## 12.6   CONTROL OF BUILDERS' SKIPS

It is necessary to obtain written permission from the roads authority to put a builders' skip on a road.[53] A 'builders' skip' is defined as 'a container designed to be carried on a road vehicle and to be placed on a road for the removal and disposal of builders' materials, rubble, waste, household and other rubbish or earth.'[54] Conditions can be placed on the permission and these can deal with siting and lighting of the skip, the care of the contents of the skip and the removal of the skip at the end of the permission period.[55] The skip must be clearly and indelibly marked with the owners' name and telephone number or address.[56] While permission is required to site the skip on a road, the 1984 Act states that an offence is committed when the owner uses it or causes or permits it to be used without permission.[57] There is a defence to a charge of failing to get permission for a skip or of non-compliance with conditions (although the 1984 Act does not specifically state that these are offences), but not to failing to mark the skip, if the accused can prove that someone else was responsible for dealing with this. The owner must also establish that the offence was committed without his consent or connivance. In such circumstances the 1984 Act states that the person responsible can be charged and convicted in place of the owner.[58] This is despite the fact that there does not appear to be statutory authority for such a charge in the first place!

48   R(S)A 1984, s 60(1)(d).
49   R(S)A 1984, s 60(1)(b), s 60(5).
50   R(S)A 1984, s 60(1)(c).
51   R(S)A 1984, s 60(2).
52   R(S)A 1984, s 60(4).
53   R(S)A 1984, s 85(1) amended by NRSWA 1991, s 168(1) and Sch 8.
54   R(S)A 1984, s 85(5).
55   R(S)A 1984, s 85(2).
56   R(S)A 1984, s 85(1)(b).
57   R(S)A 1984, s 85(1), 85(3).
58   R(S)A 1984, s 85(4).

## 12.6.1   MARKING OF BUILDERS' SKIPS

Builders' skips which are placed on a road must have specific markings and these in turn must comply with the design specifications set out in regulations, otherwise an offence is committed.[59] The markings must be clean and efficient and clearly visible to road users, except where there is a door on the skip which is open for loading and unloading and, as a result, the marks are not visible for that reason.[60] The regulations require two plates the same size and shape securely fixed at each of the outer edges of both ends of the skip, or if it is placed sideways, on the sides.[61] These are the same plates as specified in the British Standard for Rear Marking Plates for Vehicles.[62] There is a detailed design specification and a diagram for the plates in the Regulations.[63]

## 12.6.2   REMOVAL OF BUILDER'S SKIPS

Builders' skips can be removed from the road where they are causing a danger or an obstruction.[64] Whether or not permission has been granted for a skip, a uniformed police constable can insist on it being removed or repositioned, or have this done, where it is causing, or is likely to cause, a danger or an obstruction.[65] The police authority can then recover any expenses reasonably incurred in removing or repositioning the skip from the owner.[66] The roads authority can only require removal or repositioning where there is either no permission, non-compliance with conditions or if the skip is not marked with the owners name and contact details as required.[67] If this is not done within a reasonable time, the authority can attend to this itself and can also recover its reasonable expenses from the owner.[68] The police or roads authority must notify the owner that the skip has been removed, if practicable. If the owner cannot be traced or has not recovered the skip after a reasonable period of time, both the skip and its contents can be disposed of.[69] Any proceeds must be used to offset the police or roads authority expenses. The surplus should be returned to the owner unless he cannot be traced when it may be kept.[70]

The powers of a police constable or the roads authority to remove skips is without prejudice to other provisions of the 1984 Act which make it an offence for anyone to place or deposit anything in a road which obstructs

---

59   R(S)A 1984, s 60(1)(a), 60(3), 60(5), s 143(1) and the Builders' Skips (Markings) (Scotland) Regulations 1986, SI 1986/642, reg 3.
60   SI 1986/642, reg 4.
61   SI 1986/642, reg 3, Sch 1.
62   BS AU 152: 1970, para 5.
63   SI 1986/642, reg 3, Sch 2.
64   R(S)A 1984, s 86(1), (2).
65   R(S)A 1984, s 85(1).
66   R(S)A 1984, s 86(4).
67   R(S)A 1984, s 85(2).
68   R(S)A 1984, s 85(2), (4).
69   R(S)A 1984, s 86(5).
70   R(S)A 1984, s 86(6).

the passage of or endangers road users without lawful authority or reasonable excuse.[71]

## 12.7   PERMISSION FOR APPARATUS

The roads authority can grant permission to put apparatus in or under a public road or proposed public road. It can also grant permission to leave or retain the apparatus in the road or proposed road[72] and to maintain, repair and reinstate it as well as to break open and have access to the road for these purposes. Any permission must be in writing.[73] This does not apply to the apparatus of statutory undertakers or of local authorities nor where the apparatus is placed under a permission in terms of section 109 of the 1991 Act.[74] The permission can be subject to such reasonable conditions as the authority considers appropriate including those on the future cessation or withdrawal of permission and an indemnification of the authority against any claims as a result of what is being allowed.[75] The roads authority is required to give at least twenty-eight days notice before granting permission to anyone whose apparatus or plans for apparatus may be affected by it.[76] Works carried out under this permission are not considered road works within the meaning of section 107 of the 1991 Act.[77] The 1984 Act provisions do not apply to an undertaker carrying out road works within the meaning of Part IV of the 1991 Act.[78]

## 12.8   CHARGE FOR OCCUPATION OF ROAD

The Scottish Ministers and their predecessor the Secretary of State for Scotland could make regulations allowing the roads authority to charge for occupation of the road beyond a reasonable time in certain circumstances. Namely, while work or excavations are being carried out in or under a public road, while building materials or scaffolding are in a road, while anything is placed or deposited in a road, including a builders' skip and while apparatus is placed, left, retained, maintained, repaired and reinstated in or under a public road.[79] However, as is the

---

71   R(S)A 1984, s 86(3) and s 129(2).
72   A ' "proposed public road" means a new road in course of construction by or on behalf of the roads authority': R(S)A 1984, s 61(2).
73   R(S)A 1984, s 61(1) (amended by NRSWA 1991, s 168(1), Sch 8).
74   R(S)A 1984, s 61(4) (amended by NRSWA 1991, s 168(1) and Sch 8. See also Chapter 14.
75   R(S)A 1984, s 61(4) (as so amended).
76   R(S)A 1984, s 61(3).
77   R(S)A 1984, s 61(4) (amended by the Electricity Act 1986, Sch 16). For the definition of 'road works' see 14.2 below.
78   R(S)A 1984, s 61(6) (added by NRSWA 1991, s 168(1) and Sch 8).
79   R(S)A 1984, s 61A (added by NRSWA 1991, s 168(1) and Sch 8).

case with the provisions on charging undertakers carrying out road works where there is unreasonable delay, no such regulations have yet been made.[80] This is because of difficulties such as quantifying the cost of the delay, the administration which would be required to do this and the difficulties of enforcing payment. Roads authorities cannot therefore impose such charges at present.

---

80   See para 19.2 below.

# PART FIVE

# 13 Road Works Management

## 13.1 INTRODUCTION

Both the UK and the Scottish Parliament have acknowledged that it is important to have legal controls on the management of road works to ensure that they are properly co-ordinated to keep traffic flowing and also to ensure public safety while they are being carried out and afterwards.

The legal provisions on the management of road works in Scotland are contained in the New Roads and Street Works Act 1991, Part IV ("the 1991 Act")[1], and in a significant amount of secondary legislation made under the 1991 Act. The 1991 Act was recently amended by the Transport (Scotland) Act 2005 ("the 2005 Act").[2] Generally these amendments seek to improve the administration of the Scottish Road Works Register, to improve enforcement and to strengthen the provisions in relation to reinstatement. There still appear to be no reported cases on the Scottish road works provisions of the 1991 Act and only one or two south of the border on the equivalent sections for England and Wales. There is therefore currently no guidance from the Scottish judiciary as to the interpretation of the relevant parts of the legislation.

## 13.2 ROAD WORKS AND UNDERTAKERS

The 1991 Act is aimed at ensuring that road works are carried out in a way which minimises traffic disruption; that they are carried out under some sort of overall supervision and that safety and reinstatement is given priority. The 1991 Act defines 'road works' as works executed in a road for any purposes other than roads purposes.[3] This means that works carried out by a roads authority[4] itself or by a contractor acting on its behalf, including maintenance or improvement works; the erection, maintenance, alteration or removal of traffic signs; or

---

1  The Act received Royal Assent on 27 June 1991.
2  The Transport (Scotland) Act 2005 was passed by the Scottish Parliament on 29 June 2005 and subsequently received Royal Assent on 5 August 2005.
3  NRSWA 1991, s 107 (3).
4  For the definition of "roads authority" for the purposes of the 1991 Act see NRSWA 1991 s 145(1) and chapter 2.

the construction of a vehicular crossing across a footway or strengthening or adapting a footway to be used as a crossing which are all works for road purposes[5], are not covered by these provisions, while works by what are usually referred to as statutory undertakers, or contractors acting on their behalf are. A statutory undertaker operates under a statutory right, which authorises the carrying out of road works, hence the terminology.[6] However, the definition of 'undertaker' also includes a person having permission from the road works authority[7] under section 109 of the 1991 Act to carry out road works.[8] This allows road works to be carried out by a person or organisation without specific statutory authority provided permission is obtained from the Road Works Authority. The 1991 Act spells out what constitutes road works, that is placing apparatus, for example pipes, in a road, as well as inspecting, maintaining, adjusting, repairing, altering or renewing apparatus, changing its position or removing it and any associated works and in that regard the 1991 Act states that breaking up or opening the road, or any sewer, drain or tunnel under it, or tunnelling or boring under the road are associated with or "incidental to" the road works.[9]

## 13.3    DEFINITION OF 'ROAD'

The definition of 'road' for the purposes of the 1991 Act is wider than that in the 1984 Act.[10] In relation to road works, 'a "road" means any way … whether or not there is over it a public right of passage and whether or not it is for the time being formed as a way; and the expression includes a square or court, and any part of a road.'[11] Where the road passes over a bridge or through a tunnel this is also included.[12] This extended definition of a road allows for control over works carried out both in a road or in a prospective road, whether public or private and in what would not normally be considered a road, for example, a building site or a car park.

## 13.4    ROAD WORKS AUTHORITIES

Road works authorities act as regulators under the 1991 Act. They have powers and duties to deal with the control and monitoring of various aspects of road works. The definition of 'road works authorities' in the 1991 Act encompasses the roads authority where the road is a public

5    NRSWA 1991, s 145(2).
6    NRSWA 1991, s 107(4) and (5).
7    For definition of "road works authority" for the purposes of the 1991 Act see NRSWA s 108(1), (4) and paragraph 13.4 below.
8    NRSWA 1991 s 107(4) and (5). See paragraph 13.5 below.
9    NRSWA 1991, s 107 (3).
10   See R(S)A 1984, s 151(1) and Chapter 4.
11   NRSWA 1991, s 107 (1).
12   NRSWA 1991, s 107 (2).

road, and where it is not, the road managers.[13] Where a roads authority has declared that a road in their area is likely to become a public road, they are responsible for ensuring that undertakers comply with the Act and that they exercise their powers "in such a manner as is reasonably required for the protection of the road managers", which includes complying with any reasonable request from the road managers.[14] The term 'road managers' means the authority, body or person who is liable to the public for maintaining or repairing the road. If there is no one with that responsibility then it is whoever has management or control of the road.[15] The 1991 Act allows for the use of regulations to exempt road managers from the provisions which apply to them in relation to a road. As a result they are exempt from the requirement to keep a road works register[16]. No other exemptions have been granted.[17]

If a roads authority is acting as an agent of the Scottish Ministers in respect of a road for which the Scottish Ministers are the roads authority, for example, Trunk Roads, then the roads authority is the road works authority in relation to the provisions of the Act dealing with the duty to enter certain information in to the road works register and for advance notice and co-ordination of works.[18] Local authority consortia currently act as agents for Transport Scotland in partnership with the private sector for some trunk and special roads in Scotland. The private sector also has some roads management contracts and regulations allow for the Scottish Ministers to delegate some of their functions to the private sector.[19]

## 13.5   PERMISSION FOR ROAD WORKS

The 1991 Act allows a road works authority to grant written permission for any road works except those involving the inspection and maintenance of fire hydrants.[20] As already noted above[21] this permission can be granted where the person or organisation seeking to carry out the work does not have statutory authority to do so. When granting permission, the road works authority can impose such reasonable conditions as it considers appropriate.[22] The conditions can relate to payment of fees, to

13   NRSWA 1991, s 108(1) and (4).
14   NRSWA 1991, s 146.
15   NRSWA 1991, s 108(4).
16   This is likely to change given the new provisions inserted by s 19 of the Transport (Scotland) Act 2005 in respect of the Scottish Road Works Register and the Scottish Road Works Commissioner. See also paragraphs 13.6.
17   NRSWA 1991, s 108(5) and the Road Works (Registers, Notices, Directions and Designations) (Scotland) Regulations 1992, (SI 1992/2991), reg 10. These regulations are expected to be replaced by The Road Works (Scottish Road Works Register, Notices, Directions and Designations) (Scotland) Regulations 2008 which are due to come into force on 1 April 2008 (the 2008 Regulations). The 2008 Regulations will replace the changes introduced by the Transport (Scotland) Act 2005.
18   NRSWA 1991, s 108(2).
19   The Secretary of State's Trunk Road Functions (Contracting Out) (Scotland) Order 1996 SI 1996/878.
20   NRSWA 1991, s 109 and the Road Works (Permission under Section 109) (Scotland) Regulations 1996, SI 1996/3199, reg 2.
21   At para 13.2.
22   NRSWA 1991, s 109(1).

the future cessation or withdrawal of permission and to granting an indemnity in favour of the roadworks authority against claims arising from what is being permitted.[23] The permission makes it unnecessary to obtain any further consent from a 'relevant authority' or from the owner of apparatus affected by the work.[24] In addition to the roads authority itself, a 'relevant authority' includes Scottish Water[25], a transport authority or a bridge authority[26] in relation to their respective interests, although there may be a requirement to notify them in advance.[27] The granting of permission does not remove the need to obtain any other consent, licence or permission which is needed.[28] For example, the approval of Network Rail must be sought where the work involves its operational land, such as road works on a level crossing. Some apparatus also requires a licence from the Scottish Ministers before it can be used and its installation is unauthorised unless and until that licence has been granted, even if road works permission has been given.[29] The licensing requirement applies to cable television and telecommunications equipment.

### 13.5.1    NOTICE BY ROAD WORKS AUTHORITY

Notice provisions protect the interests of Scottish Water, a transport or bridge authority. Although their permission is not necessary for road works to be carried out, the 1991 Act states that, before granting permission, a road works authority shall give not less than ten working days' notice to these authorities where their interests may be affected[30]. It must also inform anyone who has given notice under the Act[31] that it intends to carry out road works and also to anyone with apparatus in the road, in each case where they are likely to be affected.[32] However, any failure to notify does not affect the validity of the permission granted.[33]

### 13.5.2    UNAUTHORISED ROAD WORKS

It is an offence for anyone other than a road works authority to carry out works without permission or a statutory right to do so unless they are emergency works, works for roads purposes or works with permission

23    NRSWA 1991, s 109(5).
24    NRSWA 1991, s 109(2).
25    NRSWA 1991, s 108(6) as amended by the Water Industry (Scotland) Act 2003 Schedule 7 paragraph 21(2).
26    NRSWA 1991, s 108(6).
27    NRSWA 1991, s 108(6) and see paragraph 13.5.1 below.
28    NRSWA 1991, s 109(3).
29    NRSWA 1991, s 109(3).
30    NRSWA 1991, s 109(6).
31    NRSWA 1991, s 109(6) (d) and s 113.
32    NRSWA 1991 s 109(6).
33    NRSWA 1991, s 109(6).

under the 1984 Act.[34] Commission of such an offence is punishable on summary conviction by a fine not exceeding level 5 on the standard scale.[35] In addition, where an offence has been committed and a person has placed apparatus in a road without consent, the road works authority has the power to direct the offender to remove the apparatus which has been illegally placed in the road and to require reinstatement.[36] Where a person has, without consent, broken up or opened a road, sewer, drain or tunnel under it, or bored under the road to place, inspect, maintain, adjust, repair, alter or renew apparatus or to alter its position or remove it,[37] the roads works authority has the power to direct the offender 'to take such steps as appear to them necessary to reinstate the road or any sewer, drain or tunnel under it.'[38] The road works authority can remove the apparatus or carry out the reinstatement itself if there is a failure by the offender to comply with any direction from the road works authority to either remove apparatus or to reinstate. The roads works authority can recover the costs reasonably incurred in doing so from the offender. It should be noted that there is no time limit for the offender to comply with the direction to make good and therefore it is likely that the road works authority will have to give the offender reasonable time and this may depend on the nature of the failure in the first place.

### 13.5.3   EMERGENCY ROAD WORKS

It is not an offence to carry out emergency road works without permission or statutory authority[39] however it should be noted that in certain circumstances, notice may be required of such works.[40] Emergency road works are defined as works which are necessary to stop or prevent circumstances which are likely to cause danger to people or property.[41] This means that emergency road works can be carried out to deal with an existing dangerous situation or to prevent one from arising, for example, to deal with subsidence or an actual or threatened landslide. It is specifically provided that this also includes the situation where the person responsible for the works believes on reasonable grounds that danger exists or is imminent.[42] If some of the work falls into the emergency category and some does not, anything that cannot reasonably be severed from the emergency work is included in the definition.[43] In any civil or criminal proceedings under Part IV of the 1991 Act the onus is on the person alleging works were of an emergency nature to prove this.[44]

34   NRSWA 1991, s 110(1) and (3).
35   Currently £5,000: Criminal Procedure (Scotland) Act 1995, s 225. These levels can be altered by statutory instrument.
36   NRSWA 1991, s 110(4).
37   NRSWA 1991, s 110(1).
38   NRSWA 1991, s 110(4)(b).
39   See paragraph 13.5.2 above.
40   NRSWA 1991, s 110(4).
41   NRSWA 1991, s 111(1).
42   NRSWA 1991, s 111(1).
43   NRSWA 1991, s 111(2).
44   NRSWA 1991, s 111(3).

## 13.6    THE SCOTTISH ROAD WORKS COMMISSIONER AND REGISTER

### 13.6.1    THE SCOTTISH ROAD WORKS COMMISSIONER

The 2005 Act created the role of the Scottish Road Works Commissioner ("the Commissioner").[45] The Commissioner is to be appointed on such terms and conditions as the Scottish Ministers' determine.[46] The Commissioner has the general functions of (1) monitoring the carrying out of works in roads[47] in Scotland; (2) promoting compliance with the 1991 Act and the obligations imposed under it; and (3) promoting the pursuit of good practice by those persons who have functions conferred on or permissions granted to them by or under the 1991 Act.[48] "Good practice" means complying with any code of practice issued or approved under the 1991 Act or any direction under the 1991 Act and complying with such practice as the Commissioner considers desirable.[49]

The Commissioner must also carry out any other functions conferred on him under either the 2005 Act or the 1991 Act.[50] Schedule 2 of the 2005 Act sets out some of the powers and duties of the Commissioner. These include the power to appoint staff, the duty to prepare accounts and the duty to comply with the Freedom of Information (Scotland) Act 2002.[51]

### 13.6.2    DUTY TO PROVIDE THE COMMISSIONER WITH INFORMATION

Previously road works authorities were under a duty to keep a register of road works containing certain information. Now it is the Commissioner who has such a duty[52] however the road works authority or an undertaker must provide the Commissioner, if required by him, with such information as is reasonably requested by him in respect of their respective functions and activities.[53] This includes any information which the authority or undertaker possesses or can reasonably be expected to acquire.[54] Where there is any dispute as to whether the information

---

45   Transport (Scotland) Act 2005 s 16. It should be noted that the Commissioner is not a servant or agent of the Crown and has no status, immunity or privilege of the Crown. Transport (Scotland) Act 2005 s 16(3).
46   Transport (Scotland) Act 2005 s 16(2).
47   "works in roads" includes road works as defined by s 107(3) of the 1991 Act, works for roads purposes as defined by s 145(2) of the 1991 Act and major works for road purposes as defined by s 145(3) of the 1991 Act.
48   Transport (Scotland) Act 2005 s 17(1).
49   Transport (Scotland) Act 2005 s 17(4).
50   Transport (Scotland) Act 2005 s 17(1).
51   Transport (Scotland) Act 2005 schedule 2.
52   See paragraph 13.6.3 below.
53   Transport (Scotland) Act 2005 s 18(1).
54   Transport (Scotland) Act 2005 s 18(2).

asked for by the Commissioner is reasonably asked for, the matter will be settled in the prescribed manner.[55]

## 13.6.3   THE SCOTTISH ROAD WORKS REGISTER

The Commissioner has to keep the Scottish Road Works Register ("the Register")[56] in such form and manner as may be prescribed.[57] Any person who has a duty to enter information in the Register will be given access to the Register by the Commissioner for that purpose.[58] However the Commissioner will be entitled, subject to the necessary regulations being made, to charge a prescribed fee for giving such access and different fees may be prescribed for access for different purposes.[59] All fees received must be applied by the Commissioner to keep the Register.[60] In addition to giving access to those who require to enter information in the Register, the Commissioner must make the Register, except restricted information[61], available for inspection at all reasonable times and free of charge to any person[62]. Restricted information must be made available to any person who has the authority to execute any works in a road in respect of which that restricted information is kept or, in any other case, where the person appears to the Commissioner to have sufficient interest in that information.[63]

## 13.6.4   DUTY TO ENTER CERTAIN INFORMATION IN THE SCOTTISH ROADS WORKS REGISTER

Road works authorities must enter information in the Scottish Road Works Register for each road for which the authority is responsible.[64] The form of the information to be entered and the manner in which the

---

55  Transport (Scotland) Act 2005 s 18(3). The Road Works (Settlement of Disputes and Appeals against Directions) Regulations 2008 are expected to come into force on 1 April 2008. The consultation draft regulations envisaged that such a dispute would be settled by arbitration.
56  NRSWA 1991, s 112A(1) as inserted by s 19 of the Transport (Scotland) Act 2005.
57  NRSWA 1991, s 112A(2) as inserted by s 19 of the Transport (Scotland) Act 2005.
58  NRSWA 1991, s 112A(3) as inserted by s 19 of the Transport (Scotland) Act 2005.
59  NRSWA 1991, s 112A(4) as inserted by s 19 of the Transport (Scotland) Act 2005.
60  NRSWA 1991, s 112A(5) as inserted by s 19 of the Transport (Scotland) Act 2005.
61  NRSWA 1991, s 112A(7) as inserted by s 19 of the Transport (Scotland) Act 2005. 'Restricted information' is defined SI 1992/2991. See also the 2008 regulations which are expected to come into force on 1 April 2008.
62  NRSWA s 112A (6)(b) as inserted by s 19 of the Transport (Scotland) Act 2005.
63  NRSWA 1991 s 112A(6)(a) as inserted by s 19 of the Transport (Scotland) Act 2005.
64  NRSWA 1991, s 112B(1) as inserted by s 19 of the Transport (Scotland) Act 2005.

information should be entered will be prescribed by regulations.[65] Where a road works authority is proposing to carry out works it must enter the prescribed information in the Register by a certain period prior to the start of the works.[66] In addition where the road works authority has given permission under s109 for a person to carry out works or given a direction under either s115 or s115A of the 1991 Act, it must enter the prescribed information in the Register.[67] Certain provisions under the Road (Scotland) Act 1984 also impose a duty to enter information in the register both prior to the works being carried out and on completion of the works.[68]

## 13.7   RESTRICTION ON FURTHER WORKS

Where there is a proposal to carry out substantial works in a road, the authority can restrict further works for a period from the completion of the first set of works by serving a notice.[69] 'Substantial works' are works for road purposes comprising reconstruction, widening, alteration of levels, resurfacing or non-skid surfacing of part of the road. However such works only fall within the definition of "substantial works" if in the case of a footpath, footway, bridleway or cycle track, they extend to more than thirty metres continuous length and reduce period the width of the footpath or cycle track during the construction by more than two-thirds.[70] Similarly, in the case of the road, the road works are "substantial" where they extend to more than thirty metres continuous length and the use of the carriageway is either prohibited or reduced by more than one-third.[71] The road works authority must give notice at least three months in advance of the works commencing specifying the nature and location of the works, the date on which the works will commence and the extent of the restriction. Notice is given by entering the required information in the Register[72] Copies of the notice must be given to anyone who has served advance notice of their intention to carry out works in the part of the road which would be restricted, and to any other person having apparatus in that part of the road. Scottish Water, the transport authority and/or bridge

65   NRSWA 1991, s 112B(8) as inserted by s 19 of the Transport (Scotland) Act 2005.
66   NRSWA 1991, s 112B(2) as inserted by s 19 of the Transport (Scotland) Act 2005. The period is to be prescribed by the 2008 Regulations.
67   NRSWA 1991, s 112B(3) as inserted by s 19 of the Transport (Scotland) Act 2005.
68   NRSWA 1991, s 112B(4), (5), (6) and (7) as inserted by the Transport (Scotland) Act 2005. See also Chapter 12.
69   NRSWA 1991, s 117(1) as amended by s 22 of the Transport (Scotland) Act 2005.
70   See also the 2008 Regulations which are expected to come into force on 1 April 2008 SI 1992/2991 reg 9(1)(a).
71   See also the 2008 Regulations which are expected to come into force on 1 April 2008 1992/2991 reg 9(1)(b).
72   NRSWA 1991, s 117(2).

authority must also be notified if appropriate.[73] Anyone who has given notice under section 113 of the Act that it intends to carry out road works and also anyone who has apparatus in the road must also be notified.[74] However, any failure to notify does not affect the validity of the restriction.[75] If the works referred to in the notice are not substantially started on or within a month of the specified date, the notice is no longer effective and a fresh notice has to be issued.[76] Similarly, if road works are in progress on the date specified in the notice, the notice loses its validity within one month from completion of the works.[77]

An undertaker is allowed to contravene such a restriction to carry out emergency works or where he has the consent of the road works authority and in other specified circumstances.[78] The consent of the road works authority is not to be unreasonably withheld[79]. In the event of a dispute, the matter will be settled in the prescribed manner.[80] The other circumstances in which an undertaker is permitted to contravene a restriction are when works are urgent, are carried out in response to a request for a new service or supply to a customer and the request was not received in time for the works to be carried out before the restriction took effect[81] or where works do not involve breaking up of the road and thus are relatively trivial, such as replacing manhole covers, resurfacing up to twenty square metres or replacing a lamp, columns or sign in the same location.[82] Otherwise, any contravention of a restriction is an offence subject to a fine on summary conviction not exceeding level 5 on the standard scale.[83] In addition, if convicted of an offence, the undertaker is responsible for the costs reasonably incurred by the road works authority

73  NRSWA 1991, s 117(3).
74  NRSWA 1991, s 117(3).
75  NRSWA 1991, s 117(3).
76  NRSWA 1991, s 117(4).
77  This provision is unclear in the 1991 Act but it is submitted that this interpretation appears to make most sense. However, it is not actually clear from the wording of the subsection whether it is the date specified in the notice or one month from that date.
78  NRSWA 1991, s 117(5) and SI 1992/2991, reg 9(3). See also the 2008 Regulations which are expected to come into force on 1 April 2008
79  NRSWA 1991, s 117(7).
80  NRSWA 1991, s 117(7) as amended by s 36 of the Transport (Scotland) Act 2005. Disputes are likely to be settled by the Commissioner see the Consultation Draft Regulations: The Roads Works (Settlement of Disputes and Appeals against Directions) (Scotland) Regulations reg 3 which are expected to come into force on 1 April 2008. It should be noted that there may be changes between the draft regulations and the regulations once made. See also paragraph 21.8.
81  NRSWA 1991, s 117(5)(c); SI 1992/2991, reg 9(3)(b). NRSWA 1991 s 117(8) also states that an undertaker shall not be taken to have failed to fulfil a statutory duty to provide a supply or a service if this is attributable to a restriction on further works.
82  NRSWA 1991, s 117(5)(c) and SI 1992/2991, reg 9(3). See also the 2008 Regulations which are expected to come into force on1 April 2008.
83  NRSWA 1991, s 117(6)(a). Currently £5,000: Criminal Procedure (Scotland) Act 1995, s 225. These levels can be altered by statutory instrument.

in reinstating the road.[84] The Scottish Ministers must issue or approve a code of practice to give practical guidance as to the performance by road works authority of their functions under this section of the 1991 Act. A roads works authority must have regard to such codes when carrying out their functions.[85]

## 13.8   DUTY TO CO-ORDINATE WORKS

The road works authority has a duty to use its best endeavours to co-ordinate works in roads for which it is responsible including works for road purposes.[86] This is in the interests of safety, of minimising inconvenience to road users, in particular those with a disability, and to protect the structure of the road and the apparatus in it.[87] The duty extends to works of all kinds, not just road works.[88] It includes a duty to co-operate with other road works authorities if their roads are affected.[89] In addition, the road works authority must also have regard to all the information in the Register which relates to its functions, must assist the Commissioner to comply with his statutory duties and must keep all information under surveillance.[90] The Scottish Ministers are required to issue or approve codes of practice[91] in relation to this duty and a road works authority must take these into account.[92] In addition, when having regard to the code of practice the road works authority must have regard to any guidance published under the 2005 Act.[93] The Commissioner also has powers to direct an authority to provide him with information where it appears that it is not fulfilling its duty properly. He must specify the information sought as well as the timescale for compliance.[94] When the time for compliance has expired, the Commissioner can direct the authority to take steps to discharge its duty where he considers it has not properly done so. This applies whether or not the authority has provided the requested information.[95] The Commissioner must also specify the

84   NRSWA 1991, s 117(6)(b).
85   NRSWA 1991, s 117((9). See also paragraph 21.8.
86   NRSWA 1991, s 118(1).
87   NRSWA 1991, s 118(1).
88   NRSWA 1991, s 118(1).
89   NRSWA 1991, s 118(2).
90   NRSWA 1991 s 118(2A) and s 118(2B) as inserted by s 23 of the Transport (Scotland) Act 2005.
91   See the code of practice for the Co-ordination of Street Works for Road Purposes and Related Matters. This code also deals with the duty to co-operate and directions as to timing of works. A new Code of Practice for reco-ordination of road works and works for road purposes and related matters is expected to be released in March 2008. This will reflect the changes introduced by the Transport (Scotland) Act 2005. See also paragraph 21.8.
92   NRSWA 1991, s 118(3).
93   NRSWA 1991 S 118(3A) as inserted by s 23 of the Transport (Scotland) Act 2005.
94   NRSWA 1991, s 118(4) as amended by s 23 of the Transport (Scotland) Act 2005.
95   NRSWA 1991, s 118(5) as amended by s 23 of the Transport (Scotland) Act 2005.

steps to be taken to remedy the deficiency and a deadline for doing so. There may also be a requirement for the authority to report back on what has been done and the results of taking such steps.[96] Any direction can be varied or revoked by a further direction.[97]

## 13.9 DUTY TO CO-OPERATE

The 1991 Act also imposes a general duty on undertakers to co-operate with each other in the execution of road works[98] for the same reasons as authorities are required to co-ordinate works.[99] The obligations on undertakers are similar to those for road works authorities. The undertaker[100] must have regard to the information in the Register, must assist the Commissioner to comply with his statutory duties and must keep all information under surveillance.[101] Again a code of practice must be issued or approved.[102] Compliance with this is seen as discharging the duty under the Act while non-compliance is evidence of a failure to do so.[103] Again the Commissioner has powers to issue directions[104] which can be varied or revoked by a further direction.[105]

## 13.10 ENFORCEMENT

The Commissioner can impose fixed penalties on both road works authorities and undertakers who fail to comply with the duties imposed on them by s118 and s119 of the 1991 Act respectively.[106] Notice of the penalty will be given in writing to the chief executive of either the roads works authority or the undertaker and will include the prescribed information namely (1) a note of the facts that the Commissioner has considered in imposing the penalty; (2) the amount of

96  NRSWA 1991, s 118(5) as amended by s 23 of the Transport (Scotland) Act 2005.
97  NRSWA 1991, s 118(6).
98  NRSWA 1991, s 119(1).
99  See para 13.8 above.
100 Note that in these provisions "undertaker" does not include a person having permission under s 109. NRSWA 1991 s 119(1C) as inserted by s 24 of the Transport (Scotland) Act 2005.
101 NRSWA 1991, s 119(1A) and s 119(1B) as inserted by s 24 of the Transport (Scotland) Act 2005.
102 NRSWA 1991, s 119(2) and code of practice for the Co-ordination of Street Works for Road Purposes and Related Matters. This code also deals with the duty to co-operate and directions as to timing of works. See also paragraph 21.8. See also footnote 92 above.
103 NRSWA 1991, s 119(2).
104 NRSWA 1991, s 119(2A) and s 119(2B) as inserted by s 24 of the Transport (Scotland) Act 2005.
105 NRSWA 1991, s 119(4) as inserted by s 24 of the Transport (Scotland) Act 2005.
106 NRSWA 1991, s 119A as inserted by s 25 of the Transport (Scotland) Act 2005; Scottish Road Works Commissioner (Imposition of Penalties) Regulations 2007 SSI 2007/411, which come into force on 1 October 2007. A Code of Practice for Penalties is expected to be released April/May 2008.

the penalty; (3) where the penalty can be paid; (4) the method of payment; and (5) the date by which the penalty must be paid.[107] The penalty is such amount as the Commissioner thinks is appropriate in the circumstances however the penalty must not exceed £50,000.[108] Any penalty must be paid within 36 days of it being imposed.[109] Where it is not paid within 36 days, it is enforceable as though it was a decree issued by a sheriff.[110] There is however the right to appeal against the imposition of a penalty.[111] Where the penalty is appealed, the 36 day period for payment will be suspended from the day the appeal is lodged until the day on which the appeal is determined.[112]

107  SSI 2007/411 reg 6.
108  SSI 2007/411 reg 4.
109  SSI 2007/411 reg 5(1).
110  SSI 2007/411 reg 7.
111  SSI 2007/411 reg 8.
112  SSI 2007/41 reg 5(2).

# 14 Notice and Co-ordination of Road Works

## 14.1 INTRODUCTION

Statutory undertakers are required to notify road works authorities of their intention to carry out road works in some circumstances. There are a variety of specific notice provisions depending on the nature of the road works. There are also more general requirements on the form and content of notices and regarding the service of notices.

## 14.2 ADVANCE NOTICE OF WORKS

A statutory undertaker is required to give advance notice of some works.[1] Notices are given by entering prescribed information in to the Register.[2] As a result of the information being inputted directly in to the Register, the relevant road works authority can access up to date information in order to co-ordinate roads works and other works taking place on roads. Different notice periods may be prescribed for different categories of work.[3] For example, the period of advance notice is one month. This applies to major projects and to standard and minor works in traffic-sensitive roads which involve breaking up the road.[4] The information which requires to be entered into the will be set out in secondary legislation.[5]

Once advance notice has been given the undertaker must provide such further information or take any steps required to co-ordinate with other road works including works for road purposes.[6] A failure to comply with

---

1  NRSWA 1991, s 113(1) as amended by section 19 of the Transport (Scotland) Act 2005.
2  NRSWA 1991 s 113(3A) as inserted by s 19(3) of the Transport (Scotland) Act 2005. See paragraph 13.6 for details of the Register. Previously the requirement was to give notice to the roads works authority.
3  NRSWA 1991, s 113(2).
4  SI 1992/2991, reg 6. The terms 'major projects', 'standard works', 'minor works' and 'traffic-sensitive roads' are defined in reg 2(1). See also the 2008 Regulations which are expected to come into force on 1 April 2008. See also paras 14.4 and 15.4.
5  NRSWA 1991 s 112 as inserted by s 19 of the Transport (Scotland) 2005. See also the 2008 Regulations.
6  NRSWA 1991, s 113(4) and SI 1992/2991. See also the 2008 Regulations.

any of these duties is an offence for which the offender can be fined an amount up to level 4 on the standard scale.[7]

## 14.3    NOTICE OF START DATE OF WORKS

Generally, an undertaker must give at least seven working days advance notice of any road works which involve breaking up or opening the road or any sewer, drain or tunnel under it or which involve tunnelling or boring under the road.[8] However different notice periods may apply for different categories of road works[9], for example urgent works where it would be unrealistic to expect a week's notice,[10] or where notice has been given to the undertaker in accordance with S117(1).[11] In some cases no notice may be required.[12] Notice is given by giving to any relevant authority (not being a road works authority) and to any other person who has apparatus in the road which is likely to be affected by the proposed work, a notice stating the start date and containing any other prescribed information[13] and by entering a copy of that notice in the Register.[14]

Works must not commence without giving notice if this is required nor should any work commence before the notice period has expired, unless those entitled to notice have consented to this.[15] Contravention of these provisions is an offence punishable on summary conviction by a fine not exceeding level 4 on the standard scale.[16] An undertaker has a defence if either he did not know of the position of, or of the existence of, apparatus or did not know the identity of or the address of the body or person to whom notice should have been given. This defence is only available if his ignorance was not due to negligence or to a failure to make reasonable inquiries.[17]

A notice ceases to be effective if the works are not substantially started by the end of a further period (starting on the day on which the works

---

7    NRSWA 1991, s 113(5). The maximum fine is currently £2,500: Criminal Procedure (Scotland) Act 1995, s 225. The level can be altered by statutory instrument.
8    NRSWA 1991, s 114(1) as amended by s 19 of the Transport (Scotland) Act 2005.
9    NRSWA 1991, s 114(2) as amended by s 19 of the Transport (Scotland) Act 2005.
10   NRSWA 1991, s 114(2) as amended by s 19 of the Transport (Scotland) Act 2005 and SI 1992/2991, reg 7. See also the 2008 Regulations which are expected to come into force on 1 April 2008.
11   NRSWA 1991, s 114(2).
12   SI 1992/2991 reg 7(3). See also the 2008 Regulations.
13   NRSWA 1991, s 114(3A) as substituted by s 19 of the Transport (Scotland) Act 2005.
14   NRSWA 1991, s 114 (3A) (b).
15   NRSWA 1991, s 114(4).
16   NRSWA 1991, s 114(5). Currently £2,500: Criminal Procedure (Scotland) Act 1995, s 225. The amount can be altered by statutory instrument.
17   NRSWA 1991, s 114(6).

would have started) equivalent to the notice required for that category of work. If this happens, the undertaker must serve a fresh notice before work can begin.[18]

## 14.4 TRAFFIC-SENSITIVE ROADS

There are detailed notice provisions in respect of various categories of work in traffic-sensitive roads.[19] 'Traffic-sensitive' is defined as a road designated as such under s 123 of the 1991 Act.[20] For example, the notice period for 'urgent works' is "as soon as reasonably practicable" or at least two hours of beginning the works.[21] Urgent works are those which are either necessary to stop or prevent an unplanned interruption to a supply or a service by an undertaker, such as gas or electricity, or to avoid substantial loss to the undertaker in relation to an existing service, or to reconnect supplies or services where there would be criminal or civil liability if reconnection was delayed until after the expiration of a notice period.[22] The definition of 'urgent works' includes works required to restore a supply or service to premises where there is an agreement in advance between the undertaker and the road works authority that this should be the case and the undertaker fears that people or property might be in danger unless this is dealt with immediately.[23] This might be the case where there is a serious gas leak which has interrupted supplies or a power cut in the middle of winter. 'Urgent works' also include other works which cannot reasonably be severed from the urgent works and situations where the undertaker either does not know or have reasonable grounds to believe that there are circumstances which would constitute an emergency but there is still a degree of urgency. In terms of road works, an emergency is viewed more seriously than urgent works.[24]

Minor works[25] which do not involve breaking up of the road, but could include the replacement of lamps, columns and signs, pole testing and similar works which would involve minimal breaking up the road have a notice period of at least three days.[26] Standard works and other minor

---

18    NRSWA 1991, s 114(7).
19    SI 1992/2991, reg 7(1). See also the 2008 Regulations which are expected to come into force on 1 April 2008.
20    SI 1992/2991, reg 2(1). See also paragraph 15.4.
21    SI 1992/2991, reg 7(2).
22    SI 1992/2991, reg 2(1).
23    SI 1992/2991, reg 7(2).
24    SI 1992/2991, reg 7. See also paragraph 14.9 below.
25    Defined in SI 1992/2991, reg 2 as works (not being emergency works or urgent works) whether in the footway, verge or carriageway, which are planned to last not more than three days, do not form part of a rolling programme of works and do not involve more than thirty metres of works or which normally leave less than three metres width of carriageway for traffic (or 2.5 metres width if traffic consists only cars and light locomotives within the meaning of s 185(1) of the Road Traffic Act 1988).
26    SI 1992/2991 reg 7(1).

works[27] which do involve breaking up a road both require periods of notice of not less than seven days.[28] Remedial reinstatement works (which are not defined[29]) by an undertaker, where there is no immediate danger to road users, require a minimum of three days notice.[30]

## 14.5   NON TRAFFIC-SENSITIVE ROADS

There are less stringent notice requirements for non traffic-sensitive roads as the potential for delay and disruption to road users clearly is less in such cases. Where non-traffic sensitive roads are involved, notice only needs to be given in respect of standard works and urgent works. No notice is required for minor works or remedial reinstatement works.[31] Not less than seven days notice is necessary for standard works. For urgent works, notice must be given as soon as reasonably practicable, and in any event within two hours of commencement.[32]

## 14.6   DIRECTIONS ON TIMING OF WORKS

If it is likely that works will cause serious disruption to traffic and that this could be avoided or reduced if the works were only carried out at certain times, or on certain days or at certain times on certain days, the road works authority can issue directions to undertakers on the timing of works.[33] Directions can also be issued as the works are being carried out where the road works authority considers that the subsisting works are causing delay or disruption to traffic and that could be avoided.[34] The road works authority can insist that undertakers avoid doing work during peak traffic flow, such as at rush hour in the morning and early evening. The procedure for issuing directions is detailed in regulations.[35]

The actual service of directions by the roads authority is governed by essentially the same procedures as those which apply to the service of notices by undertakers.[36] However given that notices are served by

---

27   'Standard works' are defined in SI 1992/2991, reg 2 as all works which are not emergency works, urgent works or minor works. 'Other minor works' are those which meet the requirements of reg 2 and which are excluded from the definition of 'minor works' above.
28   SI 1992/2991 reg 7(1).
29   See Chapter 17 on reinstatement.
30   SI 1992/2991, reg 7(1).
31   SI 1992/2991, reg 7(3).
32   SI 1992/2991, reg 7(3).
33   NRSWA 1991, s 115(1) as amended by s 20 of the Transport (Scotland) Act 2005.
34   NRSWA 1991, s 115(1A) as inserted by s 20 of the Transport (Scotland) Act 2005.
35   SI 1992/2991, reg 8.
36   See SI 1992/2991, regs 5 and 8. See also paras 14.2 and 14.3 above.

entering details into the Register rather than by serving notice on the road works authority, it is likely that the regulations will require to be amended.[37] Currently, the direction must be served by the roads works authority on the undertaker by endorsing it on the notice of works served by the undertaker.[38]

Where the direction is in response to an advance notice of works by an undertaker, the direction must be issued not more than ten days after receipt of the notice by the authority, otherwise the direction is invalid.[39] If it simply relates to notice of the start date of works by the undertaker, it is invalid if it is served later than one hour after receipt where the notice period is two hours, later than one day where the notice period is three days and later than three days where the notice period is seven days.[40] It is an offence for an undertaker to carry out works in contravention of a valid direction,[41] however undertakers have a right of appeal against directions.[42] Where an undertaker is prevented from providing a supply or service due to a direction issued by the road works authority, he will not have failed to fulfil any statutory duty.[43] There is a code of practice in relation to directions as to timing[44] however there is a statutory duty on the Scottish Ministers to issue or approve an updated code of practice, to reflect the changes to the 1991 Act, to give practical guidance to the road works authorities in the exercise of their powers under this section of the 1991 Act.[45] This is still awaited however once available, the road works authority must have regard to the code of practice in exercising its powers. Until the new code of practice is available, it would be prudent for road works authorities to have regard to the current code of practice.

## 14.7 DIRECTIONS ON PLACING APPARATUS

New provisions have been introduced by the 2005 Act 2005 giving road works authorities the power to issue directions on the

---

37  This is due to the amendments made to the Act by the Transport (Scotland) Act 2005.
38  NRSWA 1991, s 115(1), SI 1992/2991, reg 8(1).
39  SI 1992/2991, reg 8(3).
40  SI 1992/2991, reg 8(3).
41  NRSWA 1991 s 115(3). He is liable on summary conviction to a fine not exceeding level 5 on the standard scale. Currently £5,000: Criminal Procedure (Scotland) Act 1995, s 225. The level can be altered by statutory instrument.
42  NRSWA 1991 s 115(2A) as inserted by s 20 of the Transport (Scotland) Act 2005. See paragraph 14.8 below.
43  NRSWA 1991 s 115 (3A) as inserted by s 20 of the Transport (Scotland) Act 2005.
44  NRSWA 1991, s 115(4) and Code of Practice for the Co-ordination of Street Works for Road Purposes and Related Matters. This code also deals with the duty to co-operate as well as with directions as to timing. A new code of practice for the co-ordination of road works and works for road purposes and related matters is expected to be released in March 2008. This would reflect the changes introduced by the Transport (Scotland) Act 2005. See also paragraph 21.10.
45  NRSWA 1991 s 115(4) as amended by s 20 of the Transport (Scotland) Act 2005.

placing of apparatus.[46] If it is likely that works involving the placing of apparatus in a road will cause disruption to traffic and that this could be avoided by placing the apparatus in another road, then the road works authority can issue a direction to the undertaker not to place the apparatus in that road,[47] provided that the placing of the apparatus would avoid or reduce the disruption to traffic, it would be a reasonable way of achieving the purpose for which the apparatus is to be placed and it is reasonable to require the undertaker not to place the apparatus in the proposed road.[48]

It should be noted that such directions can be issued where it is likely that there will be "disruption". For directions on the timing of works, the test is that there is a likelihood that there will be "serious disruption".[49] It would therefore appear that there may be greater scope for road works authorities issuing directions regarding the placing of apparatus.

The procedure for giving directions on placing apparatus has still to be prescribed.[50]

It is an offence for an undertaker to carry out works in contravention of a valid direction.[51] However undertakers have a right of appeal against directions.[52] Where an undertaker is prevented from providing a supply or service due to a direction issued by the road works authority, he will not have failed to fulfil any statutory duty.[53]

A code of practice is to be issued or approved by the Scottish Ministers giving guidance on how the powers under this provision of the Act should be exercised. This is still awaited however once available in exercising the powers under this section, the road works authority must have regard to the code of practice.[54]

## 14.8    RIGHTS OF APPEAL

Undertakers have a right of appeal against both directions as to the timing of works and directions as to the placing of apparatus.[55]

---

46    NRSWA 1991, s 115A as inserted by s 21 of the Transport (Scotland) Act 2005.
47    NRSWA 1991, s 115A(1).
48    NRSWA 1991, s 115A(2).
49    Compare the drafting of s 115(1)(a) and s 115A(1)(b).
50    NRSWA 1991, s 115A(4).
51    NRSWA 1991, s 115A(6). He is liable on summary conviction to a fine not exceeding level 5 on the standard scale. Currently £5,000: Criminal Procedure (Scotland) Act 1995, s 225. The level can be altered by statutory instrument.
52    NRSWA 1991, s 115A(5). See paragraph 14.8 below.
53    NRSWA 1991, s 115A(7).
54    NRSWA 1991, s 115A(8).
55    NRSWA 1991, s 115(2A) and s 115A(5) as inserted by s 20 and 21 of the Transport (Scotland) Act 2005 respectively.

Secondary legislation will be required to make provision for appeals and also to set out the procedure to be followed in an appeal.

Consultation draft regulations have already been published[56] but have not yet been laid before the Scottish Parliament or made. However if the final regulations are based on the consultation draft regulations then it is likely that an undertaker will have twenty eight days in which to appeal a direction to the Commissioner.[57] The Commissioner will fix a date for a hearing which will be no more than 14 days after receipt of the appeal and will notify the parties of that date.[58] The Commissioner will make such arrangements as he considers appropriate for the hearing of the appeal; however both the undertaker and the road works authority will be entitled to appear or be represented and the evidence may be oral, written or such other evidence that the Commissioner considers relevant to the appeal whether or not it is admissible in a court of law.[59] If both parties agree, the appeal can be determined on the basis of written submissions.[60]

The Commissioner must determine the appeal within seven days of the hearing. He can confirm, revoke or vary the direction and his determination is final and binding on both parties. Reasons for the determination require to be notified to both parties no later than seven days after the determination is made.[61]

## 14.9   NOTICE OF EMERGENCY WORKS

Emergency road works can be carried out at very short notice. Notice is required if the works are covered by section 114 of the 1991 Act and must be given in the same way as notice for other road works.[62] However, in an emergency, the notice period is 'as soon as reasonably practicable and in any event within two hours (or such other period as may be prescribed) of the works being begun.'[63] No other period has been specified in the regulations. Notice is given to any relevant authority (not being a road works authority) and to any other person having apparatus in the road, which is likely to be affected by the works. It should state the reason to carry out emergency works or the fact that they have begun and should contain any other prescribed information.[64]

56  The Road Works (Settlement of Disputes and Appeals against Directions) (Scotland) Regulations. These are expected to come into force on 1 April 2008. It should be noted that the draft regulations may change before the final regulations are made.
57  Draft Regulations reg 5(1).
58  Draft Regulations reg 5(2).
59  Draft Regulations regs 5(3)–(6).
60  Draft Regulations reg 5(13).
61  Draft Regulations regs 5(9)–(11).
62  NRSWA 1991, s 116(1), (2), (3A).
63  NRSWA 1991, s 116(2) as amended by s 19(5) of the Transport (Scotland) Act 2005.
64  NRSWA 1991, s 116(3A) as inserted by s 19(5) of the Transport (Scotland) Act 2005.

As for advance notice of works, a notice of emergency works must be entered in to the Register.[65] Any failure to comply with these provisions is punishable on summary conviction by a fine not exceeding level 4 on the standard scale.[66] Again it is a defence to any breach if the undertaker did not know the position of, or of the existence of, apparatus, or did not know the identity of or the address of the body or person to whom notice should have been given provided his ignorance was not due to negligence or to a failure to make reasonable inquiries.[67]

## 14.10    FORM OF NOTICES

Notices must be in the prescribed form.[68] The information which is required to complete the form is that which has been or will be prescribed.[69] Such information at present includes the date of issue of the notice, the time of issue if it relates to urgent or emergency works, the expected start and completion dates for the work, the location of the work, including a national grid reference, and a description of the works including, construction methods, if known, comments on traffic management or anything else which is relevant and information about reinstatement.[70]

## 14.11    OTHER NOTICES

Any other notice required under Part IV of the 1991 Act must be in writing, must refer to the relevant provision of the 1991 Act it is issued under and can be in any form.[71]

---

65  NRSWA 1991, s 116 (3A)(b) as amended by s 19 of the Transport (Scotland) Act 2005.
66  NRSWA 1991, s 116(4). The maximum fine is currently £2,500: Criminal Procedure (Scotland) Act 1995 s 225. The level can be altered by statutory instrument.
67  NRSWA 1991, s 116(5).
68  SI 1992/2991, reg 4(1), Sch 2. See also the 2008 Regulations which are expected to come into force on 1 April 2008.
69  NRSWA 1991, s 113(3A), 114(3A), 116 (3A).
70  SI 1992/2991, reg 4(2), Sch 2. See also the 2008 Regulations which are expected to come into force on 1 April 2008.
71  SI 1992/2991, reg 4(3).

## 14.12   SERVICE OF NOTICES

Where an undertaker has to serve notice before works can begin this can be done either by delivering it or sending it by fax or electronically, or by any other manner which has been agreed by the parties.[72]

In other cases under the 1991 Act, notice can be served by delivery to the person it is addressed to or by leaving it at his address, or by fax or electronically, or by first-class post or by any other way agreed by the parties.[73] Where a fax or electronic mail is used service is deemed effective on record of satisfactory transmission, unless the contrary is proved.[74] If three attempts at service by these methods fail, notice can be given by telephone, followed by service of a copy of the notice as soon as practicable.[75] Service is to the 'proper address' which is the address (if any) which has been given for the service of notices. Otherwise service must be made at the registered or principal office of a corporation and, in any other case, it is the last known address. Different addresses can be given for different notices.[76]

---

72   SI 1992/2991, reg 5(1). Where the recipient does not have arrangements for receiving and responding to notices between 4.30pm and 8am the following day, the undertaker complies if the notice is served by 10am that day.
73   SI 1992/2991, reg 5(2).
74   SI 1992/2991, reg 5(3).
75   SI 1992/2991 reg 5(3).
76   SI 1992/2991 reg 5(4). It is expected that given the new provisions inserted by the Transport (Scotland) Act 2005 and the role of the Register, in particular that notice is served by entry information in the Register, these provisions may be amended by the 2008 Regulations.

# 15 Roads Subject to Special Controls

## 15.1 INTRODUCTION

Certain categories of road are subject to additional controls because it is vital to minimise disruption and ensure safety in such cases. These are roads which are of strategic importance, such as motorways, roads which have high and constant traffic flows, such as dual carriageways, roads which could be adversely structurally affected by works; roads which, for safety reasons, require special precautions to be taken; and busy roads.[1] They are referred to in the legislation as 'protected roads,' as 'roads with special engineering difficulties' and as 'traffic-sensitive roads.' Protected roads are the most strictly controlled and a road is only accorded this status when there is an alternative to putting apparatus in the road itself. In such cases, if it is necessary to have apparatus following the line of the road, it will normally run alongside it rather than be placed in it. It is not usual to have any apparatus in a protected road. Each of these road designations will now be considered in turn.

## 15.2 PROTECTED ROADS

A protected road is subject to the greatest degree of control by a road works authority. A protected road is defined as 'any road or proposed road which is a special road in accordance with section 7 of the Roads (Scotland) Act 1984,[2] and any road designated by the roads authority as protected.'[3] An undertaker needs the consent of the authority to place apparatus in such a road. Consent is not normally required where the undertaker is simply renewing existing apparatus, or is carrying out work under permission granted under section 109 of the 1991 Act[4] or section 61 of the Roads (Scotland) Act 1984. However, if this permission was granted before the road became protected, consent must still be sought.[6] A road works authority can only designate a road as protected if certain criteria are met.[7] The road must fulfil a specific strategic need; it must be subject to such high and constant traffic flows that being designed as traffic-sensitive would not be enough to avoid serious disruption to traffic; and there must be a reasonable alternative to

---

1   See paragraph 15.2.
2   Such roads include motorways; see further Chapter 4.
3   NRSWA 1991, s 120(1).
4   See paragraph 13.5.
5   NRSWA 1991, s 120(2).
6   NRSWA 1991, s 121(1)(a) and SI 1992/2991, reg 11. See also the 2008 Regulations which are expected to come into force on 1 April 2008.

placing apparatus which could lawfully be placed in the road.[7] Alternatives to placing apparatus in the road include placing it adjacent to the road or in a walk-through duct under the road which would allow access without disrupting traffic.

There is a specified procedure for making or withdrawing protected road status.[8] The road works authority must publish notice of its intention to designate a road as protected in one or more newspapers circulating locally and allow at least one month for objections to be made.[9]

The road works authority must also notify undertakers with apparatus in the road or who have advised the authority of their intention to execute works in the road. Local authorities, other than the road works authority itself, owners and occupiers and anyone who has lodged a written request for notification must also be notified.[10] If there are no objections, or any that are made are withdrawn, the road works authority can proceed with the designation.[11] Otherwise, a local inquiry must be held.[12] The road works authority must consider any outstanding objections and the inquiry report before making a decision on designation.[13] The road works authority can seek payment of a reasonable fee from the undertaker to cover legal or other expenses associated with the consent to place apparatus in a protected road, as well as a reasonable annual fee for administering the consent. This is in addition to any rights the authority may have as owners of the land.[14] An authority can therefore seek payment for allowing an undertaker access for placing apparatus if it owns the land next to the road in the same way as any other landowner. This is usually done by granting a servitude right (commonly referred to as a 'wayleave') for which payment is normally sought. The consent may be subject to conditions and the authority can agree to contribute to the undertaker's expense of complying with the conditions.[15]

Where the apparatus will cross the road rather than run along it, the authority can only withhold consent if there are special reasons for doing so.[16] For example, it could do so where it was not satisfied about how the apparatus was to cross the road and where it was concerned about the restrictions working on the apparatus would impose on traffic using the road. Any dispute over the withholding of consent, the imposition of conditions or the making of contributions can be settled in the prescribed manner.[17] It is likely that any such disputes will be settled by the

7    SI 1992/2991, reg 11.
8    NRSWA 1991, s 121(1)(b) and SI 1992/2991, reg 11(2), Sch 1.
9    SI 1992/2991 Schedule 1 part 1 paragraph 1.
10   SI 1992/2991 Schedule 1 part 1 paragraph 2.
11   SI 1991/2991 Schedule 1 part 1 paragprah 3.
12   SI 1992/2991 Schedule 1 part 1 paragraph 4.
13   SI 1992/2991 Schedule 1 part 1 paragraph 5.
14   NRSWA 1991, s 120(3).
15   NRSWA 1991, s 120(5).
16   NRSWA 1991, s 120(4).
17   NRSWA 1991, s 120(6) as amended by section 36 of the Transport (Scotland) At 2005. See also para 21.8 below.

Commissioner.[18] An undertaker who may otherwise be in breach of a statutory duty to provide a supply or service has a defence if it is not reasonably practicable to do so as a result of the actions of the road works authority in relation to a protected road.[19]

The authority can instruct an undertaker to remove or change the position of apparatus which was placed in the road before it was designated as protected. However, in this event the authority must reimburse the undertaker's reasonable expenses as a result of complying with this instruction.[20] The financial implications of this make it unlikely that this provision will be used very often. Again, any dispute can be settled in the prescribed manner, which again is likely to be by the Commissioner.[21]

## 15.2.1 INFORMATION ON PROTECTED ROADS

The road works authority must make certain information available regarding protected roads.[22] This information includes the date of designation, sufficient detail of the road to enable it to be identified and particulars of any consents granted for apparatus to be placed in the road. In addition, the road works authority must ensure that the road works register records the making of a designation within seven days of it being made.[23] It is thought that although the regulations will require to be amended, there will be an obligation to enter similar information in the Scottish Register within a similar timescale[24]. It must also ensure that the designation is noted in the list of public roads which it is obliged to maintain in terms of the 1984 Act.[25]

## 15.3 ROADS WITH SPECIAL ENGINEERING DIFFICULTIES

There are two situations in which roads can be designated as roads with special engineering difficulties. First, where a road has a specific engineering feature which is fundamental to its structure and integrity and which requires special precautions to be taken in planning and carrying out road works to avoid serious failure.[26] Such an engineering feature

18  Consultation draft regulations – The Road Works (Settlement of Disputes and Appeals Against Directions) (Scotland) Regulations reg 3. These are expected to come into force on 1 April 2008. It should be noted that the draft regulations may change before the final regulations are made.
19  NRSWA 1991, s 120(7).
20  NRSWA 1991, s 121(2).
21  NRSWA 1991, s 121(5) as amended by s 36 of the Transport (Scotland) Act 2005 and para 21.11.
22  NRSWA 1991, s 121(1)(c) and SI 1992/2991, reg 11(3).
23  SI 1992/2991 Schedule 1 part 3 paragraph 13.
24  See 2008 Regulations which are expected to come into force on 1 April 2008.
25  NRSWA 1991, s 121(6). As to the use of public roads, see paragraph 4.8.1 above.
26  NRSWA 1991, s 122(2) and SI 1992/2991, reg 12(1)(a).

might occur where there is peat in the road, poor ground conditions or some other feature which could affect the stability of the road. Secondly, a road might be designated as having special engineering difficulties where special measures need to be taken in planning and executing road works to avoid serious failure of an engineering structure associated with a road.[27] An example of this might be a bridge or a tunnel or a flyover.

The procedure for making and withdrawing the designation of a road with special engineering difficulties[28] does not require publication of a notice in the press, as is the case with protected roads. However, in all other respects the notification procedure for roads with special engineering difficulties is virtually the same as for protected roads with one difference, namely that there is no requirement to notify owners and occupiers of land adjacent to a road with special engineering difficulties.[29]

The authority can make the designation if there have been no objections or if any made have been withdrawn.[30] There is no provision in such cases for a local inquiry to be held as there is with protected roads.[31] Where any objection is insisted upon, the authority simply has to consider it before making the designation.[32]

A transport authority, if it has a structure which belongs to it or which it manages in proximity to the road, or an undertaker with apparatus in a road, has a right of appeal to the Scottish Ministers against a refusal to designate a road as having special engineering difficulties.[33] Presumably they would take this step to ensure that their interests were protected.

### 15.3.1    A PLAN FOR ROADS WITH SPECIAL ENGINEERING DIFFICULTIES

Road works in a public road with special engineering difficulties, which involve breaking up or opening the road or any sewer or drain or tunnel under it or tunnelling or boring under the road, (other than emergency road works) cannot be carried out until a plan and section of the works has been agreed between the parties. If this is not possible then the matter must be settled by arbitration.[34] The parties involved are the

27    NRSWA 1991, s 122(2) and SI 1992/2991, reg 12(1)(b).
28    SI1992/2991 Schedule 1 parts 2 and 2 paragraphs 6 – 13.
29    See paragraph 15.2 above.
30    SI 1992/2991, reg 12(2) and Sch 1, para 7.
31    As to the impact which the Human Rights Act 1998 might have on this area, see para 1.4.5 above.
32    SI 1992/2991, Sch 1, para 8.
33    NRSWA 1991 s 122 (3).
34    NRSWA 1991, s 122, Sch 6, para 2(1). It appears that the changes made throughout Part IV of the NRSWA 1991 by the Transport (Scotland) Act 2005 substituting arbitration with "prescribed manner" have not been carried through to the Schedules.

undertaker and each of the relevant authorities.[35] The undertaker must submit a plan and section to each relevant authority. However, the authority can accept a description of the works as sufficient as a plan or in lieu of one, whether or not this is in the form of a diagram.[36] In other words an actual plan may not be necessary. The authority must notify its approval, modification, objection (on the grounds it is on too small a scale or gives insufficient particulars) or disapproval of the plan and section[37] within a certain timescale, otherwise it is deemed acceptable. This must be given 'without avoidable delay' and at the latest within seven working days where it involves a service pipe or line, or overhead electric lines or telecommunications apparatus and, in any other case, within one month.[38] If the plan and section is either not approved or modified, the authority must give reasons.[39] If the authority objects or disapproves or imposes modifications which are disputed and which it refuses to withdraw, then the undertaker can refer the matter to arbitration.[40]

Where an undertaker has carried out works without submitting the appropriate plan, the authority can object to the works and give the undertaker a chance to enter into an agreement. If he fails to do so the authority can refer the matter to arbitration. The arbiter can issue a direction requiring the works to conform to the plan, or can seek the removal of the apparatus, provided this will not involve any undue interruption or restriction of the supply or service which the works were carried out to provide.[41]

It is an offence to carry out works without a plan and section where one is required; to fail to comply with an arbiter's direction; and to fail to carry out works in accordance with the plan and section. In each case, the undertaker is liable on summary conviction to a fine not exceeding level 3 on the standard scale.[42]

There are separate provisions governing emergency road works and those in a road which is not a public road.[43] In the case of an emergency, works can be carried out without submitting a plan provided that this is provided as soon as reasonably practicable after the works have been

35 'Relevant authorities' means a Scottish Water (as inserted by the Water Industry (Scotland) Act 2002 Schedule 7 paragraph 21(2), a transport authority or bridge authority for their respective interests: NRSWA 1991, s 108(6) and s 150(3). Also para 13.5 above.
36 NRSWA 1991, s 122, Sch 6, para 5(1).
37 NRSWA 1991 Schedule 6 paragraph 7.
38 SI 1992/2991, Sch 6, para 7(2)(b). See also the 2008 Regulations which are expected to come into force on 1 April 2008.
39 NRSWA 1991 Schedule 6 paragraph 8.
40 NRSWA 1991, s 122, Sch 6, para 8.
41 NRSWA 1991, s 122, Sch 6, para 12.
42 NRSWA 1991, s 122, Sch 6, paras 6, 12, 13. The maximum fine is currently £1,000: Criminal Procedure (Scotland) Act 1995, s 225. The level can be altered by statutory instrument.
43 NRSWA 1991 Schedule 6 paragraphs 3 and 4.

carried out. In the case of a road which is not a public road, the undertaker need only submit a plan if, following notification that works are proposed, a plan is required by the road managers, who must give notice to the undertaker of this requirement within ten working days from the date they received notification of the proposed works.

### 15.3.2   INFORMATION ON ROADS WITH SPECIAL ENGINEERING DIFFICULTIES

The information which the road works authority must make available in relation to roads with special engineering difficulties differs slightly from that required for protected roads.[44] It must note the date of designation, provide sufficient detail to enable the road to be identified, the features which justify designation and details of the authority or undertaker with an interest in the road.[45] As with protected roads, the road works authority must ensure that the road works register records the making of a designation within seven days of it being made and the authority must note the designation in the list of public roads.[46]

## 15.4   TRAFFIC-SENSITIVE ROADS

The road works authority can designate a traffic-sensitive road in one of two ways.[47] It can reach an agreement on designation with a majority of statutory undertakers who either have, or are likely to have, apparatus in the road. Where agreement cannot be reached, one or more of the following criteria must be met before the road can be designated:

1.   Traffic flow must exceed certain minima. Flow rates are specified depending on the width of the carriageway, whether it is single or dual carriageway or a one way street and whether traffic is one way or both ways. These rates assume that there will be up to twelve per cent of buses or heavy goods vehicles or both. If there are more a multiplier is applied[48]. In addition, parking must either be prohibited at certain times of day[49] or not normally take place on either side of the road during these times;[50]

---

44   See para 15.2.1 above.
45   NRSWA 1991, s 122 and SI 1991/2991, reg 12(3).
46   NRSWA 1991, s 122(5). As to the list of public roads, see paragraph 4.8.1.
47   NRSWA 1991, s 123(1) and SI 1992/2991 reg 13(1).
48   SI 1992/2991 reg 13(1).
49   Under the Road Traffic Regulation Act 1984, s 1 or 9 (as amended).
50   SI 1992/2991, reg 13(1)(a).

2.   The road must be within the area of a critical signalised junction[51] or within 100 metres of a major arm[52], or fifty metres of a minor arm[53], of such a junction, or within the area of a 'critical gyratory or roundabout system'[54], or within forty metres of a major arm, or twenty metres of a minor arm, of the approach to or exit from such a system[55];

3.   The road must be one where an order is in force under sections 1 or 9 of the Road Traffic Regulation Act 1984 which prohibits its use by vehicular traffic for more than eight hours in any twenty-four hour period, or where an order has been made under section 203(2) of the Town and Country Planning (Scotland) Act 1997. In addition, the pedestrian traffic flow is at least the specified minimum.[56]

4.   The road must be a single carriageway two way road less than 6.5 metres wide having a heavy traffic flow[57] and be a trunk road or a principal road.[58]

The road can only be designated as traffic-sensitive for the times and on the dates when one or more of these criteria are met.[59] This means that in practice, the authority is fairly limited in its powers to designate if it cannot reach agreement with the undertakers.

## 15.4.1   INFORMATION ON TRAFFIC-SENSITIVE ROADS

The road works authority must make certain information available regarding traffic-sensitive roads.[60] It is required to note the date of designation and sufficient particulars of the road to enable it to be identified. Where

51   This is defined at SI 1992/2991 reg 12(4) as meaning a traffic signal junction at which, in normal circumstances, no less than 5 per cent of peak hour vehicles on average fail to clear the junction on the first green signal. Peak hour means between 7.30 and 9.30 am and 3.30 and 7 pm.

52   A major arm is an arm of a critical signalised junction which receives more than 10 seconds of green time per cycle or which is the exit for at least 10 per cent of traffic passing through the junction in the peak hour. SI 1192/2991 reg 13(4).

53   This is to be construed against the definition of major arm.

54   SI 1992/2991 reg 13(4) defines this as meaning a gyratory or roundabout system where, in normal circumstances, no less than 5 per cent of peak hour vehicles on average are delayed by more than 20 seconds. Peak hour is defined as before.

55   Here a major arm means an arm which is used by no less than 20 per cent of the vehicles using that system. Again minor arm is to be construed against the definition of major arm.

56   ie twenty-two persons per minute per metre width during the busiest hour of the relevant day.

57   ie not less than 600 vehicles an hour.

58   See R(S)A 1984, s 5, 11(1).

59   SI 1992/2991 reg 13(1).

60   NRSWA 1991, s 123(2)(c) and SI 1992/2991, reg 13(3).

the designation is limited in nature, it must also record the times of day, days, periods or occasions when the designation applies.[61] As with protected roads and roads with special engineering difficulties, the authority has to indicate that the road has been designated as traffic-sensitive in the list of public roads[62] Similarly, the road works authority must ensure that the Road Works Register records the making of a designation within seven days of it being made.[63]

## 15.5   WITHDRAWAL OF DESIGNATIONS

An authority can withdraw the designation of a road as protected or as a traffic-sensitive road at any time.[64] In each case the authority must publish a notice of withdrawal in one or more local newspapers. It must ensure that the withdrawal is recorded in the road works register within seven days. It is thought that although the regulations will require to be amended, there will be an obligation to enter similar information in the Scottish Road Works Register within a similar timescale. There are also some further specific provisions which apply to protected roads and roads with special engineering difficulties which will be considered separately below.

### 15.5.1   PROTECTED ROADS

Where a protected road designation is withdrawn, the authority can direct that any conditions imposed on the placing of apparatus in the road remain in force.[65] The authority can also continue paying any contribution it has agreed to make to the undertaker to offset his expense in complying with the conditions.[66] Where protected road status is either applied or withdrawn, the authority may give such directions as it considers appropriate in relation to works in progress at the time.[67] Any dispute over these matters is to be settled in the prescribed manner.[68]

### 15.5.2   ROADS WITH SPECIAL ENGINEERING DIFFICULTIES

Where withdrawal of designation is proposed for a road with special engineering difficulties there must be prior consultation with the transport authority or undertaker who requested the designation. If the

61   SI 1992/2991, reg 13(3).
62   NRSWA 1991, s 123(4). As to the list of public roads, see para 4.8.1.
63   See paragraph 4.8.1.
64   NRSWA 1991, s 121(1)(b), s 123(2)(b) and SI 1992/2991, Sch 1 paras 9–14.
65   NRSWA 1991 s 121(3)(a).
66   NRSWA 1991, s 121(3).
67   NRSWA 1991, s 121(4).
68   NRSWA 1991, s 121(5) as amended by section 36 of the Transport (Scotland) Act 2005.

Scottish Ministers sought the designation they must consent to the designation being withdrawn.[69]

### 15.5.3   RECORDING OF WITHDRAWAL OF DESIGNATION

The road works authority must ensure that a withdrawal of a designation is recorded in the road works register within seven days.[70] There is no penalty specified for failure to comply with this deadline.

---

69  NRSWA 1991 s 122(4); SI 1992/2991, Sch 1, paras 10, 11.
70  SI 1992/2991, Sch 1, para 13. See also the 2008 Regulations which are expected to come into effect on 1 April 2008

# 16   Road Works Safety

## 16.1   INTRODUCTION

In addition to the controls on specific types of road works already dealt
with in Chapters 14 and 15, there are more general constraints on those
carrying out roadworks. Again, these are aimed principally at ensuring
the safety of road users, as well as at minimising any delay as a result of
road works.

## 16.2   SAFETY MEASURES

Certain precautions must be taken when carrying out roadworks to protect road users from danger. An undertaker[1] must ensure that any part of
a road which is broken up or open, or which is obstructed by plant or
materials, is adequately guarded and lit.[2] There is also a duty to make
sure that any traffic signs[3] which are reasonably required for the guidance and direction of road users are placed, maintained and, if necessary,
operated.[4] For example a sign would be operated where there is a need to
control traffic with a stop/go board. An undertaker must comply with
any directions given by the traffic authority[5] for placing, maintaining or
operating any traffic signs.[6] The power of the authority to issue directions is, itself, subject to any directions made by the relevant ministers
under section 65 of the Road Traffic Regulation Act 1984. There is also a
duty to have regard to the needs of people with disabilities when considering where to place traffic signs and how they are operated.[7]

There is a code of practice on Safety at Street Works and Road Works[8]
which gives guidance to undertakers regarding their duties. If the code

1   As to 'undertaker', see paragraph 13.2.
2   NRSWA 1991, s 124(1)(a).
3   A traffic sign is 'any object or device (whether fixed or portable) for
    conveying, to traffic on roads or any specified class of traffic, warnings,
    information, requirements, restrictions or prohibition of any description –
    (a) specifically by regulations made by the relevant ministers acting jointly
    or (b) authorised by the Scottish Ministers and any line or mark on the road
    for so conveying such warnings, information, requirements, restrictions or
    prohibitions': Road Traffic Regulation Act 1984, s 64(1), 142.
4   NRSWA 1991, s 124(1)(b).
5   'Traffic authority' is defined in RTRA 1984, ss 121A and 142 (added by the
    NRSWA 1991, s 168, Sch 8, para 78). These are the Scottish Ministers where
    they are responsible for certain roads, and local authorities for the rest.
6   NRSWA 1991, s 124(2).
7   NRSWA 1991 s 124(1)(b); Roads (Scotland) Act 1984 Act, s 120.
8   NRSWA 1991, s 124(3).

has been complied with, the undertaker is presumed to have fulfilled his statutory duties.[9] However, failure to comply with its statutory duties is an offence punishable on summary conviction by a fine up to level 5 on the standard scale.[10] In addition, the road works authority itself can take steps to ensure compliance and can recover its reasonable costs in doing so from the undertaker.[11] It is not only undertakers who can be prosecuted. Any person who takes down, alters or removes any fence, barrier, traffic sign, or light or who extinguishes a light can also be fined on summary conviction up to level 5 on the standard scale.[12]

## 16.3   DELAY AND OBSTRUCTION

An undertaker must complete certain types of road works as quickly as is reasonably practicable.[13] Failure to do so is an offence which carries the penalty of a fine not exceeding level 5 on the standard scale.[14] Such works include breaking up or opening a road or any sewer, drain or tunnel under it, or tunnelling or boring under the road.[15] Where an undertaker while carrying out road works creates an obstruction greater than or for longer than reasonably necessary, the road works authority can issue a notice requiring him to take reasonable steps to mitigate or discontinue the obstruction.[16] If he fails to comply within twenty-four hours of receiving the notice, or such longer period as specified by the authority in the notice, then the authority can do what is required and recover the reasonable costs of doing so from the undertaker.[17]

## 16.4   QUALIFIED STAFF

At least one supervisor and one of the workers (referred to as a 'trained operative') carrying out certain types of road works must be qualified to do so.[18]

Where the works involve breaking up the road, or any sewer, drain or tunnel under it, or if they require tunnelling or boring under the road, then the undertaker must ensure that they are supervised by someone

9   NRSWA 1991, s 124(3).
10  NRSWA 1991, s 124(4). The maximum fine is currently £5,000: Criminal Procedure (Scotland) Act 1995, s 225. The level can be altered by statutory instrument.
11  NRSWA 1991, s 124(5).
12  NRSWA 1991, s 124(6).
13  NRSWA 1991, s 125(1).
14  NRSWA 1991, s 125(2). The maximum fine is currently £5,000: Criminal Procedure (Scotland) Act 1995, s 225. The level can be altered by statutory instrument.
15  NRSWA 1991, s 125(1).
16  NRSWA 1991, s 125(3).
17  NRSWA 1991, s 125(4).
18  NRSWA 1991, s 126(1), (2).

who has appropriate qualifications.[19] In addition the undertaker must ensure that there is at least one trained operative on site at all times when such works are being carried out.[20] The road works authority can at any time during the works or after their completion, within a prescribed period[21] give notice to an undertaker requiring him to provide the name of the current and any previous supervisors and evidence of their requisite qualification.[22] The road works authority can request the same information in respect of each trained operative.[23] The undertaker must comply with any such notice within such period and in such way as may be prescribed.[24] Consultation draft regulations have been published but these have not yet been made.[25] However it is envisaged that any notice must be served by the end of the next working day following the completion of the works; that the names of the supervisors and/or the trained operative must be provided by the undertaker within 4 hours of the roads authority giving such notice[26] unless this period would expire after 4.30pm, in which case the deadline is 10am on the next working day; and the copy of the certificate of competence must be provided within 24 hours of the giving of the notice.[27] Failure to have the requisite supervisor and trained operative on site and to comply with any notice is an offence which is punishable on summary conviction by a fine not exceeding level 5 on the standard scale.[28]

Regulations made under the 1991 Act[29] detail the areas of competence required for supervisors and operatives and specify the awarding bodies for certificates of competence. These are The City and Guilds of London Institute, The Scottish Vocational Education Council (SCOTVEC)[30] and The Certification and Assessment Board for the Water Industry. Approval may be withdrawn from the awarding bodies if they fail to

---

19  NRSWA 1991, s 126(1).
20  NRSWA 1991, s 126(2).
21  NRSWA 1991 s 126(2B). All of the new subsections of s 126 were inserted by s 26 of the Transport (Scotland) Act 2005.
22  NRSWA 1991 s 126(1A).
23  NRSWA 1991 s 126(2A).
24  NRSWA 1991 s 126(2C).
25  Following the amendments to the Act by the Transport (Scotland) Act 2005, the current regulations, The Road Works (Qualifications of Supervisors and Operatives) (Scotland) Regulations 1992 (SI 1992/1675) will be superseded by The Road Works (Qualifications of Supervisors and Operatives) (Scotland) Regulations 2008 which are due to come into force on April or May 2008. These have already been published for consultation. However it should be noted that the draft regulations may change before the final regulations are made.
26  Note that the trigger is the giving of notice and not receipt.
27  Draft consultations regs 9–11.
28  NRSWA 1991, s 126(3). Currently the maximum fine is £5,000: Criminal Procedure (Scotland) Act 1995, s 225. The level can be altered by statutory instrument.
29  SI 1992/1675.
30  Now the Scottish Qualification Authority – this change is reflected in the regulations reg 5.

discharge their functions satisfactorily in relation to certification or registration of qualifications.[31] The areas of competence for supervisors and operatives are specified in schedules to the regulations. For example, a supervisor must have a registered certificate of competence covering areas such as monitoring signing, lighting and guarding and monitoring reinstatement using various methods and materials.[32] Similarly, a trained operative must be assessed as competent in carrying out signing, lighting and guarding and various types of reinstatement. Like the supervisor, the operative must also have a registered certificate to establish this.[33] Where a supervisor or trained operative has only a limited qualification they are restricted to the types of work for which they are certificated.[34] Qualifications from other European Community states are recognised where they guarantee an equivalent level of skill and competence.[35] Qualifications are not required either to supervise or carry out replacement of poles, lamps, columns or signs, for pole testing or other similar works which involve minimal breaking up of the road.[36] Where works do not involve breaking up the road at all, an operative only needs to have a certificate of competence in signing, lighting and guarding.[37] Certificates for supervisors and operatives expire after five years but can be re-registered for further five year periods provided the application is received within three months of the expiry date of the original one.[38] It appears that there is no limit to the number of times a certificate can be re-registered, which surely defeats the purpose of the regulations! However it would appear that the consultation draft regulations will rectify this flaw. They provide that where a certificate has expired, while it can be re-registered for further five year periods provided the application is received within three months of the expiry date of the original one, it must be accompanied by a reassessment certificate.[39] It is envisaged that there would be a two year transitional period where applications do not require to be accompanied by a reassessment certificate.[40]

31  NRSWA 1991, s 126(4) and SI 1992/1675, reg 5.
32  SI 1992/1675, reg 3, Schs 3, 4.
33  SI 1992/1675, reg 4, Schs 1, 2.
34  SI 1992/1675, regs 7, 8.
35  SI 1992/1675, regs 3, 4.
36  SI 1992/1675, regs 3, 4. It should be noted that under the consultation draft regulations, a superviser will be required to have the prescribed qualification for carrying out such works in the future.
37  SI 1992/1675, reg 4(2) and Sch 1.
38  SI 1992/1675, reg 9.
39  Draft Regulations reg 8.
40  Draft Regulations reg 8(5).

## 16.5 FACILITIES FOR ROAD WORKS AUTHORITY

The 1991 Act provides that the undertaker 'shall afford the road works authority reasonable facilities for ascertaining whether he is complying with his duties under this Part.'[41] Failure to do so is an offence.[42]

## 16.6 WORKS AFFECTING OTHER APPARATUS

An undertaker has duties if road works are likely to affect another person's apparatus. First, he must take all reasonably practicable steps to give the person an opportunity to monitor the works. Secondly, the undertaker must take all reasonably practicable steps to comply with any requirement made by the owner of the apparatus which is reasonably necessary to protect the apparatus or to allow continuing access to it.[43] It is an offence on each count for an undertaker to fail to comply.[44] The undertaker has a defence if he can show that he did not know of the position of, or of the existence of the apparatus, or that he did not know the identity or address of its owner to whom the apparatus belongs. The defence is subject to the proviso that the undertaker's ignorance was not due to negligence on his part or a failure to make reasonable inquiries.[45]

41   NRSWA 1991, s 127(1).
42   NRSWA 1991, s 127(2). Each failure to comply is a separate offence and the penalty is a fine not exceeding level 4. This is currently £2,500 current procedure (Scotland) Act 1995 s 225. The level can be altered by statutory instrument on the standard scale. It is not clear from the wording of the 1991 Act whether the undertaker can have a level 3 fine imposed for each offence or in total, although there would seem to be little point in the latter.
43   NRSWA 1991, s 128(1).
44   NRSWA 1991, s 128(2). On summary conviction an undertaker will be liable to a fine not exceeding level 4 on the standard scale. The maximum fine is £2,500: current procedure (Scotland) Act 1995 s 225. The level can be altered by statutory instrument.
45   NRSWA 1991, s 128(3).

# 17 Reinstatement Following Road Works

## 17.1 INTRODUCTION

Reinstatement following road works is a vitally important issue and is one which earlier legislation failed adequately to address. The Public Utilities Street Works Act 1950 made undertakers responsible for reinstatement. However, it also allowed undertakers and road works authorities to make agreements as to responsibility for reinstatement. In practice, this led to undertakers carrying out temporary reinstatement only and then meeting the road works authorities costs for permanent reinstatement. The result of this was very often considerable delay in making good road works. The 1991 Act makes undertakers responsible for all aspects of reinstatement. The road works authority's role is to monitor and enforce the relevant statutory provisions. It only carries out reinstatement itself as a last resort.[1]

## 17.2 DUTY TO REINSTATE

The 1991 Act imposes a duty on the undertaker who carries out road works to reinstate the road as soon as reasonably practicable after completion of any part of the work.[2] This clearly envisages an ongoing programme of reinstatement as the work progresses, rather than leaving it all until the end. Reinstatement must be carried out and completed 'with all such dispatch as is reasonably practicable.'[3] In addition, the undertaker must give the required notice not later than a day after the road works are completed and indicate whether the reinstatement carried out is permanent or interim.[4] The undertaker gives the required notice by first giving to the Commissioner a notice containing the prescribed information and secondly by entering a copy of the notice into the Register.[5] Permanent reinstatement is defined as 'the orderly placement and proper compaction of reinstatement layers up to and

1   See below at para 17.4.
2   NRSWA 1991, s 129(1), (2).
3   NRSWA 1991, s 129(2).
4   NRSWA 1991, s 129(3) as amended by s 28(a) of the Transport (Scotland) Act 2005.
5   NRSWA 1991 s 129(5A) as inserted by s 28(a) of the Transport (Scotland) Act 2005.

including the finished surface level[6] Interim reinstatement is 'the orderly placement and proper compaction of reinstatement layers to finished surface level, including any temporary materials'.[7] If permanent, any features designed to assist those with a disability must be reinstated.[8] Such features may include tactile paving which is used to alert the visually impaired to the fact that they are approaching a road crossing. If the reinstatement is interim, permanent reinstatement must then be completed as soon as reasonably practicable and in any case not more than six months after, or with the agreement of the road works authority, no more than twelve months after completion of the interim reinstatement.[9] Again the undertaker must give the required notice of when reinstatement has been carried out.[10]

Failure to comply with any of the 1991 Act's provisions on reinstatement is an offence for which the undertaker is liable on summary conviction to a fine up to level 5 on the standard scale.[11] It is a defence if the reason for delay in reinstating was to avoid hindering other works or other parts of the same works which were to be undertaken immediately or shortly after the works which were not reinstated.[12]

## 17.3   STANDARD OF REINSTATEMENT

The appropriate standard of reinstatement is specified, including the materials to be used and the quality of the workmanship.[13] This standard is detailed in the Road Works (Reinstatement) (Scotland) Regulations 1992[14] and in the code of practice.[15] The standard of reinstatement depends on the type of road or footpath involved, the nature of the roadworks and on the volume of traffic on the road.[16] Where the volume of traffic exceeds specified limits[17] reinstatement standards are agreed

6    See the Code of Practice (Code of Practice October 2003) Specification for the Reinstatement of Openings in Highways, October 2003 approved by the Scottish Ministers on 8 September 2003 (Code of Practice October 2003) – Definitions section. This code can be revised or re-issued from time to time. This version of the Code of Practice superseded the previous version dated June 1992.
7    See Code of Practice October 2003.
8    NRSWA 1991, s 129(5).
9    The Road Works (Reinstatement) (Scotland) Regulations 1992, SI 1674, reg 10. These regulations have been amended by the Road Works (Reinstatement) (Scotland) Amendment Regulations 1992 SI 1992/3062; the Road Works (Reinstatement) (Scotland) Amendment Regulations 2003 SI 2003/417 and the Road Works (Reinstatement) (Scotland) Amendment (No.2) Regulations 2003 SI 2003/512 (SI 1992/1674 as amended).
10   NRSWA 1991, s 129(4) as amended by s 28(b) of the Transport (Scotland) Act 2005.
11   NRSWA 1991, s 129(6). The maximum fine is currently £5,000: Criminal Procedure (Scotland) Act 1995 s 225. The level can be altered by statutory instrument.
12   NRSWA 1991, s 129(7).
13   NRSWA 1991, s 130(1).
14   SI 1992/1674 as amended – see footnote 9 above.
15   Code of Practice October 2003.
16   SI 1992/1674 and the Code of Practice October 2003.
17   Which is currently 125 million standard axles – SI 1992/1674 as amended.

between the undertaker and the road works authority on an individual basis.[18] The Code of Practice also recognises the possibility of innovation and the use of new materials in reinstatement, provided this is agreed in advance with the authority. An undertaker is allowed to adopt an alternative specification for materials, layer thicknesses and compaction materials to take advantage of new or local materials and/or compaction equipment provided he has the prior approval of the authority, which is not to be unreasonably withheld.[19] This represents a risk for the undertaker as he must still meet the performance standards for the specified period, regardless of whether he has used new, untried and untested methods and/or materials. Similarly, recycled, secondary or virgin materials are allowed provided that they meet the performance and composition requirements.[20]

There are different standards for interim and permanent re-instatement. Interim reinstatement must conform to prescribed standards until permanent reinstatement is carried out, while permanent reinstatement must meet these standards for a specified period after completion of the work.[21] The period begins on completion of the permanent reinstatement and usually runs for two years, three if a 'deep opening' is involved.[22] It should be noted that the period runs from completion of the permanent reinstatement rather than the giving of the requisite notice.[23] The obligations regarding interim and permanent reinstatement are extended in some cases and restricted in others where this is affected by subsequent works.[24] The regulations also identify works classified as 'immediate'. There is a slight variation between the definition of these works given in the regulations and in the Code of Practice. Essentially, immediate works involve 'the orderly replacement of excavated material, reasonably compacted to finished surface level'.[25] However the regulations provide that the finish will be a deferred set macadam[25] whereas the Code of Practice provides for a cold-laying surfacing.[26]

Compliance by the undertaker with the Code of Practice is taken to be a discharge of his duties under the 1991 Act and the regulations, while failure to adhere to it is evidence of non-compliance.[27] Such failure is an offence and the undertaker is again liable on summary conviction to a

18   Code of Practice October 2003, s 1.3.2.
19   Code of Practice October 2003 s 1.6.1.
20   Code of Practice October 2003 s 1.6.2.
21   NRSWA 1991, s 130(2). This is referred to in the Code of Practice October 2003 as 'the guarantee period': p 1, ss 1.1.3 and 1.2.
22   Code of Practice October 2003, ss 1.2.1 and 1.2.2. A 'deep opening' is basically one in which the depth of cover over buried plant or equipment is greater than 1.5 metres. Trenches which fall intermittently below 1.5m depth of cover for lengths of less than 5 metres are deemed not to be deep openings.
23   Code of Practice October 2003 s 1.2.2. cf paragraph 18.2 and NRSWA 1991 s 129(6).
24   NRSWA 1991, s 130(2) and s 132..
25   SI 1992/1674 reg 2(1).
26   Code of Practice October 2003 Definitions.
27   NRSWA 1991, s 130(4).

fine not exceeding level 5 on the standard scale.[28] There is provision in the Code of Practice for any disputes arising under it to be settled by arbitration.[29] However both the road works authority and the undertakers are encouraged to use their best endeavours to resolve disputes rather than resorting to dispute resolution.[30]

## 17.4  POWERS OF ROAD WORKS AUTHORITY

The road works authority has powers to conduct such investigations as appear necessary to ascertain whether an undertaker is fulfilling his duties to reinstate. If an undertaker has not complied, he bears the cost of the investigation; otherwise the road works authority is responsible for the investigation costs and for any reinstatement which is necessary as a result.[31] Included in the costs which may fall on the undertaker where he has failed to comply with his duty, are those of a joint inspection with the road works authority to determine the nature of the failure and to assess what remedial works are needed, as well as for an inspection by the authority of the remedial works in progress and on completion.[32] The road works authority can serve notice on the undertaker requiring him to carry out remedial works within a period not to be shorter than the period to be prescribed by regulation.[33] Different periods can be prescribed for different types of remedial works. In some cases no minimum period may apply.[34] Where there is a minimum period, the notice period cannot be any shorter than that period prescribed. If the undertaker fails to carry out the remedial works, the authority can do the work and recover its costs reasonably incurred.[35] If the authority considers there is a danger to road users it can do the work itself without giving notice and still recover its reasonable costs from the undertaker. In such circumstances, it must give notice to the undertaker as soon as reasonably practicable stating why it was necessary to take immediate action.[36]

Unlike other sections of the 1991 Act, these provisions do not make any provision for the Scottish Ministers to issue or approve a Code of

28  NRSWA 1991, s 130(5) as amended. The maximum fine is currently £5,000: Criminal Procedure (Scotland) Act 1995 s 225. The level can be altered by statutory instrument.
29  Code of Practice October 2003 s 1.11.2. Reference is made to the provisions set out in the Code of Practice for the Co-ordination of Street Works and Works for Road Purposes and Related Matters. It should be noted that this Code of Practice will be superseded with a Code of Practice which is expected to be released in March 2008.
30  Code of Practice October 2003 s 1.11.1.
31  NRSWA 1991, s 131(1).
32  NRSWA 1991, s 131(2).
33  NRSWA 1991, s 131(3) as amended by s 29(1)(a) of the Transport (Scotland) Act 2005.
34  NRSWA 1991, s 131(3A) as inserted by s 29(1)(b) of the Transport (Scotland) Act 2005.
35  NRSWA 1991, s 131(3) as amended.
36  NRSWA 1991, s 131(4).

Practice in respect of inspections. However the road authorities and undertakers have agreed that it would be prudent to have a code, albeit a non-statutory one, to cover amongst other things inspections.[37] In addition the Road Works (Inspection Fees)(Scotland) Regulations 2003 (as amended) set out prescribed fees.[38]

## 17.5 SUBSEQUENT WORKS

Where reinstatement works fail during the guarantee period the undertaker must carry out remedial works.[39] If in doing so he exceeds what is prescribed in the regulations and Code of Practice, then the subsequent re-instatement is treated as new works in terms of the guarantee period.[40] This means that the two or three year guarantee period will run from the date of completion of the remedial works.

An undertaker's responsibility for a reinstatement ceases if the roads authority disturbs it while investigating for possible non-compliance with his duties under the 1991 Act, but only where there has been no failure by the undertaker.[41] If there is a failure by the undertaker, he remains responsible. Where the road works authority has carried out the works due to default by the undertaker,[42] he is held responsible for the subsequent reinstatement. Where this exceeds the original works, the undertaker is also responsible for the new work for the full guarantee period which will run from the date of completion of the remedial works.[43]

In other situations where reinstatement is affected by subsequent works other than the remedial works, the undertaker's responsibility ceases to the extent that the reinstatement is dug out in the course of such works.[44] If the reinstatement does not comply with the required standards due to subsequent works, responsibility is transferred to whoever carried out those subsequent works.[45] The reinstatement provisions of the Act apply to someone executing subsequent works in the same way as they would have applied to the original undertaker.[46] Where successive works are carried out on a reinstatement, there is a presumption that it is the person responsible for the latest works who is liable for any failure unless they can prove that this is not the case.[47]

37  Code of Practice for Inspections October 2003, which applies to Scotland only. It should be noted that this supersedes the Code of Practice for Inspections which came in to force in England, Wales and Scotland on 1 January 1993.
38  The Road Works (Inspection Fees) (Scotland) Regulations 2003 as amended by the Road Works (Inspection Fees) (Scotland) Amendment Regulations 2007, which came in to force on 1 April 2007. The current prescribed fee is £24.
39  NRSWA 1991, s 130(2) and s 132.
40  NRSWA 1991, s 132(2).
41  NRSWA 1991, s 131(1), 132(3).
42  NRSWA 1991, s 131(3), (4).
43  NRSWA 1991, s 132(4).
44  NRSWA 1991, s 132(5), (6).
45  NRSWA 1991, s 132(7).
46  NRSWA 1991, s 132(7).
47  NRSWA 1991, s 132(8).

# 18 Resurfacing

## 18.1 INTRODUCTION

The 2005 Act gives road works authorities a new power to require undertakers to resurface a road in certain circumstances.[1]

## 18.2 POWER TO REQUIRE AN UNDERTAKER TO RESURFACE ROAD

Where an undertaker has given notice under s113 or s114 of proposed road works, or is executing road works, or has executed works and the works involve or will involve or have involved breaking up any part of the road,[2] the road works authority can serve notice on the undertaker requiring him to execute the resurfacing works specified in the notice.[3] "Resurfacing works" means any works relating to the replacement of the surface of any part of the road.[4] "Surface" includes a paved surface.[5] The resurfacing works can relate to any part of the road even parts of the road which have not been broken up by the undertaker[6] however the obligation to resurface the road relieves the undertaker of any obligation to reinstate the surface of the road.[7] The notice can be varied or withdrawn at any time by the road works authority[8] and the notice may include resurfacing works which the road works authority is under a duty, in whatever capacity, to carry out.[9] Regulations may restrict the extent of the resurfacing works which can be specified, the extent of the relief from reinstatement and the circumstances in which notices may be varied or withdrawn by the road works authority.[10]

## 18.3 POWER TO SPECIFY TIMING OF RESURFACING

Any notice served by the road works authority can require the undertaker to execute the specified works in stages and can specify the

1   NRSWA 1991, ss 132A, 132B, 132C, 132D, 132E and 137A as inserted by s 30–32 of the Transport (Scotland) Act 2005.
2   NRSWA 1991, s 132A(2).
3   NRSWA 1991, s 132A(1).
4   NRSWA 1991, s 132A(7).
5   NRSWA 1991, s 132A(7).
6   NRSWA 1991, s 132A(3).
7   NRSWA 1991, s 132A(4). See also chapter 17 on reinstatement.
8   NRSWA 1991, s 132A(5).
9   NRSWA 1991, s 132A(6).
10  NRSWA 1991, s 132A(3), (4) and (5). To date no regulations have been made. However is it expected that regulations will be made in 2009.

commencement date of the works, the times and days on which the works can be carried out and the date by which the works must be completed.[11] Regulations may restrict the power of the road works authority to impose such conditions and may require that any prescribed timescales, whether for the commencement, execution or completion of the works, are no earlier than the date on which the notice is given.[12] In addition the road works authority may also have to consult with the undertaker prior to imposing such condition.[13]

## 18.4   MATERIALS, WORKMANSHIP AND STANDARD OF RESURFACING

The undertaker must comply with any requirements prescribed in the notice in respect of the specification of the materials to be used and the standards of workmanship to be observed. The works must meet any prescribed performance standards for the prescribed period after completion.[14] Again it is likely that regulations will be made in this regard.[13]

## 18.5   CONTRIBUTION TO COSTS OF RESURFACING BY THE UNDERTAKER

Where both the road works authority and undertakers are working on an area of road in respect of which a notice has been served on another undertaker to complete the resurfacing, both the road works authority and the other undertakers must make a contribution to the costs of such works.[15] The road works authority will pay a proportion of the costs reasonably incurred by the undertaker in carrying out the resurfacing works specified in the notice.[16] Costs incurred by the undertaker as a consequence of his failure to comply with any duty under the 1991 Act will be treated as unreasonable costs.[17] Other undertakers will pay a proportion of the costs.[18] All payments, whether payable by the road works authority or the other undertakers can be paid in instalments, if prescribed, and in such manner as may be prescribed.[19] Any disputes will be determined in the prescribed manner.[20]

11   NRSWA 1991, s 132B(1).
12   NRSWA 1991, s 132B(2)(b).
13   NRSWA 1991, s 132B(2)(a). To date no regulations have been made. See footnote 10.
14   NRSWA 1991, s 132C(2).
15   NRSWA 1991, s 137A(1).
16   NRSWA 1991, s 137A(1)(a).
17   NRSWA 1991, s 137A(6).
18   NRSWA 1991, s137A(1)(b). Note that these costs do not have to be reasonable however the Scottish Minister may prescribe exemptions which are not recoverable – s 137A(3).
19   NRSWA 1991, s 137A(4).
20   This is likely to be by arbitration. See the draft regulations: The Road Works (Settlement of Disputes and Appeals against Directions) (Scotland) Regulations which are expected to come into force on 1 April 2008. It should be noted that there may be changes between the draft regulations and the final regulations once made.

## 18.6   REGULATIONS

The Scottish Ministers can make regulations to prescribe the following: (1) the information to be contained in the resurfacing notice to be served by the road works authority, including the way in which the works are described; (2) the matters which the road works authority should take into account when determining on which undertaker to serve the notice, where there may be more than one undertaker who could carry out the resurfacing works; (3) the circumstances where the undertaker is required to give notice to on the road works authority for certain prescribed events; (4) the circum-stances where the undertaker can make a payment to the road works authority in lieu of carrying out the works including the mechanism for calculating the amount of such payment; (5) the provision for appeals including the procedure to be followed; (6) the manner in which disputes will be dealt with; and (7) the application of the Roads (Scotland) Act 1984.[21] It is an offence for an undertaker to fail to comply with the regulations.[22] The first regulations to be made must be laid before and approved by the Scottish Parliament.[23]

## 18.7   CODE OF PRACTICE

The Scottish Ministers must issue or approve a code of practice giving practical guidance to the roads works authority regarding the exercise of its powers in respect of resurfacing and also to undertaker regarding the discharge of its duties in that regard. Both the road works authority and the undertaker must have regard to the code when exercising their powers or discharging their duties.[24]

---

21   NRSWA 1991, s 132D(2).
22   NRSWA 1991, s 132D(3). He is liable on summary conviction to a fine not exceeding level 4 (£2,500) where he has failed to give a notice in accordance with the regulations. In all other cases he is liable on summary conviction to a fine not exceeding level 5 (£5,000) on the standard scale: Criminal Procedure (Scotland) Act 1995 s225. The levels can be altered by statutory instrument.
23   NRSWA 1991, s 132D(4).
24   NRSWA 1991, s 132E. It is unlikely that the code of practice will be issued until April 2009 to coincide with the making of the regulations – see footnote 10.

# 19 Payments in Connection with Road Works

## 19.1 INTRODUCTION

Although the 1991 Act makes provision for payments to be made in connection with road works in a variety of situations, while all of the provisions are now in force,[1] the regulations required to implement many of these provisions have not, in fact, been made. This is because of difficulties such as quantifying the cost, the administration required and potential difficulties with enforcement.

## 19.2 CHARGE FOR OCCUPATION OF ROAD

The power to charge an undertaker for occupying the road was intended to be used where the undertaker took too long to complete the road works, resulting in road users being denied access to the road for longer than necessary. While the Scottish Ministers may make regulations which would require an undertaker to pay the road works authority for occupying the road,[2] the regulations necessary for implementation have not been made and it is submitted that it is not likely now that such regulations will be made.

## 19.3 INSPECTION FEES

Regulations have, however, been made for the payment by undertakers to road works authorities of fees where a road works authority carries out inspections of road works.[3] The fee is currently £24.00 for a charge-

---

1   NRSWA 1991 s 134 came in to force on 14 July 1992: The New Roads and Street Works Act 1991 (Commencement No.4 Order) (Scotland) Order 1992 SI1992/1671; s 133, 135–137 all came in to force on 1 January 1993: The New Roads and Street Works Act 1991 (Commencement No.6 and Transitional Provisions and Savings) (Scotland) Order 1992 SI 1992/2990.
2   NRSWA 1991, s 133.
3   See NRSWA 1991, s 134 and the Road Works (Inspection Fees) (Scotland) Regulations 2003 SI 2003/415 as amended by the Road Works (Inspection Fees) (Scotland) Amendment Regulations 2007 SI2007/4. These Regulations revoke the Road Works (Inspection Fees) (Scotland) Regulations 1992, SI 1992/1676 (amended by SI 1998/1029).

able inspection of works which involve the excavation or reinstatement of any part of a road.[4]

An undertaker who has permission to carry out road works under section 109 of the 1991 Act[5] can be charged a fee for inspection of works, or a phase of works, subject to a maximum of thirty inspections where the estimated number of units of inspection in a year is less than 100.[6] If the estimate is 100 or more then the undertaker can be charged for random inspections of not more than 10.5% of each phase of works or not more than 30% of the estimated total.[7] This latter provision also applies to statutory undertakers as well as to those granted permission under section 109 of the 1991 Act.[8] The regulations define a 'unit of inspection'[9] and 'phases of work'.[10] It is envisaged that there will be inspections during excavation, during reinstatement and at several points after reinstatement including three months before the end of the guarantee period of either two or three years.[11] There are provisions for calculating the number of units of inspection.[12] Where an undertaker has not previously executed any road works, the undertaker must provide the roads authority with an estimate of the number of units of inspection for that year which is to be updated quarterly to reflect the actual number of inspections.[13] If the undertaker fails to provide this information, the roads authority can charge for as many inspections as it considers appropriate until the information which is provided.[14]

It is not clear how any dispute arising out of the regulations would be settled as there is no provision either in the 1991 Act or in the regulations referring the matter to arbitration.[15]

## 19.4   LIABILITY FOR COSTS

The 1991 Act allows the road works authority to recover certain expenses from undertakers incurred as a result of road works. The cost of a temporary prohibition or restriction of traffic or the cost of using an alternative route during road works may be passed on to the undertaker.

4    SI 2003/415 as amended.
5    As to which see para [13.5] above.
6    SI 2003/415, reg 3(2)(a).
7    SI 2003/415, reg 3(2)(b).
8    SI 2003/415, reg 3(2)(c). See para [13.2] above for a discussion of the difference between an 'undertaker' and a 'statutory undertaker'.
9    SI 2003/415 as amended reg 3(3).
10   SI 2003/415 as amended, reg 3(4).
11   SI 1992/1676, reg 3(4). See also para 17.3 above.
12   SI 2003/415 regs 5–9.
13   SI 203/415 reg 7.
14   SI 2003/415 reg 8.
15   Previously the regulations provided that any dispute would be referred to arbitration. NRSWA 1991 s 158 only applies to those sections of the 1991 Act which state whether they are to be settled by arbitration. NRSWA 1991 s 134 is silent.

These do not require regulations for implementation and the relevant sections of the Act are in force.

### 19.4.1   TEMPORARY TRAFFIC REGULATION

If as a result of road works an authority makes an order or issues a notice under section 14 of the Road Traffic Regulation Act 1984 temporarily prohibiting or restricting traffic, the whole cost can be recovered from the undertaker. This includes the cost of notifying the public if necessary and of providing traffic signs.[16]

### 19.4.2   ALTERNATIVE ROUTE

If traffic is diverted as a result of road works, the undertaker can be made to indemnify the authority for the associated costs. This power can be exercised when the use of a road is restricted or prohibited as a result of works and traffic then uses a lower classification road. Payment can be sought for any sums reasonably incurred by the roads authority to strengthen the road, in so far as it is done with a view to and is necessary for the purpose of being used by diverted traffic, and to make good any damage as a result of it being used as a diversion.[17]

## 19.5   CONTRIBUTIONS FOR LONG TERM DAMAGE

The Scottish Ministers have the power to make regulations requiring an undertaker executing roadworks to contribute to the costs incurred, or likely to be incurred, by the road works authority in the reconstruction or resurfacing of the road.[18] To date, no such regulations have been made.[19]

---

16   NRSWA 1991, s 135.
17   NRSWA 1991, s 136. As to the classification of roads, see NRSWA 1991, s 136(2) and R(S)A 1984, ss 11 and 51.
18   NRSWA 1991, s 137.
19   It is submitted that it is unlikely that regulations will be made given the resurfacing provisions inserted into the 1991 Act by the transport (Scotland) Act 2005.

# 20   Apparatus in a Road

## 20.1   INTRODUCTION

This chapter deals with the duties and liabilities of undertakers in relation to apparatus in a road. It also considers the special provisions which apply where works for road purposes are likely to affect apparatus.

## 20.2   LOCATION OF APPARATUS AND DUTY TO INFORM

The parts of the 1991 Act which would require an undertaker to keep a record of the location of his own apparatus and to advise where they discover another undertaker's apparatus, either where it is not supposed to be or in the wrong place, are not yet in force.[1]

## 20.3   DUTY TO MAINTAIN APPARATUS

An undertaker with apparatus in a road has a duty to maintain it to the reasonable satisfaction of both the road works authority and any other relevant authority.[2] In maintaining the apparatus, the undertaker must satisfy the roads works authority as to the safety and convenience of people using the road (including those with a disability) as well as in respect of both the structure of the road and the integrity of the road works authority's apparatus in the road.[3] He must also satisfy any other relevant authority (for example a bridge or transport authority) as regards any land, structure or apparatus of theirs.[4] Both the road works authority and any other relevant authority must be given reasonable facilities by the undertaker to check that these duties are being met and that the apparatus is being maintained accordingly.[5] In this regard, 'maintenance' is defined as 'the carrying out of such works as are necessary to keep the apparatus in efficient working condition (including the periodic renewal where appropriate); and includes works rendered necessary by other works in the road, other than major works for roads purposes, major bridge works or major transport works.'[6] These major

1   NRSWA 1991, ss 138, 139.
2   NRSWA 1991, s 140(1).
3   NRSWA 1991, s 140(1)(a).
4   NRSWA 1991, s 140(1)(b).
5   NRSWA 1991, s 140(1).
6   NRSWA 1991, s 140(2).

works are excluded because they are the subject of separate provision.[7] If the undertaker does not facilitate the necessary inspection by the road works authority of relevant apparatus, the road works authority can carry out such works as are necessary to enable them to inspect the apparatus which can include breaking up or opening the road.[8] The road works authority can use this power where it has cause to believe that the apparatus has not been maintained due to subsidence or disturbance of the road surface.[9] 'Relevant apparatus' is specified in The Road Works (Maintenance) (Scotland) Regulations 1992 SI 1992/1673.[10] It includes manhole covers and chambers, tunnels or other structures affecting the integrity of the road's structure. If the apparatus has not been properly maintained, the road works authority can carry out emergency work to remedy the situation[11] and the undertaker will indemnify the road works authority in respect of its reasonable costs incurred in doing so[12], both for the investigation and the work itself. Before doing so, the road works authority must serve notice on any other relevant authority stating the general nature of the necessary works.[13] Other relevant authorities have the same powers to act in any situation where their land, structures or apparatus are affected.[14] These provisions do not exclude any other way of securing compliance with the duty to maintain apparatus.[15]

## 20.4   LIABILITY FOR DAMAGE OR LOSS TO APPARATUS

An undertaker is liable for damage or loss caused to others as a result of carrying out road works or as a result of an "event" caused by the carrying out of roads works.[16] 'An event' occurs if he causes an escape of gas, electricity, water or other supply or service which causes an explosion, ignition, discharge or other event.[17] In any of these situations he must compensate the road works authority and any other relevant authority for any loss or damage suffered.[18] He must also compensate any other person who has apparatus in the road for the reasonable expense of making good any damage to that apparatus.[19]

---

7    See NRSWA 1991, s 143 and s 144. See also paragraph 20.5.2 below.
8    NRSWA 1991, s 140(3).
9    NRSWA 1991, s 140(3) and SI 1992/1673, reg 3.
10   SI 1992/1673 reg 2.
11   NRSWA 1991, s 140(4).
12   NRSWA 1991, s 140(5).
13   NRSWA 1991, s 140(6).
14   NRSWA 1991, s 140 (1), (3) and (4).
15   NRSWA 1991, s 140(7).
16   NRSWA 1991 s 141(1).
17   NRSWA 1991, s 141(2).
18   NRSWA 1991, s 141(1)(a).
19   NRSWA 1991, s 141(1)(b).

This liability is strict as it arises whether or not there has been negligence by the undertaker or anyone whom he is responsible for[20] and is notwithstanding the fact that he is acting in pursuance of statutory duty.[21] However, the undertaker is not held liable for damage or loss attributable to the misconduct or negligence of either the person suffering the damage or loss, a person for whom he is responsible or a third party.[22] This does not exonerate the undertaker from any liability which he would otherwise be subject to.[23] This could allow a third party, for example, to pursue a claim against an undertaker based on common law negligence.

## 20.5   WORKS FOR ROAD PURPOSES AND THE PROTECTION OF APPARATUS

The 1991 Act allows certain steps to be taken to protect apparatus likely to be affected by works for road purposes. The steps which require to be taken depend on whether the works are major or not.

### 20.5.1   APPARATUS AFFECTED BY WORKS FOR ROADS PURPOSES

Where works for roads purposes are likely to affect apparatus in the road, the authority executing the works must take all reasonably practicable steps to give the owner of the apparatus reasonable facilities to monitor the works. The authority must also comply with any requirement of the owner which is reasonably necessary to protect the apparatus or to ensure access to it.[24] 'Works for roads purposes' are defined in the Act[25] as meaning works for the maintenance of the road, works of improvement,[26] the erection, maintenance, alteration or removal of traffic signs or the construction of a crossing for vehicles across a footway or the strengthening or adaptation of a footway for use as a vehicle crossing. Each failure to comply is a separate offence which is punishable by a fine not exceeding level 4 on the standard scale.[27] An authority has a defence if it can show that its failure was as a result of it not knowing the position of, or of the existence of, the apparatus or the identity or address of the owner, provided this was not due to negligence on the authority's part or to a failure to make reasonable inquiries.[28]

---

20   Defined in NRSWA 1991, s 141(5) as either his contractors or employees or employees of his contractor.
21   NRSWA 1991, s 141(3).
22   NRSWA 1991, s 141(4).
23   NRSWA 1991, s 141(6).
24   NRSWA 1991, s 142(2).
25   NRSWA 1991 s 145(2)
26   As defined in the R(S)A 1984, s 151.
27   NRSWA 1991, s 142(3). The maximum fine is currently £2,500: Criminal Procedure (Scotland) Act 1995 s 225. The level can be altered by statutory instrument.
28   NRSWA 1991, s 142(4).

## 20.5.2   APPARATUS AFFECTED BY MAJOR WORKS FOR ROAD PURPOSES

Where major works for either road, bridge or transport purposes may affect an undertaker's apparatus, reasonable steps must be taken to ensure that any protective measures which are necessary are put in place and that the work itself is carried out efficiently and avoids unnecessary delay.[29] The onus is placed on both the appropriate authority (roads, bridge or transport authority) and the undertaker both of whom need to identify any measures which are necessary either as a result of the works or to facilitate the works.[30] They are then required to agree a specification of the measures and who is to undertake them, as well as to co-ordinate the implementation of the measures and the works themselves.[31]

'Major works for roads purposes' are defined in the 1991 Act[32] as meaning those carried out by the roads authority where the road consists of or includes a carriageway and which involve a) road reconstruction or widening; b) substantial alteration of the level of the road; c) the provision, alteration of the position or width, or substantial alteration in the level of a carriageway, footpath or cycle track in the road; d) the construction or removal of a road hump;[33] e) the creation of a new access over a verge or footway;[34] f) the provision of a cattle grid in the road or related ancillary works, or g) tunnelling or boring under the road. A code of practice gives guidance to authorities and undertakers on how they should discharge their duties.[35] The 1991 Act provides that disputes between the authority and the undertaker in relation to these duties shall, failing agreement, be settled in the prescribed manner.[36] It also provides that failure to comply with any agreement or with the arbiter's decision made in settlement of the dispute renders the party in default liable to compensate the other for any resultant loss or damage.[37]

---

29   NRSWA 1991, s 143(1).
30   NRSWA 1991, s 143(1)(a).
31   NRSWA 1991, s 143(1)(b), (c).
32   NRSWA 1991 s 145(3).
33   As defined in R(S)A 1984, s 40.
34   In exercise of the power contained in R(S)A 1983, s 63.
35   NRSWA 1991, s 143(2). See also *Measures Necessary Where Apparatus is Affected by Major Works (Diversionary Works)* (June 1992). This code of practice may be revised or re-issued from time to time.
36   NRSWA 1991, s 143(3). as amended by s 36 of the Transport (Scotland) Act 2005. Disputes are likely to be settled by the Commissioner: See the Draft Regulations: The Roads Works (Settlement of Disputes and Appeals against Directions) (Scotland) Regulations reg 3. These are expected to come into force on 1 April 2008. However there may be changes between the draft regulations and the final regulations once made. See also paragraph 21.8.
37   NRSWA 1991, s 143(4).

## 20.6  SHARING OF COSTS OF DIVERSIONARY WORKS

The cost of taking necessary measures in relation to apparatus in consequence of the works or in order to facilitate their execution, referred to as "diversionary works"[38] is shared between the appropriate authority[39] and the undertaker where the latter's apparatus is affected by major works for roads, bridge or transport purposes.[40] The regulations which govern this are quite complex and specify both what costs are allowable and the proportion to be paid by each party.[41]

"Allowable costs" are defined as the sum of all the reasonable costs incurred in executing the diversionary works except (1) costs incurred in preparing the initial set of plans and estimates in relation to those diversionary works; and (2) any costs in respect of apparatus placed in the road after the undertaker has been notified not more than ten years before of authority's intention to carry out major works involving bridge replacement or, where any other works are involved, not more than five years before.[42]

If the authority initiates the major works and the undertaker carries out the diversionary works as a result, the authority has to pay the undertaker his allowable costs.[43] If payment is made by a lump sum in advance of the works or, where the estimated duration of the works is longer than three months, the parties agree that the payment can be made by instalments while the work is ongoing, the authority is liable for a reduced percentage of the allowable costs.[44] In all other cases the authority is liable for the whole of the allowable costs.[45]

If the authority carries out the diversionary works itself then the undertaker is liable to pay a percentage of the allowable costs.[46] In this case there are two categories of costs which will be disallowed. First, costs for the provision of adequate space in the structure of a bridge or

---

38  The Road Works (Sharing of Costs of Works) (Scotland) Regulations 2003 SSI 2003/509 reg 2.
39  A roads, bridge or transport authority.
40  NRSWA 1991, s 144(1).
41  NRSWA 1991, s 144(2). See The Road Works (Sharing of Costs of Works) (Scotland) Regulations 2003, SSI2003/509 which revoked The Road Works (Sharing of Costs of Works) (Scotland) Regulations 1992, SI 1992/1672. The latter will still apply where a formal notice to proceed with major works was served prior 18 November 2003: SSI2003/509 reg 10(2).
42  SSI 2003/509 reg 2, 6(3).
43  SSI 2–3/509 reg 3.
44  SSI 2003/509 regs 3 and 8. In the case of major transport works the reduced percentage is 92.5% of the allowable costs; and in all other cases the reduced percentage is 52.1.
45  SSI 2003/509 reg 3.
46  SI 1992/1672, reg 4. In the case of major transport works 7.5% of the allowable costs; and in all other cases 18% of the overall costs.

bridge strengthening to accommodate the undertaker's apparatus.[47] Second, costs in respect of apparatus placed after the undertaker has been notified not more than ten years before of the authority's intention to carry out major works involving bridge replacement or, where any other works are involved, not more than five years before.[48]

The undertaker is liable for the whole allowable cost where works are initiated and carried out by the authority and his apparatus is moved at his request solely because of a change in the road's construction involving a relatively minor alteration in the depth.[49]

If neither the authority nor the undertaker initiates the major works[50] then the proportion of the cost payable depends on who carries out the diversionary works; if it is the authority, then those provisions will apply.[51] If it is the undertaker, then those provisions will apply.[52] However in calculating the cost of diversionary works, any sums recoverable from either a third party for whom the works are carried out or from the authority itself are taken into account in favour of the undertaker, whether or not the sums are actually received.[53] Where diversionary works (whether by the undertaker or the authority) results in betterment of the undertaker's apparatus or in postponement of the need to renew it, this is taken into account in the authority's favour. In both instances, the amount is calculated in accordance with the code of practice.[54] Where an authority can recover their costs for carrying out diversionary works from a third party but the works have been carried out by the undertaker, the authority has the right to recover the undertaker's costs in taking those measures from the third party and the authority will account to the undertaker for any sum received.[55]

After the diversionary works have been completed, if there is any balance payable in respect of the allowable costs, the person to whom the balance is due will issue an invoice to the other party which must be paid within 35 days.[56] If the original payment by the authority was more

---

47   SSI 2003/509 reg 6(1). Note the terms of reg 6(2). Notwithstanding reg 6(1), the allowable costs will include the cost of any ducts, pipe bays, hangers or other provision for housing or supporting the apparatus within the structure of the bridge and the cost of providing adequate space or strength to accommodate future apparatus.

48   SI 1992/1672, reg 6.

49   SI 1992/1672, reg 4(2). See also the Code of Practice entitled "Measures Necessary where appartus is affected by Major Works (Diversionary Works) dated June 1992.

50   For example where the authorised undertaker under a Private Act or an undertaker on behalf of a funder or developer initiates the major works.

51   SSI 2003/509 reg 3.

52   SSI 2003/509 reg 4.

53   SI 1992/1672, reg 5(4).

54   See SSI 2003/509 reg 7 and the Code of Practice.

55   NRSWA 1991 s 144(3).

56   SSI 2003/509 reg 8(2).

than the actual allowable costs, the undertaker will refund the excess to the authority within 35 days.[57]

The cost sharing regulations do not apply to permission to execute road works under section 109 of the 1991 Act, to consent to place apparatus in a protected road under section 120, or to the cost of removal or alteration of the position of apparatus in a protected road in terms of section 121.[58]

---

57   SSI 2003/509 reg 8(3).
58   SSI 2003/509 reg 9.

# 21 Administration of Road Works

## 21.1 INTRODUCTION

There are a number of administrative provisions in the 1991 Act relevant to road works and these are dealt with in this chapter.

## 21.2 CIVIL LIABILITY AND OFFENCES

Where the 1991 Act creates a criminal offence in relation to road works in Scotland[1] this is without prejudice to any civil liability.[2] This means that someone convicted of an offence under the 1991 Act could also find themselves sued for damages in the civil courts in appropriate cases. It is also an offence to continue to fail to comply with a duty in respect of road works after being convicted of an offence under the 1991 Act.[3]

## 21.3 FIXED PENALTY OFFENCE

The 2005 Act makes provision for certain offences to be fixed penalty offences. The Commissioner can impose penalties on road works authorities and undertakers who fail to comply with sections 118 and 119.[4] Fixed penalties can also be imposed for certain offences under the Act.[5] Schedule 6A to the Act sets out those offences which are subject to fixed penalties. At present offences under the following sections will be fixed penalty offences: sections 113(5), 114(5), 116(4) and 129(6).[6] However the list can be added to or amended[7] provided that the order to do so is laid before and approved by the Scottish Parliament.[8] Schedule 6B sets out provisions for fixed penalty offences. Fixed penalty notices can be given by an authorised officer of the road works authority and

---

1 For example carrying out non-emergency road works without permission, failing to give advance notice of road works where required, contravention of a direction on the timing of road works or failure to reinstate after road works etc. See further Chapters 13 and 14.
2 NRSWA 1991, s 154(1).
3 NRSWA 1991, s 154(2).
4 NRSWA 1991, s 119A
5 NRSWA 1991, s 154A
6 Schedule 6A to the 2005 Act
7 NRSWA 1991, s 154(3)
8 NRSWA 1991, s 154(4)

should contain the prescribed information.[9] The penalty must be no more that 30% of the maximum prescribed fine for the offence and must be paid within 29 days beginning with the day on which the notice is given, although this period can be extended by the roads works authority if it is appropriate to do so.[10] If the penalty is paid within 15 days beginning with the day on which the notice is given, then a discounted amount is payable.[11] If the penalty is not paid by the end of the period for payment, proceedings can still be commenced.[12]

Consultation draft regulations have also been published which amend some of the provisions of Schedule 6B however at this time the regulations have not been made.[13]

## 21.4   OFFENCES BY CORPORATE BODIES AND PARTNERSHIPS

A director, secretary, manager or similar officer of a corporate body (or someone holding himself out as such) can be convicted of an offence under the 1991 Act, in addition to the corporate body, if he consented, connived, or was guilty of neglect in relation to the offence.[14] The same principle applies to partners who can be held individually liable in the same circumstances in addition to the partnership itself.[15] It should be noted that notwithstanding the provisions in the 1991 Act in relation to fixed penalty offences,[16] such an offence will not be a fixed penalty offence in this case and any officer or partner will still be guilty of an offence and liable for prosecution.[17]

## 21.5   COSTS AND EXPENSES

Where the 1991 Act permits recovery of costs and expenses for taking any action,[18] administrative expenses, including staff costs and over-heads, can be reclaimed.[19] Although the Scottish Ministers have the

9    NRSWA 1991 Schedule 6B paragraph 3
10   NRSWA 1991 Schedule 6B paragraph 4
11   NRSWA 1991 Schedule 6B paragraph 5(2). The discount is up to 25% of the maximum prescribed fine.
12   NRSWA 1991 Schedule 6B paragraph 6.
13   Consultation Draft Regulations: The Road Works (Fixed Penalty) (Scotland) Regulations. The Road Works (Fixed Penalty) (Scotland) Regulations are expected to come into force on 1 October 2008. However it should be noted that there may be changes between the draft regulations and the final regulations being made.
14   NRSWA 1991, s 166(1).
15   NRSWA 1991, s 166(2).
16   See paragraph 21.3 above.
17   NRSWA 1991 s 154A(2) as inserted by s 34 of the transport (Scotland) Act 2005.
18   Eg where there has been unacceptable delay and obstruction in carrying out certain categories of road works or where reinstatement fails and in both cases the authority must carry out the work itself: see paras 16.3 and 17.4.
19   NRSWA 1991, s 155(1).

power to make regulations to provide for how such amounts should be calculated none have yet been made.[20] Any dispute over whether costs and expenses can be recovered for carrying out work or taking other steps or the amount recoverable is to be settled in the prescribed manner.[21] Where there is a dispute over liability to reimburse or indemnify or pay costs that may also be referred to dispute resolution but not disputes as to the payment of a fee or to a right to compensation or to a contribution to make good long-term damage to a road or to a contribution to costs of resurfacing by undertakers.[22]

## 21.6   SERVICE OF NOTICES AND DOCUMENTS

Any notices served in respect of road works must be in the prescribed form.[23] The method of service for notices and other documents is also prescribed.[24]

## 21.7   TIME

Where a time period is expressed as being from or before a given date, the date itself is excluded from the calculation in computing time for the purposes of the road works provisions of the 1991 Act.[25] Notice given after 4.30 p.m. on a working day is treated as being given on the following working day. A 'working day' excludes Saturday, Sunday, Good Friday, Christmas day or a bank holiday.[26]

## 21.8   SETTLEMENT OF DISPUTES

It is envisaged that regulations will be made to prescribe the manner in which certain disputes will be settled.[27] There will be two ways in which disputes will be settled, either by the Commissioner or by arbitration.[28]

20   NRSWA 1991, s 155(1).
21   NRSWA 1991, s 155(3) as amended by s 36 of the Transport (Scotland) Act 2005. Disputes are likely to be settled by the Commissioner: Consultation Draft Regulations: The Roads Works (Settlement of Disputes and Appeals against Directions) (Scotland) Regulations reg 3. See also paragraph 21.7
22   NRSWA 1991, s 155(3).
23   NRSWA 1991, s 156 and SI 1992/2991 reg 4. See also the 2008 regulations which are expected to come into force on 1April 2008.
24   NRSWA 1991, s 156(2), SI 1992/2991 (amended by SI 1997/1505) reg 5.
25   NRSWA 1991, s 157(1).
26   NRSWA 1991, s 157(2). Bank holiday means a day which is a bank holiday under the Banking and Financial Dealings Act 1971 in the locality in which the road in question is situated: s 157(3)
27   NRSWA 1991 s 157A. It is expected that these regulations will come into force on 1 April 2008. However it should be noted that there may be changes between the draft regulations and the final regulations being made.
28   NRSWA 1991 s 157A(a) and (b)

Consultation draft regulations have been published however they have not yet been made.[29] It is likely that disputes will generally still be settled through arbitration but that disputes under sections 117(7), 120(6), 121(5), 143(3), 153(3) and Schedule 6 will be dealt with by the Commissioner.[30]

Although there is no obligation on the Scottish Ministers to produce a code of practice in relation to dispute resolution and appeals, a draft code of practice has been consulted on.[31]

## 21.9    ARBITRATION

Where arbitration is used to settle any dispute under the 1991 Act this means a reference to a single arbiter appointed by agreement between the parties. If they cannot agree then a sheriff will appoint the arbiter.[32] Where a point of law arises in an arbitration, the arbiter may state a case to the Court of Session in Edinburgh. Alternatively, he may be directed to state a case by the court. The court's decision is final unless leave is given to appeal to the House of Lords[33] and in such circumstances the court may impose terms as to expenses or other matters as it sees fit.[34]

## 21.10    INCONSISTENT AGREEMENTS

Any agreement which attempts to regulate roadworks is invalid if it is inconsistent with the provisions of the 1991 Act.[35] However, this does not affect an agreement to waive or vary a right conferred on a relevant authority provided this is not inconsistent with the future operation of the Act.[36]

## 21.11    REGULATIONS AND CODES OF PRACTICE

Before making, amending or revoking any regulations under the 1991 Act there is an obligation on the Scottish Ministers to consult with persons considered by the Scottish Ministers to be representative of the interests of undertakers, roads works authorities and other persons as

---

29  Regulations: The Road Works (Settlement of Disputes and Appeals against Directions) (Scotland) Regulations. It is anticipated that these will be released in March 2008.
30  See paragraphs 13.7, 15.2, 20.5.2, 21.3.
31  Draft Code of Practice for Dispute Resolution and Appeals
32  NRSWA 1991, s 158(1).
33  NRSWA 1991, s 158(2).
34  NRSWA 1991, s 158(3).
35  NRSWA 1991, s 159.
36  NRSWA 1991, s 159(2). It is difficult to work out what this actually means in practice.

the Scottish Ministers think appropriate. The same applies in relation to the issuing, amending or revoking of codes of practice.[37]

## 21.12    APPLICATION TO THE CROWN

The Crown is bound by the road works provisions of the 1991 Act,[38] but this does not authorise any criminal proceedings against anyone acting on its behalf.[39]

---

37    NRSWA 1991, s 163A
38    NRSWA 1991, s 167(4).
39    NRSWA 1991, s 167(5).

# 22   An Introduction to Road Traffic Regulation Orders

## 22.1   INTRODUCTION

The existence of a public right of passage over a road[1] does not mean that members of the public are entitled to use it as they see fit. The right of passage may be regulated by the local roads authority. Such regulation may derive from the authority's power to re-determine the means of exercise of the public right of passage.[2] It may also derive from the terms of a Road Traffic Regulation Order. Most of the urban road network is regulated by traffic regulation orders covering measures such as parking, loading, waiting, banned turns, bus lanes or access restrictions. Such measures are essential in city centres where demand for road space exceeds the capacity of the road network. Traffic regulation orders enable a roads authority to manage the available road space, which is usually done in accordance with the aims and objectives of their local transport strategy.

## 22.2   LEGAL FRAMEWORK

The Road Traffic Regulation Act 1984 empowers a local traffic authority to make Traffic Regulation Orders.[3] An authority is entitled to make an order, if it appears to them to be expedient to do so:

   a)   to avoid danger to persons or other traffic using the road or any other road, or to prevent the likelihood of any such danger arising; or

   b)   to prevent damage to the road or to any building near the road; or

   c)   to facilitate the passage on the road or any other road of any classes of traffic;[4] or

   d)   to prevent unsuitable vehicular traffic from using the road having regard to the character of the road or adjoining property; or

   e)   to preserve the character of a road where it is specially suitable for use by persons on horseback or on foot; or

1   See Chapter 4.
2   Section 1 of the R(S)A 1984.
3   Section 1 of the RTR Act 1984.
4   See Schedule 5 to RTR Act 1984 –classes of vehicle.

f)     to preserve or improve the amenities of the area through which the road runs; or

g)     for air quality purposes[5]

This is a wide ranging power enabling local traffic authorities to make an order to address matters such as road safety, amenity or damage prevention. Section 2 of the Act then sets out a range of measures that may be included in an order. Essentially, it allows the prohibition, restriction or regulation of the use of a road, or any part of the width of the road, by vehicular traffic or classes of vehicular traffic.[6] These prohibitions/restrictions/regulations may be imposed generally or subject to exceptions. The exceptions may be at all times or at specified times/days/periods. Without prejudice to the general power contained in Section 1 of the Act, Section 2 goes on to set out specific measures that may be included in an order. These are:

a)     requiring vehicular traffic or specified classes[7] of vehicular traffic to proceed in a specified direction, or prohibiting it from so proceeding;

b)     specifying the part of the carriageway to be used by such traffic proceeding in a specified direction;

c)     prohibiting or restricting waiting/loading/unloading;

d)     prohibiting the use of roads by through traffic;

e)     prohibiting or restricting overtaking.

The order may also include a provision to specify through routes for heavy commercial vehicles[8] or to prohibit or restrict the use of heavy commercial vehicles in specified zones or roads.[9] The authority may make these provisions relating to heavy commercial vehicles if they consider it expedient to do so to preserve or to improve the amenity of their area or some part of parts of their area. The provision of taxi stances is covered by a separate statutory process.[10]

## 22.3   RESTRICTIONS ON TRAFFIC REGULATION ORDERS

In some situations, the effect of an order may have significant impact on pedestrians or certain classes of vehicles. Section 3 (1) of the Act imposes certain restrictions on the authority to ensure that these more onerous measures are not imposed without due consideration. So, in terms of Section 3(1), an authority may not make an order that would have the effect of:

5    Environment Act 1995 – Section 87 paragraphs (a) to (c) of subsection (1).
6    See footnote 4 on classes of vehicles. Section (2)1 provision on vehicular traffic also applies to pedestrians – see Section 2(3) of the Act.
7    See footnote 4.
8    Section 4(a).
9    Section 4(b).
10   Civic Government (Scotland) Act 1982 s 19.

a)    preventing at any time access for pedestrians, or

b)    preventing for more than 8 hours in any period of 24 hours access for vehicles of any class, to any premises situated on or adjacent to the road, or to any other premises accessible for pedestrians or vehicles of that class from, and only from, the road.

The 'get out' clause for the authority is that, in any particular case, they are entitled to take a decision that the Section 3(1) restriction should not apply to their order[11] if they are satisfied – and they must state in the order that they are so satisfied – that terms of Section 3(1) should not be applicable. The statutory test is that they must be satisfied that Section 3(1) should not apply to their order on one or more of the following grounds:

a)    to avoid danger to persons or other traffic using the road to which the order relates or to any other road; or

b)    to prevent the likelihood of any such danger arising; or

c)    to prevent damage to the road or to buildings on or near it, or

d)    to facilitate the passage of vehicular traffic on the road, or

e)    to preserve or improve the amenities of an area by prohibiting or restricting the use of the road or roads in that area of heavy commercial vehicles.

The safeguard for operators or drivers of vehicles who would be adversely affected by the disapplication of Section 3(1) is that the consent of the Scottish Ministers is required before the order can be made.[12]

A traffic regulation order may not therefore prevent access at any time for pedestrians[13] nor regulate the speed of vehicles on roads.[14] An order may provide for its provisions to be signed on street if the traffic sign or character is of the type authorised under Section 64 of the Act.[15] Any such traffic sign is deemed to be lawfully in place unless the contrary is proved. An order may make provision for the issue and display of certificates or other means of identification of vehicles which are excepted from the restriction in the order.[16] An order may also make provision for the issue, display and operation of devices for indicating the time at which a vehicle arrived at, and the time at which it ought to leave, any place in a road in which waiting is restricted in the order.[17]

---

11   But only in so far as it relates to vehicles.
12   Schedule 9, Part II, Paragraph 13 (1) (a).
13   Section 3(1)(a) of the Act.
14   Section 3(3) of the Act – See Part VI of the Act for provisions on Speed Limits.
15   Section 4(1) of the Act.
16   Section 4(2) of the Act.
17   Section 4(3) of the Act.

A person who contravenes a traffic regulation order, or who uses a vehicle, or causes or permits a vehicle to be used in contravention of the order, shall be guilty of an offence.[18]

## 22.4    SCHEDULE 9: SPECIAL PROVISIONS

### 22.4.1    MINISTERIAL DIRECTIONS IN RELATION TO TRAFFIC REGULATION ORDERS

The Scottish Ministers have a reserve power[19] enabling them to make a direction either:

a)    requiring the local authority to make an order for a specified purpose and for the order to come into operation before the expiry of a specified period; or

b)    prohibiting the authority, either generally or without the consent of the Scottish Ministers, from making or bringing into operation an order with respect to specified matters or a specified area.

The Scottish Ministers have no power to call in a draft order which an authority intends to make; nor, in general, does an order have to be confirmed by the Scottish Ministers once it has been made by the local authority.[20] This reserve power enables the Ministers to intervene by Direction either before an order has been made by the authority or, if made, before it comes into operation. For instance, under Regulation 14 of the 1999 Regulations[21] there is provision for referral of a draft order with supporting documents to the Scottish Ministers. This referral would provide an opportunity for the Ministers to issue a Direction if they considered it appropriate to do so. If an authority fails to comply with a Direction issued by the Scottish Ministers under Part 1 of Schedule 9 then the Ministers may make the order to secure the object of the Direction. There is provision for recovery of expenses incurred by the Ministers in making the order to secure the object of their Direction.

### 22.4.2    MINISTERIAL CONSENT REQUIRED

If an authority proposes to make an order[22] containing any one of the following provisions, then they must obtain the consent of the Scottish Ministers, subject to the certain exceptions.[23]

18    Section 5 (1) of the Act.
19    Schedule 9, Part 1, Paragraphs 1 and 2.
20    Note that the consent of the Ministers is necessary in the circumstances specified in Part II of Schedule 9.
21    The Local Authorities' Traffic Orders (Procedure) (Scotland) Regulations 1999 Statutory Instrument 1999 No 614 (S.38) as amended.
22    Orders under Sections 1, 9, 19, 29, 32, 35, 37, 38, 45, 46, 49, 83(2) and 84.
23    Schedule 9, Part II, Paragraph 13(2) and (3) set out the exceptions.

a)   A provision prohibiting or restricting the use of the road as to prevent, for more than 8 hours in any period of 24 hours, access for vehicles of any class to any premises situated on or adjacent to that road or any other premises accessible for vehicles of that class from, and only from, that road,[24] or

b)   A provision that applies to a road for which the Scottish Ministers are the roads authority, or

c)   A provision within a Speed Limit Order[25] applying to any road a speed limit of less than 30 miles per hour, or

d)   A provision varying or revoking, within 12 months of its making, any order made by or made in pursuance of a direction given by the Scottish Ministers.

The requirement to obtain ministerial consent does not apply in cases where the order contains the restriction outlined at paragraph a) above (the 8 hours/24 hours' restriction) and there is no objection (or no sustained objection) to the proposed restriction from any owner, lessee or occupier of premises such as are mentioned in paragraph a) above.

Similarly, the requirement to obtain ministerial consent does not apply in cases involving an Experimental Traffic Order[26] where the order contains the restriction outlined in paragraph a) above[27] and the effect of the restriction or prohibition would be to prevent vehicles, or vehicles of any class, being loaded or unloaded in that road or to prevent persons boarding or alighting from a bus[28] on that road, and, either:

a)   no person has objected on the ground that the order would prevent the loading/unloading of vehicles/classes of vehicles in the road and no bus operator[29] has objected to the prevention of persons boarding or alighting from the vehicle in the road; or

b)   any such person who has submitted an objection on that ground has withdrawn it.

The Minister may consent to the order either in the form in which it was submitted to him or with such modifications as he thinks fit.[30] Modification may include additions, exceptions, or other modifications of any description. This is a wide power to modify so it is of little surprise that, where the modifications appear to the Minister substantially to affect the character of the order as submitted to him, he shall take such steps as

---

24   See paragraph 22.3 above re Restrictions on TRO.
25   Section 84(1) of the Act.
26   Section 9 of the RTRA 1984.
27   Schedule 9, Part II, paragraph 13 (1)(a).
28   That is a vehicle being used in the provision of a local service within the meaning of the Transport Act 1985.
29   Operator of a local service within the meaning of the Transport Act 1985.
30   Schedule 9, Part II, paragraph 16 (1).

appear to him to be sufficient and reasonably practicable for informing the local authority in question and other persons likely to be concerned.[31]

The Minister may by order add to or remove from the orders for which his consent is required by paragraphs 13 and 14 of Part II of Schedule 9 of the 1984 Act.[32]

## 22.5   PROCEDURE FOR TRAFFIC REGULATION ORDERS

The general power to make Regulations with regard to the procedure to be followed by the traffic authority in making an order is contained within Part III of Schedule 9 to the 1984 Act. The current Scottish Regulations are the Local Authorities Traffic Orders (Procedure) (Scotland) Regulations 1999 as amended.[33] ("The 1999 Regulations").

The 1999 Regulations apply to orders proposed to be made under the following provisions of the 1984 Act:

Section 1:          general power – see paragraph 22.2 above

Section 9:          experimental traffic orders

Section 19:        regulation of use of roads by public service vehicles

Section 29:        prohibition of traffic on roads to be used as playgrounds

Section 32:        provision of parking places

Section 35:        provisions as to use of parking places

Section 37:        general scheme of traffic control

Section 38:        parking place to be used as a bus or coach station

Section 45:        designation of paying parking places on roads

Section 46:        charges at and regulation of designated parking places

Section 49(2):   designations orders – revocation and effect

Section 49(4):   management of parking places in emergency and other circumstances

Section 83(2):   restricted roads

Section 84:        spend limits on roads other than restricted roads

---

31   Schedule 9, Part II, paragraph 16 (2).
32   See Road Traffic Regulations Act 1984 (Amendment) Order 1993, SI 1993/35 and Road Traffic Regulations Act 1984 (Amendment) Order 1999, SI 1999/1608.
33   The Local Authorities' Traffic Orders (Procedure) (Scotland) Amendment Regulations 2002 (SSI 2002 No 31); The Local Authorities' Traffic Orders (Procedure) (Scotland) Amendment Regulations 2005 (SSI 2005 No 338).

## 22.5.1   PROCEDURE BEFORE MAKING THE ORDER

*Statutory Consultation*

The first stage in the procedure is two fold. There is a general require-ment[34] to consult the Chief Constable for the area before making any order by virtue of (1) any of the provisions listed above or (2) the provisions of Section 61 of the Act (Loading Areas). In addition there is a requirement to consult the bodies listed in the Table contained within Regulation 4 of the 1999 Regulations. These bodies are:

1. **The other traffic authority** where the order appears to the promoting authority to be likely to affect traffic on roads of the other authority;

2. **The appropriate Crown authority** where the order relates to, or appears to the promoting authority to be likely to affect traffic on a Crown road;

3. **The concessionaire** where the order relates to, or appears to the promoting authority to be likely to affect traffic on a road subject to a toll order;

4. **The service operator and the appropriate Passenger Transport Authority** where the order relates to, or appears to the promoting authority to be likely to affect traffic on a road on which public passenger transport services are provided;

5. **The Chief Officer of the appropriate NHS Trust** where it appears to the promoting authority that the order is likely to affect the passage on any road or place of ambulances;

6. **The Fire Authority** where it appears to the promoting authority that the order is likely to affect the passage on any road or place of fire fighting vehicles;

7. In all cases, **The Freight Transport Association, the Road Haulage Association** and such other organisations (if any) representing persons likely to be affected by any provision in the order as the authority thinks appropriate.

As a matter of policy most traffic authorities maintain a wider list of con-sultees including bodies such as community councils, taxi organisations, cyclists' groups, motorcyclist groups, heritage organisations, Royal Mail, Utilities and retail associations.

The method of consultation is not prescribed. There is no statutory form of notice and no specified period within which to invite responses from the consultees. The requirement is simply to consult the persons speci-fied in the Table before making an order and to carry out the consulta-tion exercise before publication of the proposals in terms of Regulation 5. In practice, each traffic authority will have its own approach to this

---

34   Schedule 9, paragraph 20 of the Act.

consultation exercise. In some cases, the authority will forward a map outlining the proposed traffic measures together with an explanation of the authority's reasons for proposing to make the order. They may not forward the draft schedule and articles, as these documents may not have been prepared at this early stage in the process. The time allocated to the consultees may vary from authority to authority but a reasonable period should be allowed. This may be a period of 28 days or longer depending on the circumstances. What is important is that the period of time and the information provided to the consultees should be sufficient to allow a meaningful consultation exercise to take place. A meaningful exercise will establish the preliminary views of professional users of the road network and other stakeholders in advance of the public deposit of the draft order, which in turn should minimise the risk of an objection to an order by a consultee.

## 22.5.2   PUBLIC DEPOSIT OF THE DRAFT ORDER

Having carried out the statutory consultation exercise, the next stage involves the publication of the proposals by public notice and the public deposit of the draft order. It is usual practice for officers to obtain formal Council approval[35] to proceed to the public deposit stage even if, in some cases, that approval is within the scope of their delegated powers.

The publication requirements are set out in Regulation 5 of the 1999 Regulations. They involve:

(a)   Publication of a statutory notice[36] at least once in a local newspaper;

a) Taking such other steps as the authority consider appropriate for ensuring that adequate publicity about the order is given to persons likely to be affected by its provisions. These steps may include (i) publication of a notice in the Edinburgh Gazette; (ii) display of notices on street; or (iii) delivery of notices or letters to premises, or premises occupied by persons, appearing to the authority to be likely to be affected by any provision in the order.

(b)   Making specified documents available for inspection in accordance with Schedule 3 to the 1999 Regulations. The specified documents at this stage are:

a) a copy of the order as drafted or made as the case may be;

b) a copy of the relevant map;[37]

c) if the order is varying or revoking a previous order, a copy of that order and its relevant map;

---

35   This approval may be given under the Council's scheme of delegated powers.
36   Notice to contain the particulars set out in part I of Schedule I to the 1999 Regulations.
37   See paragraph 22.9.1 below on Relevant Map.

d) a copy of a statement setting out the authority's reasons for proposing to make the order;

e) if it is an experimental order, a copy of a statement setting out the authority's reasons for proceeding by way of experiment;

At the same time as the authority carries out the publication of their proposals as outlined above, they must also send a copy of the statutory notice to each of the consultees.[38]

## 22.5.3 OBJECTIONS

The authority must allow a period of at least 21 days[39] from date on which the statutory notice is first published for the submission of objections to the draft order. Some authorities allow a period of 28 days so that any publication error can be corrected in the next edition of the local newspaper without delaying the end date for objections. Any person may object to the making of an order before the end of the objection period.[40] There is no restriction on persons who may wish to object. They may or may not have some direct relationship with the affected road. The objection must contain a written statement of the grounds of objection and it must be sent to the address specified in the statutory notice.[41] It may not be clear whether or not a letter constitutes an objection. It may be prudent to apply a precautionary principle in the interpretation of objections. If there is any doubt as to whether or not a submission constitutes an objection, the authority might consider writing to the author to ask whether or not they wish their letter to be treated as an objection.

## 22.5.4 PUBLIC HEARING OF OBJECTIONS

The 1999 Regulations make provision for the holding of hearing in connection with a draft order.[42] In most cases, the decision to hold a hearing is discretionary but in specified cases, a hearing is a mandatory requirement.[43] The cases in which a hearing must be held are as follows:

(a)   Where there is a sustained objection by any person to:

a) a draft order which has been promoted under section 1, 37 or 45 of the Act and which contains a provision which prohibits, or has the effect of prohibiting, the loading or unloading of vehicles in any road either at all times or for any period of time unless such period falls wholly between 0700

---

38   Regulation 6.
39   Regulation 7(3)(a).
40   Regulation 7(1).
41   Regulation 7(2).
42   Regulation 8.
43   See the Local Authorities' Traffic Regulation Order (Procedure) (Scotland) Amendment Regulations 2007.

hours and 1000 hours or between 1600 and 1900 hours in any day, or

b) an experimental order which contains the above provision and which is proposed to be made within 6 months of the date on which a previous experimental order containing a similar provision as respects that road ceased to be in force.

(b)    Where there is a sustained objection by a person who provides a relevant service on any road to which the order relates to:

a) an order under section 1, 37 or 45 of the Act which contains a provision for requiring vehicular traffic generally, or vehicular traffic of any class, to proceed on a road in a specified direction, or from prohibiting such traffic from so proceeding, or

b) an experimental order which contains the above provision and which is proposed to be made within 6 months of the date on which a previous experimental order containing a similar provision as respects that road ceased to be in force, or

c) an order under section 19 of the Act which provides that any road shall not be used either at all times or for a limited period or periods in the year by public service vehicles or such vehicles of a specified class.

(c)    Where the order requires the consent of the Scottish Ministers[44] and he has indicated that he is not willing to consider giving his consent to the making of the order until a hearing has been held by the authority in connection with it.

If the authority decide to hold a public hearing in connection with a draft order, or if a hearing is mandatory for the reasons outlined above, then arrangements have to be made to appoint a reporter to conduct the hearing. The hearing will be conducted by an independent person appointed by the authority from a list of persons complied by the Scottish Ministers.[45] This list will be provided by the Directorate for Planning and Environmental Appeals.[46] The appointed reporter will conduct the hearing in accordance with the Code of Practice.[47] This Code appears to have been written to facilitate minor hearings of perhaps a few days' duration with a few issues to be considered. The Code is ill equipped to deal with major hearings lasting for several weeks/months to consider a suite of complex inter-related orders. For instance, the Code provides a target for the hearing to take place within 12 weeks of the date on which it is known that the case is to be heard at a hearing. The earliest that an

44    Under paragraph 13 of Schedule 9 to the Act.
45    Regulation 8(2).
46    Formerly the Inquiry Reporters Unit.
47    The Local Authorities Traffic Orders (Procedure) (Scotland) Regulations 1999 – Code of Practice – Procedure for Hearings issued by the Scottish Executive under cover of a letter dated 20 December 1999.

authority can take that decision is when they consider the report on the objections received during the public deposit period. After the decision has been taken to hold a hearing, the authority has to write to each objector to ascertain whether or not the objector wishes to be heard at the hearing. There then follows a period during which the authority has to set out their Statement of Case "containing full particulars of the case they wish to make at the hearing"[48] together with their response to objections lodged. Likewise participating objectors need time to prepare their written case in response the authority's case. In the recent example of the extension of the Controlled Parking Zone in Edinburgh, the number of letters of objection/representation exceeded 10,000. It would not have been possible to process that number of objections in a 12 week period.

A particular issue about the operation of the 1999 Regulations and the Code of Practice is that the intention of the Code is to set out a procedure embodying "the rules of fairness and natural justice".[49] The Code goes on to set out a procedure for fair disclosure and advance notice of the respective cases to be presented to the reporter. However, the right to appear at the hearing is not restricted to those parties who submitted timeous written objections during the public deposit stage. Regulation 10(2) provides that 'any person interested in the subject matter of the hearing may be heard in person or be represented by counsel or a solicitor or other representative". Regulation 10(3) provides that any person so interested may, whether or not he proposes to appear at the hearing, send written representations for the consideration of the Reporter at the hearing. Each of these provisions has the potential to derail the programme for the hearing. The only safeguard is the Reporter's power to refuse to hear any person or to consider any representation if he is satisfied that such representations are frivolous or vexatious or that the views have already been adequately stated by some other person at the hearing.[50]

## 22.6   MAKING AN ORDER

Before making an order, the roads authority must take into consideration all of the objections made during the public deposit period unless the objection has subsequently been withdrawn by its author. If a hearing has taken place, the authority must also take into account the Reporter's report and recommendations.[51]

The making of the order usually involves a decision of the authority to make the order with the Council's Solicitor then making arrangements for its execution and signature. In taking this decision, the authority will take into account all relevant considerations including:

48   Code of Practice – paragraph 5.
49   Code of Practice – paragraph 2.
50   Regulation 10(4).
51   Regulation 12 – see paragraph 22.9.3 below on notice of making order.

- Their reasons for proposing to make the order;

- The representations made by the statutory consultees together with the response to those representations from the authority's technical and other advisers;

- The objections lodged during the period of public deposit of the draft order together with the response to those representations from the authority's technical and other advisers.

## 22.7   MAKING AN ORDER WITH MODIFICATIONS

Apart from three exceptions, the authority is entitled to make the order with modifications, which may be in consequence of any objections or otherwise.[52] The three exceptions are:

a)   If any of the modifications would involve a departure from the order in the form to which the Minister or the Crown authority has given consent; or

b)   If any of the modifications would involve a departure from the order in the form to which the Minister has directed the authority to make the order in terms of Schedule 9[53] to the Act; or

c)   If any of the modifications would extend the application of the order or increase the stringency of any prohibition or restriction contained in it.

This last exception is likely to be the most common one in practice. The effect is that the authority may only modify an order if the modification is less stringent or covers a lesser area than originally included in the draft order. This stringency test should be applied to each proposed modification.

If the Minister proposes to consent to an order with modifications that appear to him substantially to affect the character of the order as submitted to him, then before the authority may make the order, they must take such steps as required by the Minister to alert affected parties to the proposed modifications. These steps might include advising persons likely to be affected by the modifications, giving those persons an opportunity to make representations in connection with the modifications and ensuring that the authority considers any such representations.[54] The Minister may ask for the representations to be forwarded to him for his consideration.

---

52   Regulation 13 (1).
53   Paragraphs 1 and 2 of Schedule 9 to the Act.
54   Regulation 13(2).

## 22.8   REFERRAL TO THE SCOTTISH MINISTERS

If there has been a mandatory hearing of objections[55] and the authority decides to make an order in a form which includes any provision at variance with the recommendations of the Reporter, the Regulations provide for the transmission of specified documents to the Minister before the order is made.[56] The referral procedure involves:

(a)   Forwarding the following documents to the Minister;

    a) a copy of the order as proposed to be made;

    b) a copy of the relevant map;

    c) a copy of the Reporter's report and recommendations;

    d) a statement of the authority's reasons for not accepting the relevant recommendations

(b)   At the same time as referring the above documents to the Minister, the authority must write to each person who objected to the order and has not withdrawn his objection to advise them of the referral of documents to the Minister;

(c)   The authority may not make the order before the expiration of one month from the date on which the above listed documents were sent to the Minister, unless the Minister gives the authority earlier notification that he has no observations to make about the order.

If the Minister wishes to intervene he has the power to direct that the authority does not make the proposed order.[57]

## 22.9   THE FORM OF THE ORDER

### 22.9.1   THE RELEVANT MAP

The authority must prepare a 'relevant map' in connection with the order.[58] The relevant map must accord with the provisions set out in Schedule 5 to the Regulations. Those provisions are that the map must clearly indicate by distinctive colours, symbols or markings:

a)   each road to which the order relates;

b)   where the order prohibits the use of a road by all vehicles or vehicles of a particular class, the alternative route available for those vehicles;[59]

---

55   By virtue of Regulation 8(1)(a) or (b).
56   Regulation 14.
57   See Schedule 9 and paragraph 22.4.1 above.
58   Regulation 15.
59   If an alternative route exists – amended by SSI 2005 No 338 regulation 2(4).

c)    where the order does not relate to a road, the location of the
site or other place to which the order applies and the
relationship of that site or place to adjacent roads or premises.
For instance, the order may relate to off street parking
accommodation.

The text of a Section 38 order[60] (parking place to be used as bus or coach
station) must make specific reference to the relevant map, with the map
being made as part of the order. Otherwise, it is not obligatory for the
order text to refer specifically to the relevant map or for the map to be
made a part of the order.[61] If the map is neither specifically referred to in
the text of the order nor made a part of the order, it shall be for
illustrative purposes only. Accordingly, the detail on the map shall not
prevail over the actual text in the order if there is any discrepancy
between the map and the text.[62]

As well as preparing the relevant map, the Regulations impose a requirement on the authority to keep a relevant map in connection with an
order. This requirement is necessary because there is a related requirement regarding public inspection of documents.[63] In cases in which an
order is to be varied or revoked, the authority must place on public
deposit that order and its relevant map. Consequently, the authority
must retain a copy of the relevant map with its order.

The Schedule 5 requirements as to the relevant map do not apply:[64]

(a)    if the order provides *only* for the revocation of the provisions
of a previous order. So there is no requirement to prepare a
relevant map for a revocation order although there is a
requirement to place the relevant map of the order being
revoked on public deposit in accordance with the Schedule 3
procedure.

(b)    if the order relates only to a parking place and provides only
for a variation of any one or more of the following matters:

a) the charges for the use of the parking place;

b) the time limits applicable to such use;

c) the classes of vehicle which may be used in the parking
place;

d) the conditions applicable to the use of the parking place by
vehicles.

---

60    1984 Act.
61    Schedule 5 paragraph 1(2) to the 1999 Regulations.
62    Schedule 5 paragraph 1(3) to the 1999 Regulations.
63    Under Schedule 3 to the 1999 Regulations.
64    Schedule 5 paragraph 1(4) to the 1999 Regulations.

## 22.9.2   DATE OF THE ORDER

The order must specify the date on which the order is made by the authority.[65] It must also specify the operative date, that is, the date on which the order comes into force. If there are different operative dates for different provisions of the order, then each of the operative dates must be specified. The operative date cannot be earlier than the date of publication of the statutory notice[66] in the local newspaper.

No order can be made after expiry of two years beginning with the date on which the statutory notice of proposals is first published.[67] The application of this 'two year' rule can be problematic in complex cases involving one or more orders, such as orders relating to a traffic management scheme or a controlled parking scheme. If the proposals are contentious and attract a significant number of objections, it may be difficult to process those objections through a public hearing in the two year period. Moreover, it might encourage a filibustering approach to defeat the proposals on time/process alone. On the other hand, a time limit ensures that any order promoted by an authority is timeously dealt with to avoid public confusion about proposed traffic measures. In order to address this difficulty, the Regulations were amended in 2005[68] to allow the Scottish Ministers to extend the two year period on application by the authority. The two year limit will not apply where an application has been made by the authority to the Scottish Ministers.[69] This application should be made to the Scottish Ministers before the expiry of the two year period. The Scottish Ministers may then extend the two year time limit for a period not exceeding 6 months, as the Minister considers appropriate. The Ministers may grant up to four further extensions to the authority.[70] If the Ministers refuse to grant an extension, then no order shall be made after the later of (1) the expiry of the two year period[71] or (2) the date falling one month after intimation to the authority of the refusal.

## 22.9.3   NOTICE OF MAKING THE ORDER

Once the authority has made the Order[72], they have to follow the process set out in Part IV of the 1999 regulations to publicise its making. The steps[73] to be taken are:

   a)   to give written notice 'forthwith' to the Chief Constable;

65   Regulation 16(1).
66   Publication under Regulation 17.
67   Publication under Regulation 5.
68   Scottish Statutory Instrument 2005 No. 338 – The Local Authorities' Traffic Orders (Procedure) (Scotland) Amendment Regulations 2005.
69   Regulation 16(4).
70   Regulation 16(5).
71   Specified in Regulation 16(3).
72   See para 22.6 above on making the order.
73   Regulation 17.

b)    to give written notice to each objector[74] of the authority's reasons for making the order in spite of the objection;

c)    within 14 days of making the order, publish once in a local newspaper[75] a notice of making the order;[76]

d)    if considered necessary, within the same period, a similar notice in the Edinburgh Gazette;

e)    the public deposit for a six week period of the order and related documents in accordance with the requirement of Schedule 3;[77]

f)    if the order relates to a road, to take such steps (forthwith) as are necessary to secure the erection of traffic signs to ensure that adequate information as to the effect of the order is given to road users;

g)    to maintain such traffic signs for so long as the order remains in force;

h)    in cases of variation or revocation orders, to remove or amend affected traffic signs, as appropriate

i)    where the road is a Crown road, consult with the appropriate Crown authority before the erection of any traffic signs.[78]

## 22.9.4   MAKING AN ORDER IN PART

The authority is entitled to make an order in part thereby giving effect to some of the proposals to which the order relates whilst deferring a decision on the remainder.[79] if an order is made in part, the authority may subsequently deal with the remaining proposals in any, or any combination, of the following ways:[80]

a)    abandon them;

b)    defer a decision on them;

c)    make an order or orders giving affect to them in whole or in part.

Where an authority defers a decision[81] on any proposals, it may subsequently deal with those deferred proposals in any of the three ways

---

74   Who has not withdrawn their objection.
75   Circulating in the area in which any road or other place to which the order relates.
76   Notice to contain the particulars set out in Part III of Schedule 1 – subject to application of Regulation 19.
77   To the 1999 Regulations.
78   Regulation 17(1)(g).
79   Regulation 18(1).
80   Regulation 18(2).
81   Regulation 18(2)(b).

listed above. If the authority decides to make a subsequent 'part' order under (c) they do not have to re-start the statutory procedure under Parts II, III and IV of the Regulations.[82] However, the notice of making the 'part' order must indicate the proposals (if any) in the original order that have been abandoned or deferred.[83] In cases of an order for measures that had previously been deferred, the notice must also give particulars of the title and date of every previous order made in relation to the same order as originally proposed.[84]

Regulation 13 sets out restrictions and prohibitions regarding modifications to an order.[85] For the purposes of Regulation 13(2) (Ministerial consent to an order with modifications), a part made order is to be treated as an order made with modifications.[86]

## 22.10   CONSOLIDATION ORDERS

A consolidation order is one that revokes and re-enacts the provisions of a number of orders into one new order without introducing any new provision. As there is no new provision, a simplified procedure applies to consolidation orders.[87] There is no requirement to undertake a statutory consultation exercise,[88] publication of the proposals,[89] notice of the proposals[90] or processing objections.[91] There is also a simplified procedure for the notice of making the order.[92]

## 22.11   CERTAIN VARIATION ORDERS

There is provision for a simplified procedure for certain types of variation orders. The simplified procedure is the same as the procedure for consolidation orders,[93] as outlined above. The types of variation orders are:

   a)   Where the sole effect of the variation is to include an exemption in respect of a disabled person's vehicle;[94] or

82   Regulation 18(4).
83   Regulation 18(5)(a).
84   Regulation 18(5)(b).
85   See paragraph 22.7 on Making Order with Modifications.
86   Regulation 18(6).
87   Regulation 19.
88   Regulation 4.
89   Regulation 5.
90   Regulation 6.
91   Regulation 7.
92   Regulation 19(1).
93   Regulation 19.
94   Of the same kind as is mentioned in Regulation 4 of the Local Authorities Traffic Orders (Exemption for Disabled Persons) (Scotland) Regulations 1971.

b)    Where the sole effect of the variation is to include a provision conferring on a traffic warden functions similar to those conferred by the order on a police constable in uniform, or both such exemption and provision.

c)    Where the sole effect of the variation is to include a provision to substitute a prohibition or restriction on the use of vehicles having a maximum gross weight of 16.5 or 17 tonnes for an identical prohibition or restriction on the use of vehicles having a maximum gross weight of 18 tonnes.

## 22.12   STATUTORY APPEAL TO THE COURT OF SESSION

The RTR Act 1984 makes provision for any person who desires to question the validity of, or of any of the provisions contained in specified orders to do so by making an application to the Court of Session within 6 weeks from the date on which the order is made.[95] The grounds of challenge are that the order or any of its provisions:

a)    are not within the relevant powers, or

b)    that any of the relevant requirements has not been complied with in relation to the order.

The specified orders are any order made under Sections

1      General power

6      (Greater London orders)

9      Experimental Orders

16A   Events orders

19     Regulation of Use of roads by Public Service vehicles

32     Provision of Parking Places

37     General Scheme of Traffic Control

38     Parking Place to be used as a bus or coach park, and

Any designation order

It should be noted that the 6 week period runs from the date of making the order. However, the public notice of making an order must be made within 14 days of the making of the order.[96] So if a potential challenger is relying on the public notice to establish the date of making the order, then two of the six week period may already have passed. If the potential challenger has already objected to the order, he may receive notification of the making of the order in advance of the public notice, if the

95   Schedule 9, Part III, Paragraphs 34 to 37.
96   Regulation 17 (1)(c).

authority is prompt in issuing the statutory letter under Regulation 17(1)(b).

## 22.13   EXPERIMENTAL TRAFFIC ORDERS

If an authority wishes to carry out an experimental scheme of traffic control, they may make an 'experimental traffic order'. An experimental order may contain any provision as may be made by a traffic regulation order.[97] An experimental order shall not continue in force for more than 18 months.[98] An authority may by order direct that an extant experimental order be extended for a further period ending not later than 18 months after it first came into force.[99]

It would appear that an experimental order would be of particular value for more complex traffic schemes to allow the authority to assess the actual impact on traffic flows rather than relying on a predicted/ modelled outcome. However, the statutory procedure for making a permanent order, including a public hearing, may take up to two years. This could mean that there is only a period of a few months in which to assess the experimental scheme before the procedure for the permanent order would have to be triggered.

In the case of St Helens Metropolitan Borough Council v West Lancashire District Council,[100] the court quashed an experimental order. The court held that an experimental order will only be valid if there is a genuine and identifiable experiment designed to gather information and inform future decisions. An experimental order should not be utilised to introduce a final restriction on traffic or to overcome procedural hurdles which would otherwise arise.

## 22.14   TEMPORARY TRAFFIC REGULATION ORDERS AND NOTICES

In certain circumstances an authority may impose temporary traffic restrictions on their road network. They may do so by order[101] or by notice.[102]

### 22.14.1   ORDERS

An authority may impose temporary restrictions *by order* if it is satisfied that traffic on a road should be restricted or prohibited:

97   Section 9 of the RTR Act 1984.
98   Section 9(3) of 1984 Act.
99   Section 9 (4) of 1984 Act.
100   1996.
101   Section 14 (1) of the RTR Act 1984.
102   Section 14(2) of the RTR Act 1984.

a) because works are being or are proposed to be executed on the road; or

b) because of the likelihood of danger to the public, or of serious damage to the road, which is not attributable to such works; or

c) for the purpose of litter clearing and cleaning[103]

The order may restrict or prohibit temporarily the use of that road, or any part of it, by vehicles, classes of vehicles or pedestrians to such extent and subject to such conditions or exceptions as the authority consider necessary.

## 22.14.2   NOTICES

An authority may at any time *by notice* [104] impose temporary restrictions or prohibitions on the use of a road, or any part of it, by vehicles, classes of vehicles or pedestrians. They may do so where it appears to the authority that the restriction or prohibition should come into force without delay because it is:

a) *necessary or expedient* for works being or proposed to be executed on the road;

b) *necessary or expedient* for the purpose of litter clearing and cleaning[105]

c) *necessary* because of the likelihood of danger to the public, or of serious damage to the road, which is not attributable to such works

The authority must have regard to the existence of alternative routes suitable for the traffic affected by the order or notice.[106] An order or notice must not have the effect of preventing at any time access for pedestrians to any premises situated on or adjacent to the affected road or to any other premises accessible for pedestrians from, and only from, the road.[107]

## 22.14.3   DURATION OF ORDERS

An order may not remain in force for more than eighteen months from the date on which it comes into force[108] subject to two exceptions. The

---

103  In terms of the duty imposed by section 89(1) (a) or (2) of the Environmental Protection Act 1990.
104  Section 14(2).
105  In terms of the duty imposed by section 89(1) (a) or (2) of the Environmental Protection Act 1990.
106  Section 14(3).
107  Section 14(4).
108  Section 15(1).

first exception is where the order relates to a footpath or cycle track in which case the order may not remain in force for more than six months. The second exception relates to situations in which the order is to facilitate works on or near the road[109] and the authority is satisfied (and it is stated in the order that they are satisfied) that the execution of the works will take longer than eighteen months. In such cases the order will have a start date but no end date. The authority must revoke the order as soon as the works are completed.

There is provision[110] for the Minister to extend the period of an order (one which is in force for a period not exceeding eighteen months) for a further period not exceeding six months. The Minister must be satisfied that the authority is proposing to make a permanent order mirroring the temporary provisions but, due to the procedure for making the permanent order, the authority will not be able to make it before the temporary one expires.

### 22.14.4   DURATION OF NOTICES

If the notice was issued for the purposes of works being or proposed to be executed on the road or for the purpose of litter clearing and cleaning, it shall not continue in force for more than five days from the date of the notice.

If the notice was issued for the purposes of the likelihood of danger to the public, or of serious damage to the road, which is not attributable to such works, it shall not continue in force for more than twenty one days from the date of the notice.

## 22.15   PROCEDURE

The procedure for making temporary orders and notices is set out in The Road Traffic (Temporary Restrictions) Procedure Regulations 1992[111] as amended by the Road Traffic (Temporary Restrictions) Procedure Amendment (Scotland) Regulations 2005.[112] It is a simplified procedure in comparison to the procedure for making a permanent order. There is no requirement for consultation on a draft order or public deposit of a draft order for objections.

### 22.15.1   PROCEDURE FOR ORDERS

On or before the day on which the temporary order is made, the authority must give notice to the parties specified in Regulation 3(4) of

109 in terms of Section 14(1)(a).
110 Section 15(3).
111 Statutory Instrument 1992 No. 1215.
112 Scottish statutory Instrument 2005 No 299.

the 1992 Regulations. These parties include the Chief Constable and the fire authority. Then, within 14 days after making the order but before it comes into operation, the authority must publish a statutory notice of making the order in a local newspaper.[113] The statutory notice must state:

a)    the reason or purpose mentioned in Section 14(1)[114] for making the order;

b)    the effect of the order;

c)    the date on which the order is in force and its maximum duration

The statutory notice of making the order may also contain the alternative route or routes available for traffic, or details as to where this information may be found.

## 22.15.2   PROCEDURE FOR NOTICES

The notice must state:

a)    the reason or purpose mentioned in section 14(1)[115] for the issue of the notice;

b)    the effect of the notice;

c)    the date of the notice and its maximum duration; and

The notice may also contain the alternative route or routes available for traffic, or details as to where this information may be found.

No later than the day on which the notice is issued, the authority must give notice of it to the parties listed in Regulation 10(3) of the 1992 Regulations. Those parties include the Chief Constable and the fire authority.

---

113  Regulation 5 of 1992 Regs.
114  RTR Act 1984.
115  RTR Act 1984.

# Index

[References are to paragraph number]